THE CRAFTY COC

ERIC BRISTOW

THE AUTOBIOGRAPHY

ERIC BRISTOW MBE was the most successful darts player of the 1980s and single-handedly turned the game into a worldwide spectator sport. He won five World Championships between 1980 and 1986, five World Masters, and has won almost every tournament in the game at least once. Between 1980 and 1987 he reigned as number one in the world and in 1989 was given an MBE for his services to the sport. He currently works as a pundit and commentator for *Sky Sports* and tours Britain with other famous darts names such as John Lowe as part of the *Legends Tour*.

PAUL CARTER began his career in journalism in 1990 at the *Oldham Advertiser*. He has worked as a sports reporter for the *Sunday Times*, feature writer for the *Sun* and also at *Sky News*. In 1996 Paul joined *Sport Newspapers* and was made editor of the *Sunday Sport* in 2001. He quit in September 2007 to pursue a career as a writer. Paul has had one other book published in 2006, *Behind Palace Doors,* the story of the Queen Mother as told through the eyes of her equerry Major Colin Burgess.

THE CRAFTY COCKNEY

ERIC BRISTOW

THE AUTOBIOGRAPHY

arrow books

Published in the United Kingdom by Arrow Books in 2010

9 10 8

First published in the United Kingdom in 2008 by Century

Arrow Books
The Random House Group Limited
20 Vauxhall Bridge Road, London, SW1V 2SA

Addresses for companies within The Random House Group Limited can be found at:
www.randomhouse.co.uk/offices.htm

The Random House Group Limited Reg. No. 954009

www.randomhouse.co.uk

A CIP catalogue record for this book
is available from the British Library

ISBN 9780099532798

Typeset by Palimpsest Book Production Limited,
Grangemouth, Stirlingshire

Penguin Random House is committed to a sustainable future for
our business, our readers and our planet. This book is made from
Forest Stewardship Council® certified paper.

Printed and bound in Great Britain by Clays Ltd, St Ives plc

Dedication

For all my family, friends and supporters and especially
for my former drivers Trevor Band and Phil Dacasto
who have sadly passed away, and Bass entertainments
manager Malcolm Powell who supported me during my
lowest moment in darts.

Acknowledgements

Writing this book wouldn't have been possible without the goodwill, vision and encouragement of so many people who have helped me in my career throughout the years. I'd particularly like to thank all those involved with the BDO especially Ollie Croft and his late wife Lorna who put a great structure in place for darts to build upon; all the officials and organisers involved in the PDC, especially John Raby, without whom there would've been no PDC; everyone at Sky Sports for making darts bigger than it has ever been in its history and supporting it through its troubled times during the breakaway from the BDOs and Dick Allix who managed me for over two decades. I'd also like to thank everyone at Random House for their help in making this book happen, especially editor Timothy Andrews; Jonathan Harris of literary agents Luxton Harris; and finally Paul Carter for doing such a great job in writing the book. I also send my appreciation to all those who have shown their help, support and patience and who have backed me during my career in darts with all the ups and downs that went with it – and there were many of those.

Contents

One: Streetwise   1

Two: Pub Darts   22

Three: County Darts   41

Four: England   59

Five: The World Championship   81

Six: Jet-setters   101

Seven: Champion of the World   129

Eight: You Can't Beat a Bit of Bully   152

Nine: The Milky Bar Kid   172

Ten: Back on Top   195

Eleven: The Beginning of the End   218

Twelve: The Power   236

Thirteen: The Marriage and the Split   254

Fourteen: I Fought the Law and the Law Won   281

Fifteen: Oh Brother!   303

Sixteen: Legend   324

ONE

Streetwise

'You play like a poof!'

These were the words my dad George said to me when he first watched me play darts. I was eleven years old and he'd just bought me a board for my birthday. I was playing in my bedroom.

'I can't take you down the pub if you play like that,' he said.

I'd never played darts before, but three weeks later I was getting regular three-dart scores of a hundred plus. The trouble was I had a unique style of throwing that in my dad's eyes looked suspect. It involved standing to the side and holding the dart lower down the barrel so my little finger rested on the tip of it. This hindered my throwing action. To overcome this I raised my little finger in the air so there was no contact with the point.

'You look like a little posh boy holding a china tea-cup,' he said.

'Give it a rest, Dad,' I said to him. 'This is the way I play, and this is the way I'll always play.'

He didn't like it, but it was a style that gave me five World Championships, five World Masters, two *News of the World* titles, four British Opens, three Butlins Grand Masters and numerous Open wins in Sweden, Denmark and North America, plus a host of other titles – and pretty soon everybody was copying my throwing style. As soon as I got good there were thousands of other players in pubs and clubs up and down the country all playing with raised pinkies. They thought they could be great darts players just by lifting up their little finger. What a bunch of wallies!

I was born in Ward 6, Hackney Hospital, East London, at 5.50 a.m. on 25 April 1957, and weighed a healthy, though not huge, six pounds. My mum Pamela was a telephonist in the City and Dad was a plasterer. Mum was the rock in our family, she was the one who pushed me and encouraged me, and she always stood up for me whenever I got into any trouble, which was quite often. My dad was a bit quieter. He had his routine: the occasional trip down the bookies, the pub on a Sunday afternoon, that sort of thing. We lived in Stoke Newington, where you learnt at an early age that life on the streets was tough. I know it's a bit of a cliché but in my case it was true. After the Second World War Stoke Newington, like many run-down areas, suffered at the hands of urban planners who tore down the slums and replaced them with housing estates. These quickly became a magnet for crime. I was lucky in that I lived in a big three-storey Victorian house. It'd be worth a fortune now because Stoke Newington, like most places in the East End, has been yuppified. However, it was slap bang in the middle of these new housing projects.

On the bottom floor of our house lived my nan, we lived on the middle floor and at the top was my Auntie Ethel. Nan smoked Kensington cigarettes all her life and when I was a kid I used to sneak into her living room and steal a few, like you do when you're young. Later on, when I'd made it at darts and was on good money, I lived with the guilt of stealing her fags so I'd use my winnings to buy her packets of two hundred, which I'd take round to her house, together with a crate of Guinness. She drank Guinness every night.

In those early days one thing a young boy had to do, living in London's East End, was learn to survive. Stoke Newington was tough and you had to be streetwise to get on. When I was a teenager I got in with a gang. My crew was known as the Oxton Boys. We were petty thieves getting up to mischief, but we were mere foot soldiers compared to the bigger gangs, of which the main one at the time was the Richardson's. They were the governors on our patch and were led by Charlie Richardson. You didn't mess with them: you avoided them at all costs and if you crossed them you left the country: either that or you'd end up dead. They were also known as the Torture Gang. Their 'speciality' was pinning victims to the floor with six-inch nails and removing their toes with bolt cutters. Other tortures included whippings, cigarette burning, teeth being pulled out with pliers, and electrocution into unconsciousness. The electrocutions were inflicted by an old Army field telephone which acted as a generator. The victims had the terminals attached to their nipples and bollocks and were then forced into a bath of cold water to enhance the electrical charge. Afterwards, if they were too badly injured, they'd be sent to a doctor who'd been struck off the Medical Register. If you saw a member of the Richardson Gang you put your head down, kept yourself to yourself and behaved. It was as simple as that. They used a pub just round the corner from where we hung out.

I always walked the streets with a claw hammer stuffed down the front of my trousers in case of any trouble. Everywhere I went I took it with me. That claw hammer became my best friend. It got me out of some sticky situations because you never felt totally safe walking the streets of Stoke Newington. Your worst enemy could always be lurking in the shadows or around the next corner. Our gang were a handy bunch, if a little small-time. I got in trouble with the police on lots of occasions for thieving, or beating people up or stealing cars. We loved the Mini Cooper S. If we saw one of those we'd have it. They were great, really nippy.

My first brush with the law came when I was thirteen. I'd borrowed a couple of monkey wrenches from a friend and was trying to steal money from a telephone box. There were two Turkish lads and myself. The police caught us red-handed and I had to appear at juvenile court, but I got away with it thanks to Mum. She'd been advised by the police to make me admit the crime, but she was having none of it. She got £40-worth of legal aid and a solicitor who established that the phone box had been tampered with before I and my two accomplices had got to work with the wrench. My brief got this fact by cross-examining a police sergeant who you could see going bright red in the face as he realised I was going to walk away free and innocent. Then I got nicked for joy-riding. Three of us had stolen a car, but the idiot driving it couldn't get out of third gear. We were being chased by the cops and had to abandon it. If you're being chased by the cops you really need someone who can drive. One of us got caught and grassed on the others. I remember a copper coming to my house and saying to me: 'You're going down this time, son.'

I got away with that as well when the police decided not to press charges. It had something to do with the driver being the son of a policeman, which was handy.

At weekends four of us would go out stealing. A local menswear shop was a particular favourite of mine. It was designed so the main window handles were on the outside. By hanging on the handle and pulling it down I could open the window, climb in and help myself to whatever I wanted. I did this about half a dozen times. Then, one night I was walking past, saw that nobody was about and pushed my fingers under the handle and took a tight grip to pull it open. All of a sudden I felt a shock of pain running through my hands. The shop owner, tired of my pilfering, had used sticky tape to fix razor blades under the handles. I was badly cut; my hands were a mess.

A tobacconist shop was another favourite. Attached to the door was a tinkling bell which rang when a customer walked in. I was a big lad, so it was easy for me to open the door slowly and grab the bell so that it didn't ring. Then I slipped inside and helped myself to as many fags as I could physically carry. By the time the shopkeeper realised some of his stock was missing I was long gone. I was particularly good with a knife, and if ever there was a small gap between a door and its frame I could get a blade in there and flip the lock. Sheds were a particular speciality. I could get in any shed.

One thing our gang prided itself on was cleanliness. We used to break into people's houses and we never damaged a thing. We were good thieves and we did a job properly. If we were going through a chest of drawers, we started at the bottom and worked our way up; that way we didn't make a mess of the place. We'd never soil the beds or urinate up the walls the way they do now because we had respect for the houses we were robbing.

We were in a house at lunchtime one day, and all of a sudden the distinctive waft of cooking came floating up the stairs. While I and a couple of others were rifling through bedroom drawers, downstairs our partner in crime was cooking. I shot down and confronted him. I was furious. 'What the fuck are you doing here?' I said. 'Let's get everything and get out, you daft sod, before we get caught.'

The smell was so good and so overpowering, however, that we all sat down to a full English breakfast, which was a rare treat back then in the late sixties – and because we were good thieves we even washed the pots and put them back where we found them afterwards. I bet the people who owned the home didn't even realise we'd made a meal when they got back.

The guy who cooked it got nicked off us by another gang shortly after that, for the simple reason he was small and pencil thin. In London around that time most of the Victorian houses had small manholes outside where the coal was poured in. When they came to deliver it, they would simply pull the manhole up and tip the coal in. when this gang of black lads saw my little mate, they took him from us to get down these coalholes. He couldn't argue with them: he had to do it or they would have put him in hospital.

So he was taken to someone's home where they had one of these holes outside. He had to slide down into it and follow the tunnel inside the house to a flimsy wire shutter that opened to access the coal. He kicked this shutter open, climbed out, went to the front door and let the lads in. That was him done then and he'd walk off down the street, absolutely filthy. However, these lads weren't just petty thieves; they were doing proper jobs. They were going in with vans and emptying the houses of everything. All people had to do to stop this happening was have a metal grate with a lock fitted on the outside hole, but people didn't think.

Everywhere our gang went we came across brainless idiots: people who just didn't have a clue. Most people deep down are basically wallies. A pal and I went to work for one down the market. He sold rollers that rubbed fluff off your clothes. Customers could buy one for fifty pence. We were working for this geezer who said he'd pay us two pounds a day to sell these things. So we said, 'Yeah, no problem, all right, when do we start?' It was easy money to us. We got to the market and he gave us a big bag of these rollers to sell, and when we'd sold them he got another bag out of the van and we sold them as well. They were flying out. This bloke was coining it in; we were making him stacks of money. Then this guy gave us the keys to the van and told us to look after things while he went for a cup of tea. What a stupid idiot. He didn't know us from Adam, and we knew that; that's why we went to the van, got about eight bags of these rollers and walked with them to the other end of the market where we started selling them for twenty-five pence each, undercutting him by half. We'd sold out in no time, made twenty times the amount he was paying us for a day, and scarpered.

When we didn't rob and pilfer we'd more often than not be fighting. A typical night out, for example, was us going down to the Tottenham Royal, which was a nightclub. It was where I made my England darts debut funnily enough, and was situated right opposite a police station of all places. One night when we went – I was fifteen but looked a lot older, so I never got asked for identity in these places – it all kicked off. There was a balcony which looked out on to the dance floor, and people were being picked up and thrown over the rail, landing thirty feet below. There were bodies sprawled everywhere; it looked as if a war had broken out.

There was one particular nutcase nicknamed Cappa, who used to go to the old North Bank and fight with Arsenal, he was a lunatic. He was tooled up this night, only he didn't have a knife or anything like that, he had a plane, a plane you use to smooth wood, which he used that night to plane the top of a poor guy's head. This bloke was stumbling about with this plane through his skull, in agony. I was convinced he was going to die and we had to run like hell to get away from the place before the police arrived.

I used to go and watch Arsenal and see Cappa on the terraces, but I never fought, even though violence was really taking off in football. I was never a hooligan for the simple reason that I went with my dad. Dad was a big Arsenal fan and I used to go to nearly every game with him. I was fourteen when they won the double in 1971 and we went to every home game, every away game and every FA Cup game except the final. Dad went to the final on his own. I watched it on television at home with a couple of mates and tried to spot him in the crowd of one hundred thousand. But my dad isn't stupid: he got near the ground and somebody wanted to buy his ticket off him for the equivalent of four week's wages, so they went to a nearby pub, Dad sold it to him, and he spent the rest of the afternoon in there watching it on telly.

When he came home I said: 'I couldn't see you on TV.'

'I wasn't there, son,' he replied and laughed.

Why we could only get one cup final ticket was simple: we only bought one match-day programme between us. There were tokens in these programmes and if you went to every game you would cut them out and keep them to get your ticket if Arsenal got to the FA Cup Final. So Dad got the ticket. I wasn't that bothered anyway; I supported Chelsea. Arsenal were a better team but Chelsea, with players like Peter Osgood and Charlie Cook, had more flair, plus I liked the colour blue. When

I was fourteen I went on my own across London to watch them lose 2–1 to Everton. I vowed never to go again, they were rubbish that day, but I still went with my dad to see Arsenal.

In the 1971 FA Cup semi-final they played Stoke City at Hillsborough in Sheffield. Me and my dad got off the train and walked down a big hill. The problem was Stoke were red and white and so were Arsenal, but Dad and I never twigged this. Walking to the ground we saw this sea of red and white in a great big park, so we headed straight for the middle of it, thinking they were Arsenal fans. When we got there all you could hear was ''Allo, duck' and 'How are you, duck?' We'd walked into the middle of Stoke's main firm, and all they wanted to do was find a couple of Arsenal fans and beat them up. Dad whispered in my ear: 'Keep walking. Don't say a word.' We walked all the way through them in silence, which was hard for me because I do like to natter.

It ended 2–2 and the replay was at Villa Park, which gives a great comparison of football in the early-seventies and now. At Villa Park they were doing repair work on the end where the Arsenal fans were. There were thousands of us standing on debris, bricks, every-thing. Now they'd have to close that stand for safety reasons, but then they didn't give a monkey's. It was dangerous as well. When we scored people could have broken their ankle and got trampled in the surge forward that followed. Some fans did fall on the bricks and rubble and hurt themselves quite badly. The St John Ambulance staff were kept very busy that day.

If it wasn't the poor state of the stadium you had to contend with, there was always the police who treated soccer fans like mad dogs. You could find yourself trampled on by a horse, hit over the head with a truncheon or basically just pushed out of the way by coppers with absolutely no respect for anyone. After the game Dad and I went outside, and as we were walking along he fancied a steak and kidney pie which he bought from a van and ate. There was litter everywhere, you couldn't see the floor for aluminium pie cartons, and all the bins tied to lamp posts were full to overflowing. So Dad threw his on the floor, only for a copper to approach him and say: 'Pick it up!' All the bins were bursting and when Dad looked on the floor he couldn't tell which one was his because it was just a sea of silver. This copper was just being stroppy and was probably itching to give my dad a belt. So Dad swallowed his pride and picked one up: it could've been his but probably wasn't. He went over to an overflowing bin and perched it precariously on top of this mountain of silver. It was a joke. What was that all about? There was rubbish everywhere and a couple of hours later they would have sent in the vans to pick everything up. I felt like smacking this copper; I really wanted to punch his lights out for humiliating my dad like that. Give a man a uniform and he becomes a different person, and that applies to quite a few policemen.

These were only minor setbacks to our overall enjoyment. Dad and I used to go everywhere together on the train to all the away games. I always used to see this young lad, he must have been about ten or eleven, and he went to every game home and away but he never had a ticket, and never had a railway ticket either. He'd just get on the train and dodge his way to the final destination. I'd always see him in the ground later. How he did it I will never know. He had no money. There'd be him and two of his pals in a train toilet and when the ticket collector came round one would come out, leaving the rest inside. I think they're a bit wise to that one now, but back then it happened all the time.

The big thing at that time was to nick somebody's scarf and bring it back to the pub. So, for example, if Arsenal were playing Liverpool, all the hooligans would go fighting and bring Liverpool scarves back to the boozer as trophies. I just remember thinking how stupid it all was – they were hitting people they didn't even know and the ones they were hitting could've been nice people but they didn't know any better and if you're brought up that way then that's it, that's the way you are. They were a product of their surroundings.

When I started playing darts on a Saturday, that's when the football stopped, but back home in Stoke Newington there was still the gang. There were still fights, we still went on the rob and things were no different. What changed everything for me came shortly after my sixteenth birthday. Me and the lads had a bit of trouble in a pub called the Queens. There were about seventeen of us, and we slaughtered this bloke and his mate inside the pub. The mate scarpered, but this guy simply refused to go down. We just couldn't beat him, even after we'd hit him with chairs, bottles, pool cues, anything we could lay our hands on. It was a trouncing, but he just stood in this corner and took it, and while he took it he kept saying, 'You've picked on the wrong bloke here, lads.'

I'll always remember that. They were like famous last words: 'You've picked on the wrong bloke.' His eyes were bloody, his head was ripped to pieces, his nose was shattered, and he was bleeding profusely, but he was a tough guy, and eventually he got out of the place. We just carried on enjoying ourselves in the pub and thought nothing more of it.

Then, a week later, one of our gang, Dum Dum, who had helped beat him up, was walking along the street when a car came screaming up to him and knocked him flying. It was a classic hit and run. He was left with two broken legs and a broken arm and was in a wheelchair for months.

Another week went by, and then another of the gang who was in the pub that night got jumped as he was walking along on his own. They put him in hospital;

he was in a right mess, stitches everywhere. He was lucky to survive. All I could think when I heard about this was that this was no coincidence, that whoever that guy was, yes, we had definitely picked on the wrong bloke.

Less than a week later, another one of our lot got done, so there were three down. If you've ever seen the Shane Meadows film *Dead Man's Shoes*, in which a paratrooper returns home to exact revenge on the tormentors of his younger brother and picks them off one by one, you'll know what it was like. A few of the lads were scared because they didn't know who they were up against, or who this bloke was in the grand scheme of things, and more terrifyingly for them they didn't know when and who he was going to strike at next. Unfortunately their fear didn't rub off on me. I know no fear, that's my problem. Pull a gun on me and I won't give a damn. I have no idea whether any of the others got taken out.

I was getting good at darts by then, I was earning money from it, I had a great life, was having fun and all of a sudden I could see the world opening up for me. I didn't need the hassle that came with being in a gang. I was on enough money to have a decent life; I didn't have to rob cars or houses to survive. Suddenly I remember thinking: I'm legal, I'm legit. So I left the gang behind; those days were over. Or so I thought.

*

After making the decision to leave the gang I also left home and went to live with a mate called Eddie. He had a flat about two streets away from where I lived with my mum and dad. I wanted to move out because, as with most youngsters, I craved independence and being able to do my own thing. I've always been like that.

So I was with Eddie and we were having a whale of a time, going out, pulling women every weekend and bringing them back to the flat. Everything was going fine until he committed the cardinal sin: he went to a pub nearby that wasn't our local and glassed some geezer in a fight, cutting him badly and leaving him scarred for life. I found out about this, and I also found out who he'd glassed and said to him: 'Eddie, you've messed with the wrong family there, mate.'

The guy he'd glassed was a big-time gangster with a big-time crew who were a nutty lot you didn't mess around with, so I made the decision to move back home right away. I didn't even hang around to take all my stuff with me; I left a lot of it there. Three or four days later I still hadn't gone round to collect my stuff, and that's when the dad of this bloke who'd been glassed came round to Eddie's flat with three of the bloke's brothers. You had to get up four flights of stairs to get to the flat. There were two flats to each floor; and Eddie's was at the top. Eddie was in when they came and he heard them kick in the front door downstairs. Luckily for him the flat opposite his was vacant. This meant the door had been left open, so Eddie grabbed a hammer – it was probably my hammer that I normally took everywhere with me as protection – and went in. All that was left in there was a big old wardrobe that was part of the fixtures and fittings. Eddie climbed into it and shut the door, but not completely or he would have been locked inside, and he waited. He heard these blokes go into his flat, open the window and throw all his belongings and personal possessions out on to some spiked railings four floors below. He later told me: 'I was worried my heartbeat would give me away. I felt sure they'd hear it because it was really hammering against my chest and going bang, bang, bang.'

When they'd thrown everything out of his window on to the spikes they went into the vacant flat, and as if by a miracle they didn't check the wardrobe. If they had they would have found Eddie with hammer in hand and his heart going nineteen to the dozen. I've no doubt he would've followed the rest of his belongings on to the spiked railings below and probably wouldn't be here today. Or if he was he would've been left severely paralysed. If I'd have stayed in that flat they would've thrown me out of the window as well. However, they just walked around the two flats, someone said, 'No one's in here,' and they were gone. If they'd have just opened the wardrobe door Eddie would've been a dead man. You didn't mess with the wrong families back then. As soon as this happened he packed his bags and moved to Las Vegas. He was a dead man walking in London. He's still there now, working as a croupier, and has a few properties. The minute that happened he was gone and he's never come back.

I always wonder what would have happened if I hadn't ended up playing darts. I'd probably have ended up in prison or drifted into big-time crime. Darts was my salvation. I tried to get the gang into darts when I was sixteen which was a big mistake. We formed a team and we might as well have called ourselves The Lunatics because they were potty. We played my league team, the Arundel Arms, who I threw for a couple of nights a week when I first started out. My lot wanted to fight them when we lost. That was an embarrassing moment. Their idea of a darts match was to play, have a load of beer and then beat up the opposition. It didn't last; it couldn't last for the sake of my career.

So I left, and didn't see most of them again, except that when I was seventeen I did get invited to the wedding of one of our top lads, a bloke called Sully. What a disaster that was. All the boys were there and it was a bit of a reunion. Unfortunately on the bride's side of the family was a rather large contingent of lads, many of whom had been involved in run-ins with our lot, including yours truly. As the beer began to flow and the day progressed so tempers got fraught, and one of our gang decided he was going to fill in this bloke who he didn't like. They weren't doing anything wrong but they sensed trouble so they managed to get a police van on standby outside, just in case a fight needed breaking up. It was the sensible thing to do. I'd had enough. I didn't want any trouble and could tell there was a big fight brewing, so I decided to go. The last thing I wanted to do was fight at a wedding and spoil someone's big day. However, by the time I got outside half the force in London had been tipped off that there was going to be a mass battle between a known gang and some other lads and they were ready to go in, round up our boys and nick them. When they saw me come out of there they must have been rubbing their hands in glee. As soon as I got about a hundred yards down the road a police van started following me. I knew they were going to do me so I tried to run but got caught. Back at the station the duty officer took my belongings. It was obvious what they were going to do, they were going to take me down to the cells and give me a beating, so as soon as I handed over my jacket to this officer I decked him with one punch; logic told me that as I was going to get done over I might as well hit one of them. That was it; they dragged me to the cells and about half a dozen of them laid into me. They beat me so hard my nose exploded and there was blood everywhere. After it was all over they called in a doctor to check me out.

'What happened to you?' he said.

'I fell over,' I mumbled through thick lips.

Saying that meant that they didn't charge me. It was no good saying I'd been beaten up because they would've thrown the book at me. I left that police station not knowing if Sully's wedding ever did erupt in violence, the people there knew nothing of the beating, but knowing that this sort of life – doing things wrong and getting in trouble with the law – was something that just didn't give me a rush any more. Darts was where I got my buzz now. I need a buzz and a thrill – they get me through life and make it enjoyable. Without that adrenaline rush life is not worth living. In the early days it was being with the gang and living every day on a knife edge. By the time I was in my late teens it was the arrows that did it for me and gave me my main focus.

Years later I did meet up with Sully again. I was the World Champion by then and I was doing *The Cockney Classic* at Truman's Brewery in London for ITV. I did darts and Steve Davis did snooker. My mum had bumped into Sully and a guy called Hursty who used to live with him and was also an old friend of mine, so she invited them to come and meet me after the programme. Sully was still married, had four kids and was running a removal business. They came and joined me and all these top nobs from ITV who took us for an Indian. As we sat with producers, directors and quite a lot of top executives I said to them, 'Did you enjoy it?' It was the first time they'd been to a televised darts match.

'It was brilliant, great,' Sully said.

'Well why don't you come next year?' I replied.

'OK,' said Sully.

'I can't,' said Hursty quite loudly. 'I have to go up the Old Bailey next month. I'm getting a seven to ten stretch for armed robbery.'

You couldn't have scripted it any better. All these execs and producers nearly choked on their curries and you could see the blood draining from their faces. The whole place went so deathly quiet you could have heard a pin drop, apart from the sound of the ITV bosses taking nervous gulps, that is. It was left to me to break the silence.

'You never bloody change,' I said, and roared with laughter.

But that was the last time I ever saw him or my old crew. By the time I was World Champion those days had been left far behind.

TWO

Pub Darts

Right from the start I loved playing darts. At school I was always good at maths; my maths got me into Hackney Downs Grammer School when I took the eleven plus exam. Darts was an extension of this. I'd spend hours working out different permutations to finish on, all that sort of thing. An early way I practised was to throw a dart at the board and if it hit twelve I'd have to put the other two darts with it. I just tried to follow the line of my first throw. Doing this got me good at hitting numbers all around the board and I became nuts about the game in no time, so much so that when I was fifteen I'd call for my mate Eddie Rayson, who lived round the corner from me and who was also a good darts player, and we'd be in the pub at eleven in the morning and play darts until three. Then we'd go for something to eat and be back in the pub for six and play until closing time. I should have been at school, but they let me leave six months early, well before my sixteenth birthday. There was no point in staying: I wouldn't have passed any exams because I didn't do any work. I was just mad at school, nuts. I told the teachers I didn't need an education because I was going to play darts, so that's why they signed me off for the last six months and told me I could go home.

I never liked school; I hated it. I got a new bike off Mum and Dad for my first day and rode the two miles there, chained it up by the playground and at the end of lessons when I went to fetch it someone had nicked the front wheel. That annoyed me intensely. I had to walk the whole two miles home with a one-wheeled bike. Then, three days after starting I got the cane for beating up another boy. It was the quickest time from starting school any newcomer had been caned. After that I just thought sod it, school wasn't for me.

If there were tests or exams I'd do my best to get out of them. In January 1971, we were due to have a German test. I'd learned so little German that I made the decision I had to get out of it at whatever cost. So I and a few others hatched a plan to scupper it: I phoned Scotland Yard from a call box and told them a bomb had been planted at school and was due to go off at the exact moment the test was due to start. Chaos ensued as pupils were evacuated to the safety of the school playground and the fire brigade and police arrived en masse. There were five of us behind the hoax, all chuckling away to ourselves. Thirty minutes later we went ashen-faced as our names were read out one by one on the school loudspeaker and we were told to report to the headmaster's office. Someone, I don't know who, had found out what we did and grassed on us. We got bollocked but we didn't get the cane, which amazed me, and still does to this day.

I was always getting caned by the headmaster Alec Williams. One time I put a thin book down the back of my trousers as padding.

'It is the first time you have used this book to good effect,' Williams said drily, which made me laugh.

Then I was thwacked.

Another time, as I was being caned on the hand, I asked: 'Can't you hit harder?'

Williams launched himself at my hand as hard as he could, only for me to move my hand away at the last minute. The cane smashed down on the table and split.

By the time I was fourteen I was refusing to be caned and the teachers were beginning to realise I was a lost cause. Darts was my escape. I used to play all the kids in school at darts for money and beat them, which was understandable considering how much better I was. Soon nobody would play me: they all knew they were on to a loser straight away. So I played 'ten pence up the wall' which is a game where whoever got their ten-pence piece closer to the wall was the winner and could keep their opponent's money. I was as good at that as I was at darts and would often leave school at the end of the day with five to ten pounds in ten-pence pieces. I used to walk to school with a mate called Brian, who was part of my gang, though he tended to avoid trouble, and on the way home I'd buy him a portion of fish and chips out of my winnings.

I had lots of gambling schools going, anything in which I could win a bit of money, anything apart from actual school work. Even going to school was a way of getting into a scam. In the morning I'd nick two pints of milk off somebody's doorstep, but I'd make sure I never did the same doorstep twice. As I drank them I didn't think anything of it. There was no guilt. It was thieving, but it was just the way you were brought up around those parts. Nobody made you feel as if you were doing anything wrong. It was just part of life.

Things really started changing for me when I got to fourteen. Every Saturday I'd go with my dad to the bookies. That's how I got my first pair of tungsten darts. Back then I played with brass darts – tungsten were too expensive – but on this particular day dad had a £5 each way accumulator on six races, and the first five came in with the sixth horse being placed. He'd backed them singly as well, so he'd won a tidy sum. With the winnings we got two buses to the darts shop. I took my brass darts to be weighed. They were fat little things and came in at 21.8 grams. I got a pair of tungsten ones for the same weight but with a much more slender barrel. They were a relatively new thing, and I'd tried some out a couple of weeks previously: a machinist called Harry who threw for my local had a set. I had picked them up and thrown 180. I knew instantly I had to get some. They were a revelation; they just felt right when I held them. My dad was watching and decided to get me to the dart shop to buy some at the first opportunity. They transformed my game forever. My averages shot up.

I always remember Dad saying to me when I was young, 'Everybody is good at something. It's just finding out what they are good at.' To that end he took me to pitch and putt to see whether I was good at golf, he took me to play snooker, I went boxing; he did everything with me really. At school I captained the football team and was a decent cricketer. But darts was what I was really good at.

When I first started, I played in my bedroom for hours against my old man and we had some close games. Dad was a good darts player in his time, but he had no bottle. He was brilliant on the floor, but put him on a stage and he would go to pieces, which was sad really because he was quite a thrower. He couldn't have been a pro, but he could've been a decent league player. By the time my twelfth birthday came I was beating him, and I was beating him by two or three hundred points in games of 1001. A few months after my fourteenth birthday he came into my bedroom on a Sunday morning and said to me: 'Right, son, when you've got yourself washed and dressed I'm going to take you down the pub.'

It was one of those rights of passage moments between a father and his boy. At half past ten that morning he took me down to his local, the Arundel Arms, where he went every Sunday from eleven until two before coming back for Sunday dinner at two-thirty. We were the first to arrive and the first on the dart board. Back then you played for sixpence a game and while I played my dad other people came and chalked their name up to play the winner. I beat Dad and played another bloke for sixpence. I beat him and then played from eleven until 2.15, never losing a game. I ended up walking home with a pocketful of sixpences and knew I had found my road in life. One thing that puzzled me though was that when I beat my dad he never chalked his name up for another game. He loved playing darts and had spent most of his Sundays on the pub dart board. Instead he just sat down now with a couple of mates in a corner, chatting and drinking, but I could see that every now and again he was looking up to see how I was doing and having a little chuckle to himself because I was making all this money. It must have made him very proud because I killed every bloke I played.

Soon a lot of the pub regulars were getting fed up with me and wanted to knock me down a peg or two. They'd offer me a game of darts for a fiver or a tenner. Most people, if they could play darts the way I could play, would have snapped their hand off. Not me. I used to wind them up and say, 'Look, you're not good enough to play me for money, so go away.' That used to rile them even more, and when they were riled it was easier to take more money off them.

They'd snap back: 'What do you mean, I'm not good enough?'

'You're not,' I'd say, 'you're simply not good enough to play me for money, now go away.'

That would make them even angrier, so they'd up the ante. I knew I had got them then, and when I beat them they would have no excuses. They couldn't get the hump with me because I'd just say: 'I told you that you weren't good enough to beat me.' I'd get them with this every single time.

Sundays became a ritual for Dad and me. He took me down the pub every Sunday. There was one poor bloke in there who was quite good at darts and offered to play me for sixpence. I gave him the usual nonsense about him not being good enough and ended up playing him for a pound. I beat him, turned to him and said, 'See, I told you you were rubbish. I told you that you weren't good enough to play me.'

My dad was in the corner drinking and thinking: Here we go again. This bloke wanted to double it up to two pounds, and no matter how rubbish I said he was, he just wouldn't let go. So I beat him, and I beat him, and I beat him and eventually he ended up owing me £256.

I said: 'I'm not playing you for £512.'

When was it going to stop? The bloke was gone, he was begging me: 'Please, just one more game, just one more game.'

And I said: 'No, no, bollocks to you.'

I took everything he had off him in the pub, which was thirty or forty quid. He paid me a few twenty quids over the next couple of months and that was it. I never did get the full amount.

When I was fifteen I played for the Arundel's dart team. Three of our team were deaf and dumb. There was a family of them and I used to love them. They were great people, and strong as an ox. If you have something wrong with you, you seem to build up on other things. These guys were huge. Nobody messed with them, and because of this nobody messed with our team and that was a good thing because it kept me out of trouble. There was one league, we played 1001, and it was an eight-man team. They put me first man. I used to have to start on a double, so I started on double six. That got me off straight away and bang I'd be murdering the opposition.

Away from the pub I was working. I had a number of jobs, all in a short space of time. I was at MFI for a while, sometimes selling in the shop and other times delivering goods in a van. I worked with a bloke called Ron who was nutty as a fruitcake. He had about six kids and his wife didn't have one of them in hospital. He firmly believed a woman's place was in the home, and more specifically in the kitchen, and shortly after she'd given birth upstairs he'd say to her, 'Right, well done love, now pop down to the kitchen and make me a nice cup of tea.' He was old school. She may have had the baby but he still expected his dinner on the table at half past five and his shirts washed and ironed.

I also worked in the City as a proofreader for the newspapers. I had to make sure the spellings were right and commas were in the right place, that sort of thing. I did that for two or three months then quit, mainly through boredom. Another job I had was at a clothing factory, bringing the cloth from the vans. This was where I met Sully. We used to go in to work on a Friday or Saturday in our baggiest clothes, nick a suit, put it on underneath and walk out with it at the end of the day. I must have been the only fifteen-year-old in the country with thirty-five suits in his wardrobe. Another lad who worked there was the real pro. He'd steal suits, wear them, then walk into offices carrying a briefcase and looking the works. The people there didn't bat an eyelid because he looked so smart. They thought he was a businessman who'd come to see their boss. Once inside he'd start rifling through the desks, taking whatever he could. I saw him come out of places with all sorts of things, including people's lunchtime sandwiches. He would've made a fortune today with laptops and things like that to steal. At the factory I was the cloth room boy, and if the cutters wanted to make suits upstairs they'd tell me to bring up a thousand yards of this or that. I'd take it up there and they'd cut the suits in the cutting room.

I was earning twelve quid a week when I was fifteen, but by that time I was playing a tournament on a Friday and more often than not I'd win it and get fifty pounds. Then I'd play another tournament on a Saturday, maybe a singles tournament for sixty pounds, and another on a Sunday for say forty pounds. I was winning one or two of these every other weekend, so that was the end of the jobs. What was the point of working all week for twelve pounds when I could earn about fifty pounds a week playing three days of darts? I became a full-time darts player and hustler, making money from the darts tournaments and from the people who challenged me at these tournaments or in the pub – this could have been at pool as well because I was also good at this game and I won quite a bit of cash playing that too. I played darts in a Monday league, Tuesday league, Wednesday league, Friday league and for one called the Loughton League. In this league was a team from the Bank of England and we played them at their main HQ. Every year it became a bit of a jolly boys' outing for the pub and we'd get coachloads of supporters coming to watch us, not because we were good or they wanted us to win, but because the bar was subsidised and you could get things like double vodkas for five pence or a pint for two pence. It was party night for them, regardless of whether we won or lost. They couldn't give a toss about the darts if truth be told. They didn't go to any other away games.

In the summer the leagues finished, and that was when my attention turned to girls. I met my first love, Pauline, when I was sixteen. She was beautiful, and she thought I was magic. We hit it of straight away and had a brilliant time. Then, towards the end of summer, the Monday league restarted so I couldn't see her that night, a little later the Tuesday league began, then the Wednesday league, and she said to me, 'When can I see you?'

'How about next summer?' I replied.

She may have been my first love but darts came before everything – and that was the problem. I couldn't have any relationships with girls because I just didn't have the time; the only love affair I had was with darts. I'd meet girls, sleep with them and they'd ask me, 'When am I going to meet you again?'

'You ain't,' I'd reply.

Darts was much more important. Nothing intruded on my darts. When I worked for MFI I'd barely started the job before quitting. Their busiest day was Saturday and I'd be travelling on Friday night to play darts on a Saturday so I told them I couldn't work then.

My boss said, 'If you don't work on a Saturday you're sacked.'

'I'll get my cards now then,' I said, 'because I'm off,' and that was the end of that.

I played for the Arundel Arms for about eighteen months and then the whole team moved to another pub close by called the Red Lion. We had a nice little room at the back of the pub where we could play darts and practise. At the front, in the main bar, it was chaos. On a Thursday the place would be heaving with Irish – in those days you got paid every Thursday, so they'd be in the front drinking and our lads would be in the back playing darts. Every week these Irish lads would kick off. There'd be mass brawls inside the pub and on the pavement outside. Then they'd be back at the bar minutes later, bloodied and bruised with their arms rounds each other, knocking more booze back! Because of this the turnover of landlords was high. Some just couldn't cope – and added to this many of them would end up getting robbed or beaten up by the customers. Our darts champion Brian Kearney, who was a good mate of mine but has now died, used to get in with a new landlord and help serve behind the bar. Once he'd got on friendly terms, and he did this to every landlord who worked there, he'd take him out for an Indian, and while they were at the restaurant Brian's accomplices would be in the boozer robbing it. It was the norm: every few weeks we'd be playing darts and you'd hear Brian say, 'I'm going for an Indian tonight, lads.' I'd say, 'For Christ's sake, here we go again.'

One bloke came in, yet another new landlord, and he had these two big Alsatian dogs with him, fierce beasts they were, but I never got to see this guy. He moved in on a Tuesday and announced to the whole pub, 'I've heard same of your landlords here have been done over a few times. Well, you won't fucking do me with these two Alsatians here.'

The following night word got round that the new landlord thought he was a bit of a hard nut, so this geezer walked into the pool room, took the cue off a bloke who was playing, walked through to the front of the bar where the new landlord was serving and smacked him straight across the top of his head with it. He split his head right open and fractured his skull. As the landlord lay slumped on the floor his attacker said to him, 'Where are your fucking dogs now, pal?'

The Alsatians were locked in the back. They couldn't exactly roam around the bar. This poor bloke only lasted a day and a half.

Not all the landlords before that were bad. We had this great couple come in who were gay. They were fantastic and within days of them arriving we had the cleanest pub in London. They were there with their feather dusters and cleaning cloths, a bucket and a mop. The pub didn't have a speck of dust in it all the time they ran it. One of these lads had a false arm. All our darts team knew about it, apart from Brian. We were all in the pub one night having a bit of after-time and Brian got a bit rough with this gay and started pulling him about. He was having a laugh, but going a bit over the top, as he was inclined to do when he'd had a few beers. He ended up pulling this gay by the arm and it came off in Brian's hand. Brian just stared at this arm in bewilderment. His face went white and his mouth opened but no words came out. He honestly thought he'd pulled this bloke's arm off. He looked at it for about half a minute and said, 'What the fuck?'

The rest of us were gone. I was on the floor rolling about with laughter. It was the funniest thing I have ever seen. In the end the one-armed gay landlord said, 'Give me my arm back,' snatched it off Brian and put it back in the socket. Brian looked at him like a dog does when it's trying to understand his owner, his head tilting one way and then the other. I was desperately trying not to wet myself.

But Brian was the Red Lion. He was its main character, the guy you always looked forward to seeing when he walked through the door, and he sorted out a few problems there.

We had this old bloke in the pub and he was a real nasty sod, a bit mean like TV's Steptoe. On Thursday nights, when the Irish came to the pub with their money, four of them would play cards. Every week they went through the same routine: they'd play cards, drink, drink drink, fight, fight, fight, make up, go to the bar, large vodka, large vodka, large vodka, large vodka, and back to the card table. This old bloke was the pot man, which meant he collected the empties in return for a couple of free pints. When these Irish got so pissed they didn't really know what they were doing, or when they were fighting each other, this old bloke would pinch one of their vodkas and down it in one before putting the glass back on the table. Brian, who occasionally worked behind the bar at this time, spotted this old sod doing it, so he got a vodka glass and filled it with white cleaning fluid and put it to the right of where this pot man normally stood at the bar. Sure enough this old sod spotted what he thought was an untouched double vodka, picked it up and downed it in one. His face said it all. He was in agony, it burnt his mouth and his throat and he only just managed to open the toilet door to throw up. There was spew and excrement all over the place. It nearly killed him, but it did teach him not to steal anyone's drink again.

Brian also taught this other bloke a lesson. He was a white witch, a real weirdo who played darts for us, and he had this dog which he kept in the back of his van and never let out. This mad dog wasn't treated right. It'd get a tin of dog food and some water in the back of the van, and would be left in there twenty-four hours a day, seven days a week. Its muck would be thrown out of the van into the road. This used to upset me, so I'm glad he got his comeuppance. Brian got him because he was a greedy sod. He played in the Thursday league for us and at the end of the game the sandwiches came out. This bloke would take more than his fair share, and then if there were four sandwiches left at the end he'd grab them all and stuff them down his throat. This happened week after week until Brian decided enough was enough. He got some toothpicks, snapped them into pieces and put the little bits in the sandwiches, warning the rest of us not to touch them. This white witch immediately went for these sandwiches, started chewing them, and screamed as a toothpick went straight through the roof of his mouth. There was blood everywhere. He was in agony, desperately trying to prise this pick out of his mouth but having no luck. He had to go to hospital in the end. It taught him never to steal the sandwiches again.

Later in life Brian became a train driver, but that did him in. A couple of people jumped in front of his train on two separate occasions and psychologically he couldn't handle it. He had to go and give evidence to an inquest and talk about the ordeal in front of the grieving family. It traumatised him for life; he was never the same bloke. It broke him mentally.

The rest of the guys I played with were just normal fellas. There was Les Rothwell who was happily married with a couple of kids; Robbie Tarr, who worked in a printing factory; a clever bloke called Clive Jennings who ran a bookies; and a lad called Nigel who worked on planes, testing the stress on wings – I could never work out how aeroplanes wings didn't snap off mid-flight and I nearly wet myself during one bumpy flight, but he said to me, 'What are you worrying about? It's impossible to snap a wing off a plane. It doesn't happen.' Comforting words, but I still haven't fully conquered my fear of flying.

Then there was our treasurer Tony Miles, a lovely old bloke who couldn't play darts but used to love coming out with us. He was a wealthy businessman, so we knew we could trust him with the money. In all the pubs in the league each player would pay their subs every week, and anything the team won would be shared out at the end of the year – but every year you could guarantee at least two or three treasurers from other pubs would run off with the money. Our treasurer was retired and wealthy and didn't need our cash, so we knew he'd never do a runner. A black toe did for him in the end. His toe went black and he ignored it. By the time he went to the doctors they had to take it off, but found gangrene had spread to his leg so amputated that below the knee. However, it just carried on going up and up and up, until eventually he died. What a stupid way to go. If you have a black toe, you sort it out.

Finally there was me, the madman of the team. At seventeen I began to believe I was going to get somewhere in the darts world and I began to tell people I was going to be world champion. That became my sole aim. I was probably a bit too flash for my own good, but I was the main man in our league. I was number one on the team, their best player.

Unfortunately, coming into the last game of the season I wasn't number one in the Super League in terms of games won, and there was a prize for the player who won the most games. Although I'd played twenty-seven games of singles – which was one leg of 301, start and finish on a double – and had won all of my games, so too had another guy called Keith Duffy. We had to play his team, the Jerry House, in the last game of the season. It was nine players to each team and each opposing player is paired off at random by their names being drawn out of a hat. I knew this Duffy would beat any other player on our team apart from me, and I didn't want to share first prize with him, so I was desperate to draw him. First out of the hat was Duffy. Second out of the hat ... Bristow. The place erupted. This would be the play-off to decide the best player in the league, and I murdered him. I let everyone know I was the best and it was a fantastic feeling, but I was a small fish in a very large pond, and I wanted to conquer that larger pond. Two significant developments were to help me in this, the British Darts Organisation, otherwise known as the BDO, and television.

The BDO was founded in January 1973 by Ollie Croft and his wife Lorna, together with three others – Sam Hawkins, Jim Sweeney and Martin O'Sullivan – in the front room of Ollie's home in Muswell Hill. It was made up of sixty-four member counties in Britain, and organised tournaments – and still does – for grassroots players right the way up to professional level. It set all the rules from the size of the throwing oche to the height and dimensions of the board. The whole system was built on a pyramid structure and players worked their way up. The pinnacle was the World Masters, which preceded the World Championship. Other major tournaments included the various Open events, the World Cup and many others, which soon began to attract the interest of the TV executives together with sponsors and, as a result, bigger prize money for the players.

This was where it was at, and by the age of seventeen I was going places. The BDO and television came at exactly the right moment for me. Darts was taking off. It was big business.

THREE

County Darts

At seventeen, money and fame proved too tempting so I stopped playing local league darts and concentrated more on cash tournaments and playing Super League. Every weekend I'd be playing these tournaments, desperate to win first prize which in some cases was over £500, a lot back then, and all the while playing the big-name players for money beforehand so that I had something to fall back on if I got knocked out.

One tournament I played in was at Gatwick with another new player on the scene called Bobby George. Bobby was a confident 29-year-old floor layer, yet to achieve notoriety by coming on stage wearing a crown and cloak and holding a candelabra in his teeth to the sound of Queen's 'We Are the Champions'. Bobby and I played in the pairs tournament. This was the first time we'd been paired together, and because he was a mate I was looking forward to it. I went up to the oche and threw my first dart, which bounced out, threw the second and that bounced out, then threw the third which bounced out too. I just stared at the board, I couldn't believe it. Bobby had his head in his hands. Next it was his turn. He went bounce out, bounce out, bounce out. I couldn't comprehend what was going on. It was incredible.

'We've scored sod all with six darts,' I said.

'Don't worry, son,' Bobby replied. 'We can only get better from here.'

I was shell-shocked. I'll tell you now, that will not have happened anywhere else in the world. In the history of darts nobody has got six bounce outs on the trot. It's just not going to happen. It wasn't a bad board either, and it wasn't as though we were throwing bad darts, we were just hitting the wires. We got over it, however, and went on to win, and since then we've always been close pals. I like straight-talking blokes, blokes who don't talk about you behind your back, and Bobby would never do that. He is very honest.

We made arrangements to go to the Sussex Open shortly after that. It was £500 for the winner, and there were twelve hundred players in this place. To give us a better chance of winning good money we decided to split it if either of us won. On the day Bobby came to pick me up – I never drive, I can't even drive now, I like a drink you see so what's the point in driving? I'm probably the only bloke in Britain who had a fleet of cars but could never drive any of them – and I immediately realised he was suffering from a monumental hangover, which wasn't a great start. I got to his van and it was filthy inside. He'd put a plastic sheet on the passenger seat for me to sit on so I didn't get my clothes dirty. I was carrying my shirt to play in which was all clean and ironed and on a hanger, but when I got in the van there was nowhere to hang it without it getting dirty so I had to hold it up with one hand for the whole journey.

He got us there in one piece – after telling me he'd had no sleep because he'd been at a family party all night. This is typical Bobby: he didn't need to go to the Open, but because he'd made a promise to pick me up he went. He always honoured his promises, despite being wrecked on the day. When we got there Bobby went straight to the bar and had a couple of beers to try and sort his head out.

'You still look like shit,' I told him, just before he was about to go on. Then he went up to the oche and got beaten first round. That was not supposed to happen. He was one of the favourites like me, but he was totally and utterly gone from the night before. As soon as his match finished he said to me: 'I'm going for a kip.'

So off he went for a sleep and I played all day until I got down to the last eight. The last eight played on-stage, rather than off-stage where the knockout boards were lined up. Off-stage you play almost shoulder to shoulder with other competitors. There's more room on stage, which I liked. There was a table where you could put your beer and fags and it was much more civilised. I breezed through to the final, playing sublime darts, and halfway through the final I heard a loud voice shout, 'Go on, my son!' It was Bobby, who after seven hours had woken up and was now feeling as fresh as a daisy. I won it and in those days you got paid in cash. I had £500 and of course I had to give Bobby half of this. He was rubbing his hands together and going, 'Lovely jubbly.'

I couldn't believe it. I didn't know whether to laugh or cry. As we drove off from the venue I said to him, 'That has got to be the easiest £250 you have ever earned in your life. You drove me here, lost your game and drove me back.'

Bobby just started laughing and said, 'Don't worry about it, son. Next time I'll pull you through,' and that was the way he was and always has been, a favour for a favour. There is nothing crooked about Bobby.

We did a charity event shortly after that for a bloke's widow. Her husband had been decapitated in a horrific car accident. He wasn't insured and had left her with one or two debts, so a few darts players got together and held a charity bash to help her out. After the event Bobby said to the organiser, 'How much did we raise?'

'Over £500,' this guy replied.

'Great,' said Bobby, and he was really chuffed.

A few weeks later he bumped into the widow and she thanked him for what he'd done. 'Those two hundred pounds will come in really handy,' she said.

'Two hundred pounds,' Bobby replied.

'Yes, two hundred, thank you very much and thank all the players when you see them.'

With that they said goodbye – only Bobby didn't go home, he went straight to this organiser's house.

He knocked on the door and the organiser's wife answered. She said he was out and didn't know when he'd be back. 'That's OK,' said Bobby, 'I'll wait for him inside.' And he went in her house, parked himself on her sofa and waited for six hours until this bloke came home.

Suffice to say he got the extra £300 and went round to this woman's house to give it to her, apologising profusely for what had happened. The poor old girl was overwhelmed.

That's Bobby. He doesn't like dishonesty; you have to be straight with him.

Seventeen was when it all started to happen for me. When I wasn't playing at exhibitions and Opens I was playing Super League darts for a pub called the General Picton at King's Cross and aiming to get enough wins, and points, to get me into the county side; that was the next step up the BDO ladder towards my dream of becoming World Champion. My life was darts, darts, darts. It was a total 100 per cent commitment. Super League was on a Monday, but you didn't have to play Super League every week. For sixteen weeks I'd play in a tournament at Hersham Social Club where the weekly winner would pick up a prize. Dad and I would get the train from Waterloo to Weybridge and walk the half mile to the club. After it had finished we'd get the last train back to Waterloo and walk the remaining eight miles home, often with a prize like a bread bin or a Teasmade that I'd won. We got pulled up by the cops one night.

They said: 'Where did you get that from, and why are you walking round with it under your arm at midnight?'

I told them, 'I won it playing darts.'

'Yeah, right,' they said. But they didn't nick us for some reason. Nine times out of ten they probably would have, though.

Although I was earning money from darts it wasn't enough for Dad and me to get a cab home, so we used to walk, but that was the norm then. I used to walk to King's Cross every Friday night with a guy called Andy Pascoe. He lived in Walthamstow and would get a cab to my house in Stoke Newington, get out, and we'd walk the seven miles to King's Cross. Then we'd play in the pairs, more often than not win the prize money, have an Indian to celebrate, and walk back to my house where he'd get a cab home. I hated wasting the money I had on cabs, I'd got better things to spend it on, and all that walking kept me fit, which was an added bonus.

Playing darts as often and as well as I was doing meant

it didn't take me long to rack up enough points to make the county side, and I was picked for London B. This was a big step up for me. I knew all I had to do was win a couple of B games and they'd put me in the full county side, which, naturally, was London A. I'd already beaten the majority of the A squad, so I knew it was only a matter of time before I'd get in. My first county game with the B side was at Southall Labour Club in London where we played Devon B. We had a twelve-man team and there were twelve singles games of the best of three legs, 501 each game. I was down as last man on and thought that as I wouldn't be playing for another three hours I'd cheer the lads on. As I sat at the side watching we went one–nil up, two–nil, three–nil, four–nil, I was shouting 'Go on' and getting quite excited. This was good stuff. These lads were playing sensationally.

However when it got to five–nil and then six–nil I began to think: I hope somebody loses here. It was starting to play on my mind. County sides didn't do clean sweeps, ever! And if they were going to do one tonight, guess whose job it would be to nail it in the last game? As soon as it got to seven–nil I thought: Sod this, and went back on the practice board. I was getting worried thinking: Somebody for God's sake lose and take the pressure off me to do the clean sweep. But on it went, nine–nil, ten–nil. I just kept thinking this was stupid. Nobody wins twelve–nil in county games, it just doesn't happen. Next I hear a voice announce: 'And now representing London B ... Eric Bristow.'

It was eleven–nil! The tension as I walked up to the oche was unbelievable because everybody wanted the elusive clean sweep. Up I went and I was nervous. I never get nervous playing darts – even when I later appeared in World Championship finals I didn't get nervous – but here I was sweating, which I never did. I knew that if I lost there was a good chance, a very good chance, I'd be dropped for the next game. It was as though my whole future was flashing before my eyes because the sods on my team had all won. Thankfully I won the opening leg and just needed one more to make it two–nil for my game and twelve–nil for London B. I had my chance on a 118 checkout. I went treble sixteen, double nineteen, double sixteen, thank you very much. The feeling I had was more of relief than jubilation. I've been less tense in major tournaments.

In the next London B game I won my match and was launched into the A team. They had a great set of players like Charlie Hicks, Jackie Ambler, and Dave Pithouse, and Alan Glazier who was one of the greats of the 1960s and could have been as well known as I eventually was if darts had taken off ten years earlier than it did.

The county games were brilliant because I got to see different parts of the country. You'd have the A and B sides, men's and women's teams, travelling to towns and cities all over Britain to play and go out on a Saturday night. We'd end up splitting off into different groups and then all meeting back at the hotel at the end of the evening. Some came back and had been in trouble, some hadn't. A lot of people don't like Londoners, and we weren't the quietest blokes in the world so that didn't help. However, a lot of fellas didn't mess with us, like they don't mess with rugby players, because we were huge – you wouldn't want a darts player to fall on you, never mind have a fight with you.

Back then I was a lager boy. Later on I had my top-shelf nutty moments, but I never really drank spirits when I was playing county darts. I had to give up lager, though, about thirteen years ago because every morning I'd wake up and spew bile and this thick yellow muck. It was happening every time I drank the stuff. So I gave it up and swapped to Guinness.

My debut for London A was against the West of England who played at a club near Bristol. They were a great side with fantastic players like Leighton Rees, Alan Evans and Mike Butt. It was going to be a real battle and we went there to find twelve hundred people were in this place. I played Mike Butt, one of their fancied players, and won two–nil, but I played well below my game. I had an off night and finished both games on double one. London A drew that match six-all in front of the biggest crowd I had ever played in front of, but I wasn't nervous. I loved getting up there, especially when some of their home supporters started booing me. I just played up to them. It gave me a rush.

Booing was something I was going to have to get used to. And I wasn't shy. I loved the TV cameras being at certain county games. It was good for the game and it gave me a buzz knowing I was on the telly. The first TV tournament I won was again when I was seventeen. It was at the Seashore Holiday Camp in Great Yarmouth, and I was in the amateur tournament. You had to progress through to the last eight to get to play on television the next day. I killed them all. No amateur could touch me. After us was the televised Pro-8 tournament which represented the top eight best darts professionals in the country. I stayed behind for that and as their names were introduced I kept thinking: I've beaten him, I've beaten him, I've killed him, and on it went. I sat there watching players I knew I could beat playing on telly for prize money of up to £1,000 that I could have pocketed. I had practised with some of them before they went on telly and had beaten them easily. These were top professionals who resented being beaten by a young teenage upstart. I had my winnings from the amateur tournament, and they were going to earn something even if they got knocked out first round in the Pro-8. If they started getting cocky with me I'd say to them, 'Well OK, what we will do is this, if you think you can beat me. Whoever wins the game gets to keep both the cheques.'

I'd look them straight in the eyes and see fear. Then I knew I had them, I knew they were frightened of me, and in 1975 I wasted no time in telling anyone who listened how great I was going to be. I was getting lots of practice and getting better all the time because in between the Super League matches and county games the BDO would organise all these tournaments at holiday camps as well, like the one at Seashore. One of my favourites was at Camber Sands where for one week of the year the whole place would fill up with darts players. I went with my dad and got beaten in the final of the singles. I got £250 for that, and won in the four-man team event for which we each got £100. I'd earned £350 for a week's work which kept me in beer for a while. On the last day we went home on the train and that night Mum did all our washing, ready for the next morning when we'd be on a train again to another tournament, in Prestatyn.

I always remember Prestatyn because when we got there I met this gypsy boy called Kim Brown, a proper King of the Gypsies sort of bloke, a real hardcase, who was with his mate Chris. He had a tattoo across his neck with the words 'Cut Here' on it; they were a rough lot. These two came over to me while I was sitting with my dad having a drink and said, 'We want you to play this bloke for £500.'

'What you on about?' I said. 'I've only got about a hundred and fifty on me.'

But they were adamant. The guy they wanted me to play was called John Parry and he'd never been beaten. 'We want you to play him for £500,' they repeated, and they weren't going to take no for an answer.

'What happens if I lose this game?' I said.

'Nothing,' they replied.

'So if I win, you're going to give me £500, and if I lose the game you're not bothered?'

'That's right.'

'Right, I'm up for this,' I said to my dad, rubbing my hands.

But he was worried. 'You have to be careful here, son, you don't mess with people like them,' he warned, and I could see his face lined with anxiety.

'Nah, I'll be all right, no problem,' I said.

I agreed to play this guy the best out of five at 3001. They were long legs. I knew you had to be good to win long legs and no one was as good as me – as I proved. I hammered him three–nil and these gypsies gave me my £500 winnings. I was jubilant and spent the rest of the weekend getting smashed and feeling flush. I then found out that these crafty sods had won £2,500 on it. I didn't know whether to laugh or cry.

By far the biggest buzz of 1975, however, was when sixty-four of us paid £25 each to play a knockout tournament, with the winner getting all the money plus a three-week trip to America to play in darts tournaments over there with fifty-four other Brits who were making the trip. I *had* to win that tournament, and did, fairly easily, beating Alan Glazier in the final, scooping the dough and a return ticket to the States in the process.

This was to be my first taste of a jet-set lifestyle that was going to dictate my life over the next three decades. There were three tournaments to play over three weeks: one in Los Angeles, one in 'Frisco and another in Vallejo. The first words my dad said to me when I won were: 'I'm coming with you.' I was only seventeen. He wanted to look after me and keep me on the straight and narrow, so he borrowed some money and off we went. Some of the players I had beaten to get there also flew over, but they had to fund their own trip. I had my tickets paid plus $800 to spend from the money I'd won. When we arrived in LA all the darts community who lived there put us up in different houses.

Dad and I were with a couple called Malcolm and Mary-Ann Harper who had a beautiful big house with a swimming pool; I'd never seen anything like it in my life. And if the houses dwarfed the ones I'd seen at home, the darts tournaments, which were played from Friday to Sunday, were something else. There were hundreds of boards lined up and hundreds of players playing singles, pairs, mixed pairs, four-man teams, and all for money.

As the tournament progressed, and as more players got knocked out, so more of these boards became free. I was practising on one of these boards when a top player called Nicky Virachkul, originally from Thailand but with American status, said to me, 'So, you're the London Lip are you? So you think you're better than me, do you?' and all this verbal nonsense – this was before I was known as the Crafty Cockney; back then I was called lots of names, not all of them good.

I said, 'Look, you don't want to play me for money, you're not good enough to play me for money.'

My dad was at the side going, 'Leave it out, son; we've only just got here.'

He was too late. I agreed to play Nicky for $200, and Dad said, 'No, no, no, we've only got eight hundred.' His face had gone white at this point.

'Don't panic, Dad,' I said. 'I'll beat him.'

I played him best of fifteen at 501, and I beat him eight–one. My dad was elated.

Then Nicky said, 'I'll play you again, same format, same amount of money.'

Again Dad became anxious. 'Nah, don't play him again,' he said. He'd got the money and he was happy.

Nicky didn't have the cash on him so he went round his mates and raised the two hundred dollars, came back to me and said, 'Come on, I'll play you again.'

So I played him again and won eight legs to five. Now, instead of $800 dollars, we had $1,200, and we'd hardly started the three-week trip. Dad kept hold of the money. There was no point me having it because I could hardly buy anything there. I couldn't order drinks for a start because you had to be twenty-one and over to do that. So I got drinks sneaked to me: cokes with vodka in, that sort of thing.

I won the singles in Los Angeles and was runner-up in the four-man team which included Leighton Rees. Then we all packed our bags and headed for 'Frisco where we weren't put up by anyone but had to get hotels. This didn't bother Dad and me because by then we were loaded, and we got more loaded as the fortnight progressed because I won the singles in 'Frisco and was only beaten in the final in Vallejo.

It was great, one of the best three weeks of my life, but by far the biggest eye-opener for me was the American women. They were nuts, especially one group of about forty or fifty women, most of whom were married to rich Americans, but who used to spend the three weeks hopping from tournament to tournament and having sex with as many British darts players as they could get their hands on. They'd all meet up and mark their conquests out of ten. The Brits always got marked down. Most of them got one out of ten. We could hear them in the tournament bar talking about how good or bad a shag we were.

It didn't take me long to get into them. I'd be shagging this woman one night and the next night drinking with her husband. It was so free and easy it felt weird compared to the stuffiness and sexual backwardness of seventies England. I'd get women coming on to me and I'd be thinking: Hold on a minute, love, you're married; I just played your husband and beat him earlier on. The next minute I'd be shagging her and the following night I'd be going out for a meal with her and her old man, but I was seventeen and it was simply a case of 'Whatever.' At that age you get it where you can. I don't know if I got one out of ten, but then again, I didn't give a monkey's.

Everybody was at it, including players like Bobby George, who got caught out one night. It was in an LA hotel on a Friday night. We were all on a board, practising, and I could see this blonde woman eyeing up Bobby, and he was eyeing her up too. After a while the boys and I noticed he had disappeared. He was due to play and everybody was looking for him. Suddenly he appeared and he was soaking, absolutely dripping wet. Five minutes later the blonde appeared and she was sodden as well. Bobby sidled up to a group of us and whispered, 'You won't believe this, lads: I was out there giving her one on the hotel lawn and the sprinklers came on. We got soaked. They were everywhere these things, we couldn't escape them.'

The rest of us were in stiches, trying to picture Bobby desperately trying to pull his pants up as the water hit him. But this woman's husband wasn't laughing. He had obviously twigged what had happened and was giving Bobby the eyeballs from across the room. I made it worse by shouting, 'Bob, do you want a drink? Nah, you look like you've had one already, mate.'

From that first American trip I came home with a very special memento. There was a bar in Santa Monica owned by an English bloke called Les. He was a millionaire who lived on Hollywood Boulevard and he had three all-you-can-eat delis to go with this pub – the darts boys loved these delis and boy could they eat. Les loved having us Brits over and would organise a party at his house for us all. In his bar he had all these shirts lined up that you could buy. They had pictures on the back and different names. I was attracted to a bright red shirt that had a picture of a policeman on it and a Union Flag. Emblazoned across it were the words Crafty Cockney. It just seemed appropriate to what I represented. The Cockney equated to my London roots and Crafty fitted because I was a cocky little so and so. So I brought five of them back home with me, went on telly wearing one and the rest is history. Those shirts were probably the best things I have ever bought.

The pub was not so lucky. It was sold to an Indian guy who called it the Londoner; then it was knocked down, and now all that remains is a car park. Les's story is also tragic. After selling up he moved to Canada and made even more money, but his wife ended up killing herself. He found her in the car on his drive with a hosepipe attached to the exhaust. To be fair she was a bit of a scatterbrain and wasn't all there in the head. He ended up moving to Mexico. I saw him recently, and he gave me a Crafty Cockney leather jacket.

I said to him, 'What a lovely present.'

'That'll be £150,' he replied.

What a cheeky sod. This is a bloke who is a multi-millionaire. I paid him for it.

There were lots of English pubs in Santa Monica and every bar we went in had these Crafty Cockney style shirts. All the darts lads loved these bars because you could get things like fish and chips, and on Sundays they did roast beef and Yorkshire puds. It was just like being at home.

That was my first taste of America. I went there with my dad, we had $800, and we came back with a lot more. For three weeks I was completely off the rails. How I won two out of three tournaments I'll never know, it was crackers, but one thing was for certain: I had played on a much bigger stage than anywhere back at home, played the best players from all over the globe, and I had stuffed them. It was time to take the next step up the ladder.

FOUR

England

In darting terms I was a freak. Most darts players mature in their late twenties to early thirties, but everything happened for me when I was a teenager. There were other good young players around, but none of them were a patch on me. I was making money from darts, spending it as fast as I made it, and all the time I was on the road playing tournament after tournament, then coming home with packets of fags and crates of Guinness for my nan. There was none of this saving up lark. There were so few people at my age with a pocketful of money and the chance to see the world that I just wasn't going to let it slip by. You have all these people who work all their lives, they save up their pensions and tell everyone that when they retire they're going to travel. Half of them don't even make it to retirement age and the ones that do tend to have health problems so they hardly leave the country. My philosophy was formed when I was seventeen and starting to be successful at darts: I was going to enjoy it while it lasted and sod the future. To a certain extent I still live to that philosophy today.

I lived for the here and now, and at that time darts was getting bigger by the month. Tournaments were being televised all over the place and TV bosses couldn't get enough of us. There was the World Masters, and Butlins Grand Masters which was in Birmingham; Anglia TV covered a tournament at the Seashore Holiday Village in Caister; all of a sudden there were about fifteen tournaments all attracting good viewing figures and with relatively good prize money on offer. In between there were the non-televised events which were still attractive, with decent payouts. Then there was the annual American three-week beano, which was basically party time, followed by Opens in Denmark, Sweden and Finland. By the time I was eighteen I was a full-time darts player who would look at his diary on the first of January and see that eighty days had been filled already with tournaments, and that was without pencilling in the exhibitions where the majority of the money was made. Also, I still had to play Super League on Mondays to get my ranking points.

My team won the Super League in 1975 and I had great averages in that and in my county games. All the averages of all the players were forwarded to the BDO, who, in April 1975, chose me to play for England as part of a fifteen-man team. I'd like to say I was jumping for joy and bouncing off the walls when I got the call-up, but I wasn't. I expected it. It didn't come as a shock to me because I was winning everything. It would have been more of a shock not to be picked. I just told my pals and we all went out to celebrate. Underneath I was proud as punch though because it's great to get an England call-up, whatever the sport. If you play tiddly-winks and you enjoy it and you get a call to represent England at tiddlywinks you have made it. It's a pinnacle.

And what a team we had! There were myself, John Lowe, Cliff Lazarenko, Bobby George, Dave Whitcombe and Tony Brown, to name but a few. We didn't get beaten very often.

Playing for England was mad. I was with the proper boys now, hardcore boys who could drink. I'm a boozer, I like a drink, and I have drunk with the best, but when it came to an important darts tournament I'd say no. I wouldn't get drunk in the week leading up to the tournament because I wanted to remain fresh – I'd save it until after, when I'd won and got the cheque. And I know when to stop. I know when enough is enough – but very occasionally I would get caught out, and the man who caught me out was Cliff Lazarenko. Big Cliff, as he is known, is a two times winner of the British Open and a four times World Championship semi-finalist, but perhaps his biggest claim to fame is his prodigious drinking ability, which still amazes me to this day. No one could compete with Big Cliff and anyone who tried to take him on, or even keep up with him, would end up a gibbering mess.

Cliff caught me on my way to the Canadian Open with him. It was twenty-four hours I'll never forget but find hard to remember. The stewardess informed me just before I boarded the plane to Canada that I'd been upgraded to first class free of charge, but I said I wouldn't go unless Cliff came with me. That was my first mistake. Suddenly we were both sitting in luxury for the twelve-hour flight, and the champagne came out. Cliff likes his champers, it's one of his favourites and he can drink it like water – so you don't give him free champagne, that's just stupid. I'd already started to think I was going to be in a bit of trouble because we'd had four or five pints in the airport bar before we flew, but off we went and it was champagne, champagne, champagne. Then we got the meal and there was more champagne, champagne, champagne. Then they ran out. There was only me and Cliff drinking it and we'd gone through twelve bottles. The stewardess told Cliff there was no champagne left, but would he like something else? That was when he started clapping his hands together.

If you know Big Cliff, you know that when he starts clapping his hands together you're in trouble. Basically you've had it, because that is a signal that he's really beginning to enjoy himself and he wants you to join in the fun. So he starts ordering drink after drink after drink: 'We'll have a Cointreau,' he said. Next it was Bailey's on ice, then Southern Comfort. He didn't bother asking me what I wanted, he just ordered for himself and then got me one – and he was ordering every ten minutes. We were heading for a place called St John which was a short fifteen-minute connecting flight from Toronto where we were landing. All I could think when the plane touched down was how the hell was I going to get through customs, because I was smashed. While Cliff put his smart jacket on and adjusted his tie, I was in the toilet splashing my face with cold water in a desperate bid to sober up. Cliff appeared as if he'd been drinking apple juice.

As we were leaving the plane we said goodbye to the stewardess who said, 'In all the years I have done this job I have never seen anybody drink like you two, it has been an unbelievable experience. It has been a pleasure serving you two gentlemen.'

I knew as soon as she said it that I was in big, big trouble. I could feel the alcohol literally swimming around my brain. I was seeing double and when I said goodbye the words wouldn't come out of my mouth properly. I just grinned at her like an idiot. It was the only thing I could think of doing.

Fortunately I managed to get through customs without any problems, we got on the connecting flight and a few minutes later we were in St John. As we reached the hotel in our taxi Cliff said to me, 'Right, upstairs, quick wash and a change and I'll see you in the bar, Brissy, in twenty-five minutes.'

'Right,' I slurred.

I had a quick shower, put my shirt on, put my darts in the top pocket and I was downstairs. The shower had sobered me up a bit but it was still only seven in the evening. We had a couple in the hotel bar, then we went for a throw in a nearby British Legion. We'd always look for these sorts of places because we knew they'd have a dart board in them.

I was still pissed. Those couple of beers in the hotel had topped me right up again. I was wrecked. I ordered a pint and stood at the oche. After a few throws I said, 'I don't feel like playing, Cliff.'

'Nor do I,' he replied. 'Fuck it.'

This was my second mistake. I should have kept on practising. We went back to the bar and Cliff was off ordering drinks for us again.

'Any heavy rock round here?' he said to the barman after a few more jars. Cliff loves his heavy rock. We were told to go to a rock bar just down the road and it was all boom, boom, boom, boom and crashing guitars. I really didn't need it, it was giving me a headache, so I started playing some guys at pool for three dollars a pop, and beating them. Every time I won I passed the money down to Cliff and he bought the drinks. I got in a rhythm after a bit, I had my second wind, and was downing beers and spirits one after the other – and all the while beating these blokes at pool. They must have been pretty poor players to lose to me, the state I was in. At the end of the night the band's singer announced, 'We'd like to thank Eric and Cliff for the drinks,' and the whole place cheered, clapped and slapped us both on the back. Cliff, with all the money I was winning, was using it to buy the band free drinks, and anyone else who happened to want one. I looked at him and said, 'You cheeky sod,' but he just shrugged.

We left and went into a couple more late-night bars and had a few more drinks, by which time I was having trouble standing up. I'd completely lost it: I didn't know what day it was, I didn't know where we were, what country we were in, or anything. We finally arrived in a bar which had eighteen optics lined up, all different spirits.

'Right, Eric,' Cliff said, 'let's finish off here. We'll go through these optics starting from the left and then we'll call it a day.'

So we had vodka and something, brandy and something else, whisky, gin, rum, Bacardi . . . and on and on it went until we had done the lot: eighteen rounds of eighteen different drinks, all big measures compared to what you're served back in England.

Then Cliff discovered there was an Indian open nearby. I don't remember anything about this at all, but I do remember waking up the next morning to go to the toilet and seeing this half-eaten curry on a chair. I don't remember buying it or eating it, and I can't believe I managed to get back to my room, but it was there on the chair.

And it stayed there for another day and a half because for the next thirty-six hours I couldn't get out of bed. Cliff knocked on my door at eight in the morning, asking if I was going down for breakfast. He was fine, but I couldn't move. I had alcohol poisoning and was shaking like a dog having a dump. Looking back I should've gone to hospital, but I dealt with it in my room – it was just water, water, water, water, water, water, one glass after the other. I did the same in Las Vegas a few years later. I had caught the gambling bug and was at the tables for twenty-eight hours drinking White Russians one after the other – but I won twelve thousand dollars so it didn't matter. When I'd finished I went to bed and passed out – another day and a half gone.

Cliff never gets hangovers. You didn't mess with Cliff when it came to drink. To watch was to enjoy. He got me again, years later, in a Tenants Pilsner TV tournament at a big Crest Hotel up in Scotland. I should've beaten Lowey in the semi-final and Cliff should have won his semi, but we both missed our darts for the double and victory and were knocked out. We were gutted and immediately hit the bar where he started ordering large Southern Comforts for us both, one after the other, bang, bang, bang, bang, bang. I don't really do spirits; I never really have done. At the end of it I don't remember going to bed. The next day the shaking dog was back and I couldn't move, save for lurching to the bathroom to drink water out of the tap. I never tried to match him drink for drink again after that. It took me days to recover from those benders, and even when I thought I was over the hangover and the poisoning I didn't feel right for a good seventy-two hours afterwards. It spoiled the darts really, because it was only when I flew home that I started to feel normal again. I wonder sometimes how my liver didn't pack in. I could've died in bed and they'd have done the autopsy, opened me up and thought: This geezer deserved to die. When a stewardess who has been in the job for a long time tells you she's never seen drinking like it in her life then you should reckon that you've won the game. But I, being an idiot, had carried on drinking for another twelve hours. It meant nothing to Cliff. He's an animal when he gets going. Drinks to him are like what a box of Pringles is to you and me. He knocks them back like we'd eat one Pringle after another after another. In a tournament in Jersey he once got forty bottles of cheap wine, put the plug in the bath, poured in the bottles, got a glass and just drank out of the bath.

There is nobody in the world who can beat Cliff for drinking. Many have tried but all have failed. We were playing an England game in Merthyr Tydfil in Wales, a mining town that was as rough as they came, and there was myself, Big Cliff, John Lowe, Tony Brown and Paul

Gosling from Cornwall in a local bar. I was the smallest bloke there at six foot two inches, boozing with four hardcore drinkers. We'd order five pints then ten minutes later another five pints, ten minutes after that another five pints. This Welsh bloke, who was sitting at the other end of the bar, was watching us and he suddenly piped up, 'So you boys think you can drink do you? You boys think you can handle your beer,' and all that sort of nonsense.

I turned to Cliff and said, 'Look, Cliff, you sort him out. I can't be arsed. I ain't in the mood for this twat.'

So Cliff, being as nice as nice can be, smiled and went up to this prat and said, 'Right, what are you drinking, boyo?'

The Welshman asked for a large brandy and lemon, so Cliff got two large ones, picked his up and downed it in one. Then he banged his glass on the table hard and asked the barman to line them up again. This Welsh bloke had been giving it plenty of verbals, so he didn't want to back down and tried to match Cliff brandy for brandy. Cliff would knock one back, bang the glass on the table, and go 'Your round.' The bloke – I may as well call him the victim – would buy the next one and the same thing happened again. Then Cliff bought a round and it went on and on for another thirty minutes at a rate of a drink every minute and a half. The rest of us just let them get on with it and talked among ourselves. I knew Cliff would sort him out. After about forty minutes we saw this guy trying to walk out of the pub, but he fell down the steps. Cliff watched him fall, turned to us, and said, 'Right, are you up for more lagers, boys?'

We then hit a disco across the road and some other bloke tried to take him on. Cliff had twelve doubles with this idiot and in the end the stupid sod didn't know what day it was.

Cliff was the daddy of drinkers, but I soon learned when to leave it alone. I've seen too many darts players hit the top shelf and they don't play any more. Initially they'd have a large brandy, just to steady their nerves before they went on stage, then six months later it would be two or three large brandies, then half a bottle of brandy, then a bottle. Where do you stop? And spirits are too easy to drink. With pints you can only drink so many – unless you're Andy Fordham who used to drink fifty-two bottles of Pils in a session. Now he can't drink any more because he has been ill. Basically he is knack-ered. If you're doing fifty-two bottles of Pils a night and you're on a ten-night tour, it's not going to do your body much good, is it?

The killers were the American tournaments which started at ten in the morning and finished at two the next morning. At two o'clock you'd have a few beers, be in bed for about three or four, and then up and ready for the next day's play which started at ten and off you went again, playing darts round the clock until two the next morning. If you were good you'd hardly be off the board and it would be a straight sixteen-hour shift; no food, just drinking, drinking, drinking, bed and up at eight to have breakfast. You'd start breakfast with a Bailey's in your coffee just to steady the shakes from the beer the night before. Then you'd have a couple of drinks before you got ready for the morning session at ten just to steady the nerves. This is something I don't miss at all. I don't think my stomach could do it any more. I don't want to drink four or five Bailey's before the start of a tournament. The adrenaline rush used to pull me through, but as soon as the last dart was thrown on a Sunday night to signal the end of the tournament it was like, Urgh! Thank Christ for that, it's over.

But then there were other Opens in Denmark and Sweden that were potentially worse. You'd go over there and the beer was stronger. Back home it was all Skol, Skona and Watney's at 3 per cent volume, but some of those beers in the Scandinavian countries were 7, 8 or 9 per cent proof, and they were cloudy. You had to be careful not to get caught by them. Six of our pints were only about three of theirs. It was vicious. If the strong beer didn't get you then Cliff might. I learned to keep away from him, or I'd go and have a drink with him for a couple of hours and that was that – but a couple of hours with Cliff could easily see you downing a dozen pints.

Funnily enough Cliff knew when to stop. You never

saw him drunk and you never saw him make a fool of himself. He was a great ambassador for darts. As was another of my England team mates John Lowe. He was a lot quieter than Cliff, but no less deadly when it came to drinking and darts. His record is fantastic. He won the World Championship in 1979, 1987 and 1993 – three different decades; he won the World Masters twice; two British Open titles and two British Matchplay championships; two World Cup Singles and three European Cup singles titles. He also played for England over a hundred times and captained them for seven years, a period when England were unbeaten.

It could have been a whole lot better for him without me on the scene. His record against me in majors was three wins and six defeats. If I wasn't around, he would have been the undisputed king of darts throughout the seventies and eighties, and that is one of the reasons why we didn't get on well initially. He saw me as this gobby young upstart out to steal his glory. The irony was that although we didn't really get on we used to play fantastic darts together in the England side, so much so that the England manager Ollie Croft paired us for the World Cups which were played every two years and which we won four times.

John and I were chalk and cheese. He was the quiet gentleman, a money man who looked after his dough, and I was a mad man who just liked to spend it. However, we were both after the same thing: we were both chasing glory. He was the only one who could stand in my way, and vice versa, and it was this that caused some resentment between us – but the good thing was it was a resentment born of rivalry. It kept us both at the top of our game. You don't want the top two in the world to be all pally, it wouldn't have looked right to the public. Even so, John was savvy enough to ask if I wanted to split our winnings during these years, and I agreed, because even though we didn't like each other we knew that if one of us went out in a big tournament, the other one would probably win it.

So we split for seven years and at the end of it John worked it out that there was about £800 difference between us, which was nothing. Then, after we stopped splitting in 1984, he played Keith Deller in the World Matchplay tournament where he managed a nine-dart finish. This was the first time it had ever been done on telly. Not only was I gutted that John was the first to do this, because I wanted to be the one, but I was doubly gutted when he won £102,000. Even at the World Championships we had been splitting the money, and now as soon as we stopped sharing the pot he went and did that. That wasn't a good moment for me.

He was a steady player; he'd go ton, ton, one-forty, ton. He had one gear and if you weren't on the top of your game he would just wear you down and put you to bed. This was how he won most games, and this is how he still wins them today. Although you could never really describe him as a one-eighty man, he never seemed to have an off day like the rest of us occasionally did.

Like Cliff he was good for the game. You could take the pair of them anywhere in the world and they would have a drink, be sociable, be nice and always looked presentable. They are professionals in every way. I was completely different. I'd see John at all these different venues, play with him, chat to him, but once it came to night-time and we were ready to hit the town he wasn't in my school. He had his own little group. Mine was the mad school, the disco school. Wherever we were, a group of us would hire limos or fancy cars to take us to the best disco in town where we'd have a bit of fun and check out the women. John and Cliff would go out for a meal and sink a few bottles of wine before going back to the hotel. If we were abroad and it was our last night my school wouldn't bother going to bed. We'd just hit a disco, get back to the hotel at about six in the morning, pack our bags and go home. Cliff and John would be all suited and booted and my lot would look in a right state.

The other main England player was Tony Brown. He really did suffer from being around at a time when there were too many good darts players on the scene, losing four times in the semi-final of the World Championship, twice to me and twice to Lowey. If it wasn't for me and John he might have had a couple of titles under his belt. He did achieve some success, however. He won the British Open in 1979 and Yorkshire Television's Indoor

League in 1979. Tony was in my King's Cross Super League team – he would come up from Dover every Monday night to play, which was a fair trek – but he just couldn't win the big tournaments on a regular basis. Eventually, in the early 1990s, he gave up darts and lives down Torquay way today. He made me laugh, though, back then because in every tournament we played he'd go on stage carrying a large bag. Out of this he'd pull a gin bottle, then a glass which he'd wipe with a cloth, then a box of chopped lemons, and finally half a dozen tonics. He'd then pour himself a G&T. It saved him a fortune in bar bills. I got on quite well with Tony because we played in the same Super League team for years. His only bad habit was that when he threw his last dart he'd move a little. I don't think this did him any favours in the long run.

I made my debut for England at the Tottenham Royal – the last time I'd been there people were being thrown from the balcony. When I got there on the day I discovered that the England team had a uniform. We all had to wear these white trousers, drainpipe trousers. I had these big boots on, with platform soles, and when I put the trousers on I looked like Coco the Clown.

I said to the team manager Ollie Croft, 'I'm not wearing these, pal.'

His reply was simple and to the point: 'You either wear these trousers or you don't play.'

That was the end of the conversation. There was no compromise, nothing. If I didn't wear them I was out. That was how Ollie ran the England team. If you didn't fit in with his way of thinking you were a goner. No matter how good your averages were, you simply wouldn't get picked. He was almost from the Brian Clough school of management in that there was only one way and that was his way. There was one guy who was good enough to play for England who never got picked because he insisted on always wearing a red sock and a yellow sock. That was the only reason why the England management team didn't select him, but would he wear normal socks? Would he hell! So he didn't play for England. Everybody is different, and I accept that, but if you are going on TV and representing your sport you don't go on with odd socks, looking like a wally. He was an idiot.

Darts was Ollie's game, and that was it. It was a case of my bat, my ball, nobody else's, and if you didn't do as he said you didn't play. That didn't mean we listened to everything he said. When we went to places like Australia and New Zealand he'd say to the players, 'I want you all in bed by twelve. No drinking after twelve.'

This used to wind us up and I'd say to him, 'Piss off, Ollie, don't talk to me like a bleeding headmaster.'

Then we'd hit the bar and Lowey and Tony Brown would be rolling with laughter.

Although Ollie was our team manager we couldn't be

managed because we were renegades. We'd have arguments with him. We were grown men who would be saying things to him like, 'We don't want to go to bed. It's too early for bed.' And he'd be adamant: 'I want you in bed by twelve. No later than twelve.' So off we'd trot to the pub until three in the morning, and four hours later we'd all be up having breakfast as nice as you like with not the merest hint of a hangover. We were professionals in darts and in drink.

On my debut I wore the clown outfit and we won. This was a great moment for me. I had longed for this – the chance to represent my country – and most of the games were in front of the TV cameras which I loved even more. I never got frightened or nervous when the telly lads turned up, and I could never understand players who did. I'd see them in the back room and in the hall before they were due to go on: first of all they'd go very quiet and then they'd go white. The only time I was ever nervous was in my youth, and it was never about darts or being on TV. It was when I used to wonder how I was going to get home in one piece, or when I had a rival gang after me. That was the hard part; that was where life was really tough. Playing for England was easy. This was what I had strived for and I wanted to be up there soaking up the adulation. Even when we played away in places like Scotland and the whole crowd was booing me and jeering and shouting obscenities at me I couldn't care less. In fact I actually liked it. We were England, they hated us, and only if we'd fallen off a chair and broken our necks would they have given us a big cheer. In their eyes the England shirt we wore meant we were worse than the devil. I used to love hitting 180s in Scotland. I'd turn round to them and they'd all be booing and I'd raise my hand, cup it to my ear and go 'What?'

The Scots were easily the most vocal, followed by the Welsh. It was and still is a win at all costs mentality with the Scots and they tried everything to put me off my game. One supporter shook my hand. When I pulled my hand away it was bleeding, and so was his. He'd put broken glass in his palm. Luckily I could still play darts. He wasn't so lucky; some of the bouncers took him outside and kicked the living daylights out of him. On another occasion a supporter patted me on the back of my head, which I thought was a little odd. Then I discovered he'd put itching powder down my collar so the game was postponed while I took my shirt off and washed it.

The supporters were out to get me because they knew I was good – everybody knew I was good – but to prove to myself just how good I was I had to win a big one. I set my sights on the Winmau World Masters. If I could win that I could say with justification that I was the best player in the world. This really was the tournament of tournaments. Not only did you have the best sixteen players in the world competing, you also had the best county players who had come through a knockout stage to qualify plus invited players from every nation across the globe. It was global darts on a massive scale, a real melting pot of talent.

In 1976 I had narrowly missed out on claiming a top-sixteen spot so had to go through the county qualifying rounds. I got beaten in the London play-off to a player I should have walloped. I played well, but he played at a level he has probably never bettered. As penance I went down to the West Centre Hotel in Fulham where the event was being staged and helped set the dart boards up. When I saw Ollie Croft I said to him, 'I'll help you set the gear up, but I'll never do this again because next year I'll be playing and I'm going to win it.'

He just smiled, but he didn't know how much I was hurting. Not qualifying killed me because I knew, despite not being ranked in the top sixteen, that I could beat 95 per cent of the players there. It was the biggest tournament in the world, it was effectively the world title, and I'd have to wait another twelve months before I could have a shot at it. I watched as John Lowe beat Welshman Phil Obbard in the final.

I may not have beaten John, but I knew I could have killed the Welshman, so I threw myself into my darts for the next twelve months and ensured I won enough tournaments to get me into the top sixteen and automatic qualification for the next World Masters which, because of its increasing popularity, had been moved to the Wembley Conference Centre. This was a buzz. I remember walking into the centre for the first time and gazing in awe at this huge room in which thirty-two dart boards had been put up with the one on the main stage reserved for the big matches and the later rounds. You could hear the whirr of the television cameras and every nationality of player was there. It was great to see players from Denmark, America, Finland, Australia and the rest, all ready for the tournament of tournaments.

Although Lowey was favourite to win it, the clever money was on me because I had been winning Opens everywhere; in Lincolnshire, Staffordshire, you name it, I won it. I won more than I lost and unofficially I knew, and the rest of the darting world knew, that I was the number one player in the world, but winning the World Masters was tough.

It was the best of five legs of 501 all the way through, but when Lowey got knocked out this opened it up for me and I got through to the final where I was up against a Yorkshireman called Paul Reynolds.

He won the first leg, which left me with a bit of a mountain to climb. In the second leg, I still wasn't at the top of my game and needed 152 to claw it back to 1–1. It was a desperate situation because he had three darts at a double, and I knew that was all he needed to what would have been an unassailable two–nil lead. But I threw sixty, sixty and double sixteen to snatch it. He was devastated; he couldn't believe it. His head went down and he never recovered from that. I won the last two legs to take the match and the title.

It was an unbelievable feeling. I had wanted to win that title so badly that I broke down in tears with relief when they gave me the trophy. I finally had a world title in the bag at a time when I was winning all the Opens but people were saying I wasn't good enough to win a biggie. Now I'd won and there were no players in front of me. I had sent a signal to all the players that I was the best in the world. When I lifted that trophy I felt as if I was standing at the top of the mountain. I had achieved everything I had ever wanted to achieve in life. What could possibly go wrong?

FIVE

The World Championship

The World Masters was the turning point for me because I had always wanted to be World Champion, and at the age of twenty I'd effectively done it. I was the top player who everyone wanted to beat. To achieve everything you set out to achieve by the age of twenty is a bit of a head mash. I didn't know where to go from there or what to aim for next. For the first and possibly only time in my life I was lost.

I moved into a mate's house shortly after the World Masters and lived there with a girl who was in the process of getting divorced and, to put it diplomatically, liked a drink or two. More specifically she liked gin, and the house soon became awash with green bottles because after a few weeks of living with her I developed a taste for it as well. I had been taken in by her beauty and now I was hitting the bottle with her in a big way. We are talking a bottle or bottle and a half a day between us. I was earning the dosh in little tournaments all over the capital and every night I would bring home two or three bottles. I'd earn about fifty pounds a week and gin only cost about two pounds a bottle so we were never short of the stuff. It was all drink, drink, drink. The darts, for the only time in my life, took second place, because after winning the World Masters I didn't think there was anything else in the game that I could do.

I really was lost for the next six to eight months. As a result my darts suffered and I was fast becoming the sort of person I associated with failure, namely these proper drinkers who can have a tankful and not look any different, the ones who have ten doubles and are normal, twenty normal, thirty normal, who you look in the eye and they look back and you think, this stuff isn't working on you, pal. That was us. It wasn't her fault. It was my problem. Nobody forced it down my throat. The worst thing was that my darts was dying a slow and undignified death and I couldn't give a toss.

After eight months of drowning in drink I heard news that darts was going to have an official World Championship. This was like a clarion call. It really did jolt me back into life like some sort of awakening. Suddenly I was back to my old self and thinking: Right, I want to be the first World Champion. I decided the only way to get myself out of this mess was to get rid of my girlfriend and concentrate on the darts again. My focus came right back because I wanted to be the first ever official World Champion of darts.

I moved out and went back to Mum and Dad's house; it was the only way of getting rid of temptation. The relationship had gone nowhere and was going nowhere. I hate to think what would have happened to me if I had stayed with her. It got to a stage near the end where I would look at myself in the bathroom mirror the morning after a heavy drinking session and see a blotchy face with red bloodshot eyes staring back at me. I started thinking this was silly for a bit of totty and I decided the next girl I dated had to be a non-drinker. It'd be a lot cheaper that way and it'd keep me on the straight and narrow. When I went home Mum and Dad welcomed me with open arms. They knew the darts was suffering. They also knew the fun had gone out of it for me because I was with a girl who wanted to do other things. I had practically given up practising while I was with her, and if I did go out and practise I invariably started downing large gins by the bucketful, as well as four or five pints of lager. Back at home I was desperate to get my game back on track.

The first World Professional Darts Championship was held in 1978 at the Heart of the Midlands nightclub in Nottingham. It was the BDO's most important tournament in the darts calendar and its importance was further highlighted when only the elite players were invited to compete in it, namely the thirty-two best players in the world. It was well organised, with a big-name sponsor in Embassy cigarettes, and you could sense that darts was about to take a step into bigger and greater things.

Embassy were great sponsors. Every player got two hundred fags for competing, and every time we went on stage there were two packets of fags waiting for us on the table, one for each player. It was great when I played Lowey because he didn't smoke so I could pick his up as well. It got better if you won the tournament. Embassy would reward the winner with six hundred fags a month for a year. The organiser Peter Dyke loved me because every time I went on telly I always called it the Embassy rather than the World Championship. When I didn't win the title in 1982 and 1983 I said to him, 'I suppose my fags go out of the window now, do they?' But he kept on sending me them, every year, for the next seventeen years, which was a nice touch.

In the run-up to the inaugural Embassy World Championship I honestly believed I couldn't lose. I looked at every invited player and knew I could beat them. It was there for the taking. The World Masters was tough because it was a best of five format so it was short and you had to be on top of your game 100 per cent of the time. The World Championship was going to be much longer. It was the best of eleven sets, five legs of 501 to a set, which suited the better players because you could afford to have an off-set or a couple of off-legs and you'd still be in there with a shout. The weaker players simply got worn down in longer games. They didn't have the stamina.

I had another reason to feel confident. A couple of days before the tournament was due to begin my dad drove me up to Nottingham and I spent a few days practising with Welshman Leighton Rees, the number one player in Wales and number three seed in the tournament. We had some close matches and were both at the top of our game. Leighton was a good friend of mine. He was born in the village of Ynsybwl and went to school in nearby Pontypridd where a teacher declared on his report card that he would be 'good only for reading the sports pages of the *South Wales Echo*'. After leaving school he found work in the store room of a motor spares company, a job he did for twenty years until becoming a professional darts player in 1976. That was when we met and instantly hit it off. At the time Leighton was due to play in a tournament in Cleveden, Ohio, with four other Welshmen, but three or four days before they were to fly out I got a call from him to say one of the players, Alan Evans, was withdrawing due to gout and would I be his replacement. I never turn down an opportunity to see the world, so I ended up sharing a room with Leighton and we hit it off instantly. We shared rooms after that for years. And when we played together in later years on the *Queen Mary*, which was berthed at Long Beach, California, we even shared the same bed. There was no funny business! They had very few twin rooms on the *Queen Mary*, because cruises were more of a couples thing, but the ones they had generally got booked. So Leighton and I had to share this massive double bed. I was saying to him, 'You behave yourself Leighton. Don't turn over in the middle of the night or I'll stick one on you.'

He pulled a girl called Debbie while we were on the ship. She was lovely, a real stunner, but she had a mate with her as well. We were on this boat for a week and they had a room, we had a room. Leighton and Debbie wanted to sleep together, so obviously I had to go with this other girl, and not only that – I had to sleep in the same room as her for a week. Believe me, I had to do it or I would have messed up all Leighton's lovemaking plans.

I concluded that I could put up with this for a week but no longer. Leighton, on the other hand, was away with the fairies. He was smitten and totally in love with his girl. I, however, was counting down the days with mine until it was all over: Thursday, Friday, Saturday, and when Sunday came I said thank Christ for that, it was the last day with her. We had a farewell dinner with them on the Sunday night before Leighton and I were due to fly to 'Frisco the next day. As we were sat there I was rubbing my hands thinking: Great, I have a week in 'Frisco on my own, brilliant. But just as the meal was finishing Debbie hit me with the bombshell. She said,

A bouncing baby Bristow –
just after my first birthday.

At junior school I always had an eye
for the birds, even then!

I may have been a smiling
first former at Grammar School,
but even at the age of 11 I knew
school wasn't for me. It was
around this time dad bought
me my first dart board.

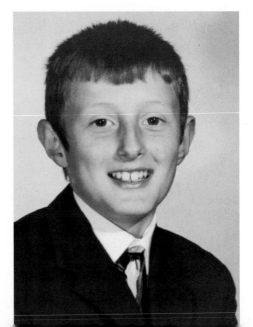

In America I'd often challenge fellow players to a darts match for money, and I always beat 'em! Now hand it over!!!

All Pals Together! The English/Welsh alliance of Leighton Rees, me, John Lowe and Tony Brown on board the Queen Mary at Long Beach, America.

The Pontins Darts
Championship held at
Prestatyn and Camber
Sands in 1975 holds
fond memories for me
because I won it.

I was 17 when I
won this trophy at a
knockout competition.
I was to win many
more over the
coming months.

Even at the age of 18 I had a large and impressive selection
of trophies under my belt.

Aged 18, young, slim and sexy! I've put on a few pounds
since then though.

The great American beano in 1976. It was three weeks of darts
and partying. No wonder Lowey looks concerned. I'm on my
way to throwing another 180.

People have sometimes called me a shady character.

The England team of 1976 sporting what I called the Coco the Clown look. Our manager Ollie Croft is in the white jacket.

On top of the world – winning the Winmau World Masters in 1977,
my first major title win.

Playing my old buddy Leighton Rees on the American tour in 1978. Bullseye star Tony Green was on the mic.

'You play like a poof', my dad once said to me. But this unique throwing style helped me to five world championships.

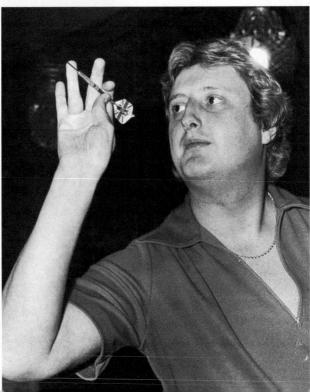

As a teenager my darts were made by Durro. This is their team. I'm in the centre with a young and good looking Bobby George on the far left.

Practising with my old pal Leighton Rees shortly before he won the inaugural Embassy World Championship in 1978.

'Anyway guys, we have some good news for you. We are both coming to 'Frisco.'

My jaw dropped. I was gutted. And after 'Frisco they came to the next one with us. I had to be with this girl for three weeks. But I performed my duty. It was all worth it in the long run because in 1980 Leighton ended up marrying Debbie and I was best man at his wedding. But when they said they were coming with us to 'Frisco my head was screaming no, no, no. I felt like the bloke in that Edvard Munch painting 'The Scream'. That was how bad the feeling was. I spent the next fortnight getting pissed up, falling into my room and waking up the next morning and thinking: Not again!

On a more positive note she was a lot easier to share a room with than Leighton because he had some mad ways. I could never clean my teeth in the basin because as soon as we got to any hotel he'd fill it up with ice and put bottles of lager in to keep them cold. It was a joke! I used to run the bathtap and clean my teeth over the tub. He was another one who liked his drink. When we stayed at Santa Monica we had a hotel right on the beach, just a short walk from the Crafty Cockney Pub where we drank and practised our darts. In the afternoon I used to leave him in the pub and go home for some kip, but he was hardcore. He didn't have kips, but instead just drank and drank and drank. I was eighteen, I could drink, but I couldn't get silly with it because my body wasn't used to it like it was with the older lot. Leighton and the boys would drink into the evening and then hit the shots. They played a game with a white spirit and a black spirit. You basically had to pour them both down your throat in one without touching the glass with your mouth. That was Leighton's game of choice. I wouldn't have got back to the hotel if I'd have played that – and the hotel was only a five-minute walk away. I can't mix my drinks. I left that to the proper drinkers like Leighton.

In the days before the first World Championship, however, we were both very careful what we drank because we wanted to be in tip-top shape for the start of the tournament. I was also watching what I ate. I had a special diet that consisted mainly of pasta because it soaked up the alcohol. On the day of the tournament I felt good, I was throwing well and everything felt in place. Leighton had been the perfect practice partner because we were still very competitive when practising together and we brought out the best in each other.

I was playing an American called Conrad Daniels in the first round. He was a virtual unknown, a rank outsider, and on paper didn't have a chance against a player of my calibre, but from the minute he stepped up to the oche I knew I was in big trouble. He was slow, really slow, and I suddenly realised I hadn't played anyone as slow as this guy before. Mentally he got to me. I didn't know if it was Monday, Tuesday or Wednesday by the time I came off the stage. One minute I was throwing quick darts, trying to speed him up, the next I was slowing them down trying to play him at his own game. What I wasn't doing was concentrating on my own game. I was thinking the wrong things and all that was going through my mind was why doesn't this guy hurry up? Consequently I lost the match by six sets to three.

It was quite simple why I lost: I was thinking negative thoughts instead of positive. Mentally I should have realised that I could murder this guy. That loss devastated me because I desperately wanted to be the first World Champion. Conrad Daniels couldn't believe it. He appeared in the next two World Championships and got beaten first round, then after that he wasn't good enough even to qualify. His only win came against me, the favourite, in 1978. I'd lost to an idiot, and it wouldn't be the last time that happened!

The tournament went on for another eight days after that. Was I miserable? Not in the least. For the remainder of the tournament I stayed in Nottingham, where in those days the gender ratio in the city was four women to every bloke. It was brilliant. I ended up pulling this lingerie model for the week and she was stunning. While I was with her I pulled a couple more in between. One night I sent this model down to the bar, telling her I had to do an interview with a local newspaper reporter. When she went down I had another girl come up to the room. I did her then went down to the bar where the model was being looked after by my dad.

'How did the interview go?' she asked.

'It went all right. It was no problem,' I replied, smiling.

I stayed the whole week in that hotel because I had paid for it upfront, I was that confident of reaching the final and winning it. When I wasn't pulling women I was watching the darts. My pal Leighton easily disposed of Australian Barry Atkinson six sets to nil in the first round to set up a clash with his close friend and Welsh team-mate Alan Evans in the second round. This was when the championship came to life. It was a classic game with both players averaging over ninety, something which was almost unheard of in those days. Evans took an early lead with a couple of one-eighties before Leighton hit the championship's first ten-dart finish, which was also the first one ever televised, and ran out the eventual winner by six sets to three. It was a great advert for darts because it was such a good match and darts' reputation as a TV sport was cemented after this.

Leighton's semi-final was a classic as well. He struggled and battled, but eventually pipped his opponent Nicky Virachkul to an eight sets to seven win which set up a final with Lowey. In my mind Lowey was always going to nick it, but I was gunning for Leighton because he was my pal. He didn't disappoint, averaging over ninety again with Lowey not far behind, to win by eleven sets to seven. It was a proud moment for Leighton. For me it was a case of going back to Stoke Newington with my dad to lick my wounds.

Back home I found all the slowest players in the league and went round to their pubs and played them all. I was determined I was never going to get caught out by a slow player again. Some of them I played for hours. I had to get the demon that was Conrad Daniels out of my mind – but looking back it was good to see me go out. I had just won the World Masters so for me to go out first round was a shock and made headline news. In a way it put darts on the map and that rooted the tournament in people's minds. If the favourite wins all the time the sport can become boring and predictable. This first ever World Championship proved that darts was anything but. I had twelve months to dwell on my failure, but I did everything in my power to put it right.

Another girl came on the scene called Lynne. I moved in with her and she drove me to all the tournaments I played in – but it didn't last. I didn't want someone with me all the time twenty-four hours a day, seven days a week. It was doing my head in. This was the problem I faced. It was a real catch-22 situation: any girl I liked had to be my driver or they would never see me because of all the darts I played and the relationship would therefore be doomed – but when they did drive me around that didn't work either because to be at the top of my game I found I had to be on my own. Girlfriends just didn't help my darts. I needed privacy and sometimes I'd crave solitude to get my head right.

This was most in evidence when I played in a three-day tournament up in Newcastle and stayed at the house of a lovely couple. The trouble was when it got to night-time I was knackered and wanted to go to bed but they wanted a few drinks with me, and because it was their house and their hospitality I felt obliged to stay up with them. I didn't like that. I hadn't liked that aspect of America when I went there for the first time. I'd play in a tournament that ended at two in the morning, get back to Malcolm and Mary-Ann's house and they would want to stay up until about four and have a drink with me. I'd be thinking: Why do I have to do this? I wanted to go to bed, get some kip and wake up fresh the next morning to have a couple of hours by the pool. That put me off staying at people's houses. I don't do it now. It's very nice to have someone invite you into their home to stay, but I don't like to feel obligated to them. It was little things like this – the girlfriends, the staying at other people's houses and the slow players – that I was determined to get right before the 1979 championship came around. And I did get them right. Years later, another slow player came on the scene called Dennis Priestley and I had no problem playing against him. The only thing was that there was a big difference between him and Daniels in that Dennis was good.

Those twelve months between the 1978 and 1979

World Championships were all about focus and preparing myself for a second pop at the world title. Twelve months on the tournament had moved to the Jollees Cabaret Club in Stoke (which was handy for me because a couple of years afterwards I moved up that way), and I was as ready as I ever would be for that championship. In my mind I was determined I was not going to let 1978 happen again and I won my first-round game quite easily against Australian Terry O'Dea by two sets to nil.

In the next round I was up against Alan Evans. There was a bit of history between us – I didn't like him and he didn't like me. The problem stemmed from Alan being one of the early faces of television darts and having some tournament success in the early to mid-seventies. He reached the final of the 1972 *News of the World* Championship, which was the first televised darts event to be shown in the UK, and he also won the 1975 British Open, which was the first televised event on the BBC. He added the World Masters title to this a few months later to make it a double winning year. He also faced Mohammed Ali in an exhibition match at the Gypsy Hill Stadium in Crystal Palace. Under the handicap rules Evans would only score points for hitting trebles. Ali was able to hit the bullseye to win the game and he proclaimed himself Darts Champion of the World. Make no mistake, in the early to mid-seventies Alan Evans was a big name. He even made it on to the

Johnny Carson Show in America, but ended up walking off, live on air, after being asked to throw darts from between his legs. Alan wasn't doing it and before he stormed off he told them so. He was right. Darts isn't a Mickey Mouse game. It's a professional sport that should be respected. I loved him for doing that. This was a big, big show and he did darts proud by walking off the way he did. However, by the time I came on the scene his star was fading. He wanted to be seen as the young pretender, he was only eight years older than me, and resented me effectively stealing his limelight. It was this resentment that sometimes manifested itself in open hostility. To put it bluntly he was a fiery little bastard who would stick the nut on you at the slightest provocation. You had to keep an eye on him. He was great friends with Leighton who was his big Welsh buddy, so you can imagine how he felt when Leighton chose me over him to be best man at his wedding.

We first crossed swords at a tournament in 1974 when an interviewer asked him who he wanted to play. He said, 'I'll have the London Lip.' This was before I became known as the Crafty Cockney. So we played the match and I absolutely killed him. I killed anybody who thought they were better than me back then. If anybody wanted to play me for money I'd get on a train and I'd be up there. For instance, a player called Brian Langworth from Sheffield wanted to play me for £500. I was up there like a shot, and soon back down to London again with the money. Alan Evans was another one who thought he was a better player. These sort of guys would galvanise me into playing much, much better and on that particular day I was lethal. I only had about twenty throws and won two games to nil. I was hitting one-eighty, one-eighty, one-forty, one-forty, one-eighty, one-forty, ton. It was relentless. I mullered him. He lost both games and still had over two hundred on the board both times. That memory didn't help him through the years to come.

So this World Championship confrontation was something of a grudge match. I was the new kid on the block and he was the young player I had usurped – and for the second year running the script went right out of the window. I fluffed it again. He beat me and I couldn't believe it.

To make matters worse I had to take part in an interview with him afterwards. He was on one chair and I was sitting on another as far away as possible. Before we did it I said to the producer, 'Do I *have* to do an interview with that dickhead?' But there was no option. We were contractually obliged to do it. So there we sat, both being as polite as we could because we were on telly, but both trying to avoid eye-contact with each other. I could tell he was elated, and I was sick, absolutely sick to the pit of my stomach, but I managed to keep a lid on things – until they asked me if I thought Evans had a chance to go all the way and win it. I could stand it no more and pointing at him said, 'He's got as much chance of winning the Embassy as you would have of finding a pork chop in a synagogue.'

Leaning forward in his chair he said, 'Well, I've got more chance than you, haven't I?'

I'll give him his due, it was a good answer, but when the cameras stopped rolling they had to send two bouncers in to keep us from tearing each other apart.

He did play lovely darts against me when he knocked me out. There was no getting away from the fact that he was well up for it. I didn't play as well, even though I was ready, and it hurt more than my exit twelve months earlier. I'd been brooding on that defeat for a year and this was my chance to put it right, and then I went and lost to somebody I didn't like. That was a double whammy. So then it was a case of waiting another twelve months.

Alan Evans didn't have much luck after that win. Leighton Rees beat him again, this time in the semi-finals, and that, effectively, was it for him and his career. He made five more appearances in the World Championship, losing to me twice in 1986 and 1987, twice to Jocky Wilson in 1982 and 1988 and to Lowey in 1983. With the exception of his 1987 semi-final loss all the others were early round exits. He died in 1999. Ironically enough we buried the hatchet in the end and became quite good friends.

The 1979 final ended up being a repeat of the one

twelve months earlier, only this time it was Lowey who came out on top, beating Leighton easily by five sets to nil. I was left to wonder if I was ever going to win that tournament. I only wanted to win it once, and I was winning everything else, so why couldn't I win the World Championship?

The good thing was there was no real time to think because the next big tournament after the World Championship was only a fortnight away and in between there were exhibitions and other matches to fit in. My diary was full. There was no time to brood. I knew my bottle didn't go at these big events, I had prepared, I wasn't drunk or anything like that. I put my failure at those first two World Championships down to one thing: it simply wasn't meant to be. I had to look forward.

I also had to look over my shoulder because, despite being favourite for the first two championships, and barring any disasters I would be top seed again for the 1980 World Championship, there were other players coming through the ranks. The one I was wary of more than any other was John Thomas Wilson, better known as Jocky Wilson. The former coal delivery man and miner made his debut at the 1979 World Championship. A spell on the dole had proved the catalyst for his darts career: it was while claiming benefit that he entered a Butlins darts competition in 1979, which he went on to win, getting £500 prize money. His success at this tournament convinced him to turn professional and go for the big money tournaments on TV. He qualified easily for the 1979 World Championship, but was knocked out by Lowey in the quarter-final. But all the time he was getting better and better. There were only two players in darts at that time who should have been winning all the tournaments and they were Lowey and me, but we both knew that pretty soon we'd be joined by Jocky and there'd be three of us at the top, fighting it out for every title. We had some monumental battles through the next decade, matches that would go down in the history of darts as all-time classics.

There was another darts player about to make a dramatic impact on my life, a woman player called Maureen Flowers. Most female darts players around this era looked like butch lesbians: they were big girls who you wouldn't want to fight, never mind have sex with, and they all had tattoos. Maureen was different. She was slim, attractive, and had lovely long blonde hair. Every red-blooded male dart player fancied her. I was no exception. I used to see her at all these tournaments we were playing in and I could feel the testosterone inside me start to surge. So I made a point of always chatting to her and we got on well. As soon as she split up from her husband all the darts players were trying to get into her. I waited for the best moment to ask her out and she said yes. To be honest I didn't think I'd get a look in, but there you go, life is full of surprises.

She was different from all the other women I'd dated

in that she could play darts and she could play well. She was the world number one women's darts player and I was the best in the men's division so I suppose it was bound to happen in the end. An added bonus was that she didn't drink alcohol; she drank tea instead. After my experience on the gin I welcomed a teetotaller with open arms. She made me laugh when I went to watch her in exhibitions and she drank tea on stage. It looked odd. She played one exhibition game with a Manchester player called Billy Leonard. He was a big name in the 1960s and early 1970s and ran a trophy business in Heywood. When I was dating Maureen I'd regularly go to watch her play exhibitions and she vice versa; effectively this was the only way we could court. When she played with Billy, instead of pints of lager and packets of fags on stage they took up a pot of tea for them. This tickled me. Billy wasn't bothered in the slightest. He'd drink whatever they brought up there be it beer, wine, water, whisky or tea.

I really didn't want a relationship with my hectic lifestyle and being constantly on the road, but with Maureen it was different. She had the same sort of existence as I did, so that made us compatible in a way. The only people who didn't really approve of me dating Maureen were my parents. They didn't like the fact that she was an older woman by six years and she had three children. However, she was a good influence on me at that time because, instead of going out chasing skirt when I was away at tournaments, I'd go back to the hotel with Maureen and more often than not have a pot of tea and some sandwiches. Maureen was also good for my darts, there's no doubt about that, because I practised with her every day and it allowed me to practise with someone good. We'd go to the pub and have proper games that were close. I'd have a couple of beers and she would have a pot of tea. Life was changing. Whenever we were away there was no late stuff any more. We'd go for a meal, I'd have a glass of wine or two or some beers, and then it was early to bed. I was turning into John Lowe!

When we started dating, however, something big was also happening in darts. The BDO, in a bid to turn itself into a world organisation, was bringing other tournaments in from all over the world to be included in the world ranking system – tournaments in Sweden, Finland, Denmark, Canada and Japan, and there were more springing up all the time. This meant one thing: we were about to see the world. I couldn't wait.

SIX

Jet-setters

As the seventies moved into the eighties darts players led the sort of life today's overpaid footballers can only dream of. When you're a footballer earning £60,000 plus a week your life is knackered. David Beckham is a prime example. He has to have security guards follow his kids everywhere to make sure they don't get kidnapped. That's not the way to be. I've had the ideal life from start to finish. I've always had a pocketful of money, and I've been able to go where I want, drink where I want, eat where I want and stay where I want. It's a lifestyle that has suited me down to the ground and I wouldn't change it for the world. Nowadays, if you're a sportsman and you earn too much money, you become a target. Take Malaysia for example – there are nutters over there who specifically target the children of rich sportsmen and hold them to ransom. The players are being punished for doing well and that is wrong. Footballers over here are also tied to the soccer season.

They can only see the world during a ten-week block from June to August.

Back in 1979 Maureen and I were going all over the place, and it was brilliant. This was in spite of the fact that almost every time I did go abroad things would happen. Our plane would nearly crash, or I'd almost get killed, or I'd save someone from a near-death experience. I got into some bizarre situations abroad. My favourite trips by far were the American beanos. They were crazy, every single one of them.

There was one 1980 tournament I went on at a huge Las Vegas hotel. When I arrived there were 2,500 darts players in this big conference room called the Space Room. They all seemed to arrive at two in the afternoon for some strange reason. The tournament didn't start until four hours later, but it was a brilliant sight to see: this hotel, this massive place, had been taken over by darts players, all in their brightly coloured shirts and all doing what every darts player does best and that's drink. Because it was a bit of a party atmosphere the beer really was flowing, so much so that at half-past ten that night the hotel ran out of beer. We'd drunk the place dry, and this wasn't your ordinary hotel, this hotel was enormous, it was some achievement.

It was also like somebody switching off the lights at a party and telling everybody to go home. Some darts players can't function without a beer inside them and pretty soon the mood was starting to turn sour, so the hotel staff called the police. They didn't know what to do; it had never been known in Vegas for a hotel to run dry. When the cops came they couldn't believe it; they were walking past us and saying to each other, 'These goddam motherfuckers sure like to drink!' So everybody and I mean *everybody* in that place hit the phones – the staff, the police, the hotel security guards, the tournament organisers. They were all ordering beer from every place you could imagine, local shops, other hotels, you name it, if it had beer that beer came to our hotel. We heard one cop screaming down the phone, 'Listen buddy, if you don't get that beer down here in one hour we're gonna have a scene on our hands, and I'll hold you responsible.'

It was chaos, complete chaos, but they managed to restock the hotel within an hour of it running dry. It was a mistake they never repeated again. The hotel staff had completely overlooked the fact that there were two and a half thousand hardcore drinkers at this place. It wasn't your old dears on the slots. These lads were having pint after pint, with double vodka chasers for good measure.

This sort of thing happened to a few places I appeared at, for instance the Holiday Village in Great Yarmouth. The people who worked these establishments just didn't realise how much these guys could drink.

Another favourite place was Penticton in Canada where I did a 29-day tour. This was paradise. I stayed at a hotel where my balcony overlooked a big lake and on either side were mountains. I sat on the balcony with a bottle of champagne and a bowl of fruit, courtesy of the hotel, and realised life didn't get much better than this. The tour finished in St John's and a guide took me to a place where the salmon went through. This part of the river was only about eight feet wide and when the salmon came, they came in a rush, millions of them. The guide said that you could literally walk on them because there were so many. It was like a bottleneck. They gave this bit of the river to the Indians in return for stealing their land many centuries ago. The Indians came in great big lorries packed with ice and just pulled the fish out of the river and threw them on to the lorry to be sold.

A great place to go was Scandinavia. Before Maureen came on the scene I used to go to Sweden and Denmark for two things: the darts and the women. In Sweden they were all beautiful blondes. I never got drunk in Sweden. I'd go on the pull instead and try and take one of them home. More often than not I succeeded, but then I'd end up staying up all night with whoever I had pulled and I'd not get any sleep, though I suppose it was better than waking up with a hangover. I had sex with some beautiful women over there, women who wouldn't have given me a second look if I wasn't a good darts player.

In Denmark we stayed right beside Tivoli Gardens in Copenhagen. Tivoli Gardens is a beautiful amusement park cum pleasure garden. The BDO put about forty of us in the Triton Hotel close by, right next to the train station and thirty yards from the red light district. Thirty yards away in another direction was the only bar in the street, the Spunk Bar. Our boys were in there like a shot; the moment we got there they were in. They wanted a beer, nothing more, but they came out just as quick when they discovered it was a hardcore gay bar full of transvestites and Freddie Mercury look-alikes dressed in leather. Everyone bolted from that place, apart from Billy Leonard, the old pro from the north, who smoked his Park Drive unfiltered and drank bitter and mild. He stayed there all the time, morning, noon and night! He couldn't have cared less about the clientele.

I went in to get him at one point because we were all going on a pub crawl and said, 'Billy, what the hell are you doing in here, mate?'

'Best pint around here,' he replied.

And he was sitting there, chatting away to this group of five or six people he thought were women, and I said, 'Billy, these are geezers dressed up as birds.'

'No they're not,' he said.

'Billy, these are blokes, mate.'

'Oh, it doesn't matter,' he replied. 'I'm only having a drink with them.' And they were his mates for the duration of the tournament. They even sold knickers and leather pants in there with Spunk Bar written on them, but I don't think Billy bought any.

We stayed at that hotel every year for the next ten years, and we had all these women darts players with us, a mixture of old ones and young ones. I used to take them to the sex shops. There was this old girl called Lily Coombs who was sixty and had been playing the game for years who approached me in a very innocent way and said: 'Eric, will you take me to a sex shop? I've never been in a sex shop before.'

I ended up taking six of them down to this place and there's nothing worse than walking around a sex shop with a load of nutty women, especially ones who are picking up giant dildos and going, 'What do I do with this, Eric?'

Lily was the worst of the lot. She'd say things like, 'Wow, I've never seen one that big. Is yours that big, Eric?'

At the opposite end of the spectrum, away from the sex shops and Spunk Bars, were the tours to the Middle East states: Bahrain, Abu Dhabi, Dubai and Qatar. These were essentially dry countries. I went with Maureen and Big Cliff and on one of our first visits, we were the guests of a nephew of the ruler of Dubai. He entertained us on his private yacht and had these two henchmen with him at all times. They were big, bigger than Cliff, and as we sat down to eat they pulled a net up from the side of the boat which was full of fish and invited us to choose one to eat for our dinner. Cliff chose one, but I waited for the last one to die and said, 'I'll have that one; he's the strongest.'

Maureen didn't like that at all. She said, 'I'll have chicken and chips!'

So the big geezers were sent all the way to our hotel, half a mile away, to get her some chicken and chips, all because Maureen was squeamish.

Although the Middle East was dry, it wasn't really. We'd heard Bahrain was the driest of the states, so Cliff smuggled in a bottle of champagne in his luggage and I smuggled in a bottle of brandy. Before we were due to play our tournament we had brandy and champagne cocktails in Cliff's hotel room. We were ready to play after that. At the tournament Cliff went on first and I went and sat with all these Brit ex-pats who said to me, 'What do you want to drink?'

'Nothing,' I replied, 'I'm all right.'

'What do you want to drink?' they said again.

'I don't want anything. I'm sick of Coke.'

'No, what do you want to *drink*: brandy, vodka, whisky, what do you want?'

'I'll have a brandy and lemonade then,' I said, my face lighting up.

As soon as Cliff finished his game I ran up to him and said, 'Cliff, Cliff, get over there with those lads, they've got booze.'

The whole audience was at it. At the end of my game I got on the microphone and announced, 'I have never seen so many happy people on Coke and lemonade in my life!' And with that they all stood up and cheered. The concept of a dry state was farcical.

It was a farce at the airport as well. We were waiting with a load of Aussies to get on a plane to take us from Bahrain to Muscat. As we queued patiently to board this sheik came along with his twelve wives and thirty-plus bodyguards, walked straight past us, straight onto our plane, and it took off. 'That cheeky sod has nicked our plane,' I said to Cliff. The Aussies were even more furious than us because they had to get a connecting flight at Muscat, which they missed because we had to wait three hours for another plane.

When we got to Muscat, Cliff was in pain and discovered that an ingrowing hair on his backside had turned septic. He'd got this huge yellow boil thing on his bum and had to go to hospital to have it lanced. The doctor told Cliff afterwards that it had been like harpooning Moby Dick. He played darts later that night, only hours after it was done. The medics had told him to lay off the booze but he was back on it. When we returned to the hotel he asked me if I'd change the padding and put a fresh one on. I said, 'I love you, Cliff, but I'm not going near that arse of yours, no way.' So he had to get some poor sod from the hotel to do it for him.

The Middle East was great. The food was all curry, curry, curry, which suited me because I'm a big fan of all things hot and spicy. I was eating it for breakfast, lunch and dinner. The place was full of Brits. They'd gone over there with the intention of working for nine months then going back home, but they got sucked into the lifestyle and the money and never went back. Some had been there for fourteen years.

It was strange playing tournaments in the Middle East because the culture was so different, but nothing compared with how weird it was playing in the Falkland Islands. The local population were odd, and probably still are. I did ten days there, playing exhibitions about eighteen months after the end of the 1982 war with Argentina. All our army boys who had been posted out there after the war to make sure the Argies didn't come back were on ninety-day tours, and every one of them was counting the hours until they could get back home. They had a Malaysian couple doing the cooking for them, who had been working four and a half years out there without a day off. I said to them, 'And our lot are worried about ninety days!'

I loved the army lads. What I didn't like were the islanders. They hated having the soldiers there, despite the fact that they had been saved by them during the Argentine invasion. One young soldier had gone missing after knocking off one of the local girls. The army lads

I spoke to reckoned the islanders had bumped him off. His body was never found.

The only exhibition I played for a mixed crowd of army boys and natives was in Port Stanley at a great big pub. Because of the hatred felt it was bound to kick off, and it did when three locals had a go at a young squaddie. I went over to this soldier's mates and I said, 'Is your pal OK?'

'Don't worry about him,' one of them said, smiling. 'He'll be fine. He can sort it out.'

The young soldier invited these three locals outside, and they all walked out of the pub, but the soldier's mates didn't go with him which puzzled me because I've always been taught that you stick together in times of trouble. I needn't have worried. This young army lad came back into the pub minutes later having done these three blokes. His mates weren't worried about helping him because they knew he could take care of himself. I was pleased because these islanders were plonkers. There were twelve hundred of them living in an area the size of Wales and basically it was a backwater. Why we ever went over there to save them I'll never know. They should have been left to the whim of General Galtieri who would probably have lined them up against a wall and had them all shot.

It wasn't all bad. The army took me to an underground bunker which acted as a missile silo, and they showed me how to knock down a plane or a ship with a rocket. It was easy, frighteningly easy. There were eight army lads stationed there, and four of them had to be awake at any one time in case of attack. Every three days or so the Argies sent a boat out and it crossed into the exclusion zone. When it did it was all hands on deck at this bunker as warning flares were sent up into the sky and the Argie boat, as soon as it saw this, scarpered. If it hadn't they would've sent one of these £900,000-a-pop rockets to sink it, and this was a game they played once, twice and sometimes three times a week.

I played at one Falklands venue where four soldiers turned up from nowhere and said to me, 'We had to see you while you were here.'

They'd been dropped onto the moorland and had to live off the land for four days, but they had their civvies in their rucksack so they got changed and went on the lash with me until the early hours of the morning. At the end of it they said, 'Don't say anything. You haven't seen us, have you?' And I said, 'No, no, no,' and off they went into the darkness.

A few hours later a boat came to pick them up. I was tucked up in bed by this time, because I had an exhibition to play later that day, and nobody was ever the wiser.

It wasn't all fun and games abroad. By 1980 I had got myself a manager called Dick Allix. They all wanted to manage me when they realised how good I was, and why not? These people are mercenaries; they want their 10 per cent cut. But Dick was the best. He used to be the drummer with a band called Vanity Fair who were one-hit wonders in the sixties with a song called 'Early in the Morning'. As soon as I signed for him he got me a deal that involved me and Maureen going to Jamaica for a ten-day tour, which was a big mistake!

On the first night we arrived late into Kingston, went to the hotel and Dick went to bed, closely followed by Maureen. I went to the hotel bar for a drink, and as I was sat there I started talking to an English bloke. He asked me what I was doing in Jamaica and I told him about the darts and then said, 'I'm going to have a couple of beers, go across the road for a KFC and then I'm going to bed.'

The bloke leaned over and whispered to me, 'Listen, son, you might go across the road, but you won't come back.'

This was only about ten o'clock at night and I looked at him as though he was some kind of nutter and said, 'What are you on about?'

'Just don't go over there, mate. Seriously, don't go over there,' he said, and I could see in his eyes that he had my best interests at heart.

So I had a couple more beers and went to bed. It was frustrating though, knowing I could have been tucking into a big bucket of chicken and chips.

In the bedroom I had a look through the window. By

this time it was pitch black outside, but I could see shadows in the darkness and no cars were stopping when the traffic lights were on red. It was a dangerous place: the drivers in these cars were too frightened to stop. We moved hotels the next day and stayed in one outside town, but the violence, or perceived threat of it, didn't end there.

Dick is into pirates so we all went on a day trip to Port Royal. That's where they lured pirates close to the shore so their ships would get dashed against the rocks. It was a pretty dull place so we decided to walk half a mile through sandy woods to get to the ocean. As we got there we saw a black kid with red Y-fronts floating in the water.

'He's brown bread, him,' I said.

Dick said, 'No he's not, he's snorkelling.'

I did a double take, looked at Dick and said, 'Well, where the fuck is his snorkel then, you dozy twat? You two better get back to the port. I'll pull him out. Now get out of here because we don't know what's happened.'

Dick and Maureen headed back and I pulled this kid out of the water and on to the sand. I wasn't going to give him the kiss of life or anything like that; he was too far gone. I just left him to dry on the beach. His clothes were nearby and as I walked past them to go back I could see a few small bushes and two black guys hiding behind them. My heart started going boom, boom, boom, and the sudden adrenaline rush made me feel dizzy. These were probably the blokes who had killed the kid, and there was no reason why they shouldn't kill me. Everything was going through my mind at this point, so I looked around for something to defend myself with. I picked up what looked like a heavy log, but it was hollow and dry and just crumbled in my hand. In the end I found a big brick and started walking. I knew these two guys were behind me, but after about a quarter of a mile they stopped following me. Thank Christ for that, I thought, and began to relax.

I got to a path and started walking along it when, from about fifty yards away, a big black lad started walking towards me. Where he came from I will never know, but he was huge, and he was walking with his mate who was also six foot eight. As we got to about ten yards from each other I said, 'All right, lads?'

One of them looked at me and sneered, 'What's the matter, man, dead boy frighten you?'

This was one of those life and death, think on your feet moments when what I said would determine whether I would see the sunset that night while sinking a cold beer or end up floating in the sea.

I looked him straight in the eye and snapped back, 'Nothing frightens me, pal,' and I walked straight through them.

I'm certain that if I'd shown any sort of timidity they would've had me, but I wouldn't have gone down without one hell of a fight. Those moments are when you know your heart is working properly. We were told the medics arrived soon after, put a tag on the dead lad, bundled him inside a large black bin-bag and threw him on the back of a lorry. Life isn't worth jack shit over there.

The whole tour seemed to lurch from one disappointment to another. I wanted to go and see Bob Marley's grave because I'm a big fan, but the tour organisers said we couldn't go because it was watched over morning, noon and night by his followers who didn't want the white man there. That riled me no end.

Part of the tour was in Montego Bay. I'd heard all the songs about it and thought this was going to be a lovely place. But it wasn't, it was just as rough as Kingston. There were all these lovely resort hotels there, but what they didn't show you in the brochures was the forty-foot-high barbed wire fence surrounding them to keep all the loonies out. It was madness.

From Montego Bay we went to play an exhibition which was held in a huge shack in the middle of a field at a sugar plantation. Inside the shack they'd put up row upon row of dart boards, but jumping between the boards were all these lizards, and the air was thick with moths. When I threw my darts I was amazed I didn't spear one mid-flight. Maureen didn't like it; it affected her game because she was beaten by this woman who was nowhere near as good as her.

We had been booked for an hour to play for the

workers during their lunch break, and at half past twelve this hooter went off and my party and I went outside the shack to see all these black workers come running over the hill towards us. There were about a hundred and fifty of them, all sprinting. I turned towards Dick and Maureen and shouted, 'In positions, men, the Zulus are coming!'

I felt like Michael Caine in *Zulu* and started shouting, 'Zulus! Zulus!' until Maureen, her face red with anger and embarrassment, said, 'Eric, shut up! Just behave yourself!'

They were packed in the shack like sardines, got their lunch and we played for them. It was good fun, and some of them were good players. Then we went back to the hotel where we had to endure constant power cuts.

The number of times during that tour that I had to have cold showers or baths, and then cut myself to ribbons shaving in cold water I wouldn't like to count, and the service at the hotels was laid back to say the least. First you got your coffee, half an hour later you got your bacon; half an hour after that you got your egg. We even took a flight on a small plane that was laid back to the point of terrifying, especially when the pilot shot the plane down the runway at eighty miles an hour for take-off and the doors either side of him were still open.

I turned to Maureen and said, 'For Christ's sake, is someone going to shut those bloody doors?'

Then, just as he was about to pull up to take off, he leant one way and closed the door, then leant the other way and closed the other door, Jesus Christ!

On the way back to England I realised how lucky I was to actually still be alive. The incident on the beach was a close call. I could've been another body in a bin-bag, tagged and thrown on the back of a lorry. I always seem to have a problem with beaches. I played a tournament in Torremolinos and took Maureen, her three children and her mum and dad. On my day off I joined them at the beach. I'd only been there a few minutes when this kid, who was swimming in the sea, stood up in the water and screamed. When I looked towards him it was as though he had a plastic head, but then I realised a giant jellyfish had wrapped itself around it and across his face. Without thinking I raced into the water, pulled him out, and with two other blokes managed to rip this thing off him. He was taken to hospital in shock. If he'd been in deep water he would've been dead; he would've panicked and most likely drowned. He was a very lucky boy. That was me finished with the sea after seeing that. I didn't go in the water again and never have done since. I stick to the pool. Why go in the sea when you don't have a clue what's in it?

One thing I couldn't avoid was planes. I survived Jamaica but I nearly didn't survive a flight on a big BA10 from Auckland in New Zealand on my way home from a tournament over there. In those days you could smoke on planes. After take-off you waited for the ding sound and the no-smoking light to go off, and then you'd spark up. We went up and were climbing no problem when suddenly there was this big boom and the whole plane shuddered. Then it levelled off, but it still carried on shuddering. Maureen was the first to panic. She said to me, 'We're flying too low; we are way too low to level off. We're going to hit something if we don't climb.' The fear in her face said it all.

Suddenly all the alarms started going off and the pilot announced, 'Ladies and gentlemen, would you please remain in your seats. We have a bit of a problem here.'

The shuddering plane started circling Auckland harbour, which is shark infested, and that's when we noticed one of the engines was on fire. Suddenly Tony Brown shouted out above the noise of the screaming passengers, 'Don't worry, we can limp home.' Then the fuel was dumped to prepare for an emergency landing.

I was desperately trying to calm my beating heart and shouted to Big Cliff, 'If we go in the water I'm throwing you out first. All those sharks will be full up after eating you.'

It was a bizarre situation. All the non-dart-playing passengers were crying and wailing and all the darts players were shouting at each other and joking as a way of trying to stay calm. I was even toying with the idea of getting my bottle of spirits out from the overhead locker and downing it in one.

Then we made it safely to the runway and ran a gauntlet of fire engines. When the plane came to a standstill they foamed the blown engine and I stood up and said, 'Right, I'm off.'

'No, no, no, we can't let you off this plane just yet,' a stewardess said.

Two hours later we were still sitting on the plane and they started serving the in-flight meal. Well, this annoyed me no end.

'I don't want a fucking meal,' I said to the stewardess. 'I just want to get off this plane.' And I added for good measure, 'You can stick your meal up your arse.' I was fuming after everything we had been through.

But they didn't let us off the plane until we had all received the in-flight meal: that way they avoided giving us a voucher for the delay, and all the pre-packed meals didn't go to waste. Basically they were money-grabbing tight-arsed sods. All I wanted was to be off that death plane.

After the meal we were all let off: the Danish dart players, the Swedish and Dutch, the English, Scottish and Welsh – if that plane had gone down it would've wiped out European darts.

Then we were supposed to wait in the airport lounge while they fixed it! I told an airport official, 'I'm not getting back on that thing. I saw what happened to the

Manchester United football team in Munich. You can stick your ticket up your arse. I'll pay for my own fare home.'

So Maureen and I booked our own flights back to Britain, arriving at Heathrow some twenty hours later absolutely knackered. The BA10 whose engine had blown arrived back safely with the rest of the players on it shortly afterwards. I had been certain that that plane was never going to get back to England and there was no way I was ever going to get on it.

The flight out to New Zealand had been equally farcical because the BDO, to save money, flew us the wrong way round the world. We went from Heathrow and stopped off at LA, where there was an eight-hour delay, then onwards to Auckland. Once there, we had another long wait for the plane to take us to Nelson, but as we were getting on they discovered the plane was overbooked by two seats. I said, 'Don't worry, me and Maureen will find our own way there.' We were the youngest so it only seemed fair.

We had to fly to Christchurch and from there get a flight to Nelson. By the time we finally arrived we had been travelling for forty-six hours. We were absolutely knackered when we got in the hotel room, so we had a shower, and then Maureen discovered there was no hair dryer and she'd forgotten hers.

It was starting to get dark now and we'd lost days, but I had to go out and buy this bloody hair dryer for

Maureen. On the way back I treated myself to a visit to the pub for a few drinks to cheer me up and bring me round a bit, I was dead beat.

We had a presentation dinner that night where all the Maoris danced in front of us, and on the following day, the Saturday, we played the World Cup where, to cap off a miserable time, I got beaten by a rat-catcher who wasn't even a full-time darts player. It still ranks to this day as my most humiliating defeat, but mentally I was shot after the exhausting flight getting there so maybe I had an excuse. Nine times out of ten I would've beaten him playing with just one dart.

The tournament was all finished on the Sunday afternoon, and we got the rest of the time to ourselves before flying back home on the Monday. We'd been doing nothing but travelling and playing darts, so when we went into town that afternoon we were looking forward to a break and the chance to let our hair down a little. Imagine how pissed off we were to find the whole place was shut. I couldn't believe it. It was a nightmare. Then we had to fly back on that dodgy plane.

I don't like flying. The only reason I fly is because I have to. I had another dodgy flight with Dennis Priestley. We were coming back from Australia and almost as soon as the plane lifted off we hit massive turbulence. Everything was banging around and flying about and all the women were screaming. Even one of the stewardesses was crying, it was that bad. I could have got up and filled her in though. This was all I needed: these stewardesses are supposed to be professionals, they're supposed to be used to this sort of thing. It was like a roller-coaster ride all the way and Dennis and I played crib to get us through it and take our minds off it. We played three games and to this day we have no idea who won because we didn't mark them down – we were just going through the motions, trying to escape the mental torture of the flight from hell.

Although I'm not keen on flying, I've helped others conquer their fears. Mark Dudbridge of Harrows, the darts manufacturers, went with me on a tour of Hong Kong and Japan. He had great trouble sleeping on planes, so I said to him, 'I'll cure you of this problem. On the way home I promise you, you'll be snoring like a baby.'

On our last night in Hong Kong the darts finished at five in the afternoon and we went out for a meal at seven. We finished it two hours later and I said to him, 'Come on, let's go out. It's our last night, let's enjoy ourselves.'

I got him back to the hotel at quarter past six the next morning and we had to leave forty-five minutes later to go to the airport. We looked like pond life, we were absolute wrecks. I told him, 'Go upstairs and have a quick shower, but *don't* sit on the bed. If you sit on the bed you won't get up.'

We got the cab to the airport, checked in and went

to the bar area where the barmaid asked me if I wanted a beer.

'Yes, I'll have a beer,' I said.

'Small or large?' she replied.

Mark looked at me in disbelief and said, 'Fucking hell!'

'Large,' I said – and she came over with a two-pint pitcher of beer, and one for Mark as well.

He said, 'I only came in here for something to do.'

We downed the pitchers of beer, got on the plane and he was away with the fairies as soon as his head touched the back of the seat. I woke him up when we got home and said, 'See, you can sleep on planes after all.'

The Far East was expensive, bloody expensive. Dick Allix organised a trip with Maureen and me to Japan and when we arrived he told us we'd have to wait three hours for the coach to come and pick us up to take us to our hotel eight miles away. I said bugger that and told him we'd get a taxi. So Maureen and I set off in a cab – and it cost us £62 to go those eight miles. Then, when we got to the hotel, we found they were charging £6 for a Coke, and this was in the late seventies! Our hotel room cost us £110 each, and to go swimming in the hotel pool cost another £10 for a special band you had to wear.

One girl called Sharon had come over from playing

in a Canadian tournament where she had been knocked out first round so didn't win any prize money. Within a couple of days all her dosh had run out, so she couldn't afford to eat, and she resorted to nicking bread rolls at breakfast to last her all day.

Despite being expensive, the food was great; it was a real eye-opener. I had everything. I ate the sushi, drank the sake, everything they served up went straight into my mouth. It could have been cat, dog, whatever. If it was on a plate in front of me I tried it. One dish they gave us was a whole duck which was presented to the table cooked and then the skin was carefully removed to form pancakes which you filled with different ingredients and ate. We had a couple of these duck skins and then they came to take the duck away.

'What's the matter with it?' I asked.

'Oh, you don't eat that,' the Japanese waiter told me. 'That gets thrown in the bin.'

'You've got to be having a laugh,' I said. 'Send it up to my room. I'll eat it later.'

One day we had a lovely fifteen-course meal and we got some good beer to drink but in tiny bottles. When the translator who ate with us asked me if I'd like some sake I said, 'No, tell him I want more of those beers. Tell him I want sixty of them.'

The translator couldn't believe what he was hearing. The beers were coming every five minutes, much to the astonishment of him, the waiters and the other people eating in the restaurant. The Japanese and Chinese can't drink lots, you see. They have a genetic intolerance to alcohol, so to watch me downing all these beers and not get drunk was a mystery to them. When the boys and I used to take these Japs out we got them absolutely rat-arsed in no time, it only took a few bottles. It's hard to get really drunk in Japan because you seem to be eating every five minutes.

At that time the men would eat at one end of the table and the women at the other. It didn't bother me, but it annoyed Maureen, especially when we'd get there and I'd jokingly say to her, 'You get over there with them lot.' She didn't like that.

They were fantastic times. We were young, we were seeing the world, and the BDO were bringing more and more foreign tournaments into the world rankings.

There was the Australian Masters. Maureen and I went as representatives of Britain and I was one dart away from going out in the first round. I was sweating, thinking: Have I really come all this way for a match that isn't going to last much longer than thirty minutes? But this guy missed the double and I went on to win the match and the tournament.

Finland held theirs in a different place every year, meaning we got to see every part of that country. However, in tournaments held in places like Boston and Chicago, where it was the same every year for eighteen years, someone like Big Cliff would walk into the hotel after a year's gap and the barman would know him by name and say to him, 'Same as usual?'

The American barmen loved having darts players around because every time you bought a drink it was customary to tip. With up to four hundred players in these bars at any one time, all drinking beer at a rate of one every ten minutes, the barmen were making an absolute fortune. Money was no object when playing abroad because everybody wanted to live it up a little.

I went to so many countries I ended up knowing them better than my own. Years later, in 1987, I was playing in an American casino when a Yank came up to me and said, 'You crazy mad Brits, shooting all those people in Hungerford.' He was referring to the Hungerford massacre when Michael Ryan shot and killed sixteen people with two semi-automatic rifles and a handgun before turning the weapons on himself.

I said, 'I've never heard of Hungerford, you dick-head. What are you on about? This is what you Yanks do all the bleeding time. It doesn't happen in England, you dozy twat. Hungerford must be in America.'

But I was wrong, even though I was right about America.

An American postman round about the same time as Hungerford happened had gone in to the Post Office where he worked and shot his boss as well as twelve others. It happened all the time in the States. For instance, I was in Hawaii with Maureen when she went out shopping. As she bought her things she was unaware that on a roof close by was a guy taking pot shots at people. He killed about eight and they never caught him. After we split I used to tell people, 'It's a shame he didn't have a pop at her. It could've saved me a lot of money.'

America was full of Michael Ryans. Later, I was in Vegas with Jane, my future wife, and we were standing outside the Flamingo Hotel when we saw a van and a car racing each other along the strip and cutting each other up. They pulled up right where we were and the guy in the car got out and went up to the van's windscreen to remonstrate. The guy inside the van simply pulled a gun out of the glove compartment and popped this guy. The bullet went straight through the windscreen.

A similar thing happened in New York. It was nine in the morning and Jane went off to shop at Bloomingdales. I was having a drink in an Irish bar in preparation for a $10,000 tournament I was about to play in. Suddenly Jane appeared, as white as a ghost and shaking. She'd been in a cab on her way to the store when a cop climbed on top of it. He pointed his gun at a van in front and shouted, 'Get out of the damn van or I'll blow your head off.'

Jane just crumpled inside the cab. She was sure that she was about to become the victim of a shoot-out. I had to get her a couple of large vodkas. She said to me plaintively, 'I only wanted to go out shopping.'

In those early heady days of the late seventies I may have been seeing the world but I wanted more: I wanted to see it as the official World Champion. The title had eluded me for two years now. Was it going to be a case of third time lucky?

SEVEN

Champion of the World

The 1980 Embassy World Darts Championship couldn't have got off to a worse start. I was drawn against a player called Tony Clark who is still playing now and recently made the last eight of the Welsh Open. Back then the result should never have been in any doubt, it was a no-brainer: I should have murdered him and fully expected to. I went into that third championship vowing that things were going to change. I was more determined than I'd ever been in my life to make my mark on this tournament and become its leading player for years to come.

He stepped up to the oche and threw his first three darts to hit 140 which was a good start. It settled his nerves and made me think that maybe I was in for a harder battle than I'd initially thought. Then I went up and threw. My first dart bounced out, the second dart did the same, and the third landed in one. I couldn't believe it. I started to think that yet again it wasn't going to be. My third World Championship had started with a score of one! The crowd was buzzing. They immediately sensed another upset was on the cards. I lost the leg but regained my composure and won quite easily after that by two sets to nil. Lowey went out in that early round, which was a bonus because he was the main stumbling block to me winning it. In the quarter-final I was drawn against Jocky Wilson.

Jocky is a lovely bloke, but he was the craziest of all of us and of any player since. He had no control over himself when he hit the bottle, and he simply didn't know what he was doing when he was drunk which, in hindsight, was a bit sad really. However, he was a fantastic darts player, even if he didn't have the most perfect throw in the world. On his last dart he used to jump in the air a little when he threw. I used to stand behind him when we played and if he needed double top, which was his double, I didn't look at the dart board. Instead I'd see him jump and for that split second think I'd got another throw. Then I'd hear the announcer say 'Game, shot,' and be left wondering how the bloody hell that dart went in when he was bouncing about as he threw it.

Although he enjoyed his darts and was right up there with Lowey and me, all he really wanted to do in life was fish. He had a couple of boats moored at Kircaldy up in Fife, where he lived, that he bought from his winnings. The highlight of his life was to go on the river in them and fish. Unfortunately he got in with some bad people; so called friends who only knocked about with him because he had a bit of money. In the end the money ran out and he lost the boats and in 1997 was declared bankrupt. It really hurt him when he lost those boats because he'd worked hard for the bit of money he had.

He now survives on a disability allowance and lives in a one-bedroomed flat back on the council estate where he grew up. It all hurt him so badly that he has shut himself off from life and become a recluse. He won't have anything more to do with the darts world. We have tried to bring him back to present trophies and things like that and to get involved on the exhibition circuit but he just doesn't want to know. Basically he hit the top shelf during his darts years, drank far too much and in 1995 got diabetes as a result. He hasn't touched a drop of alcohol since.

It's a shame what has happened because he would have been quite happy if he could've kept one of his small boats and gone fishing two or three times a week. He loved going to Canada. We went with an organiser called Ed Oliver who took him fishing for three days. Once on the lake Jocky wouldn't touch a drop of alcohol. He'd just fish all the time and never once thought of drinking. He only drank when he played darts. Then after a few drinks he would turned into this Jekyll and

Hyde character. His drink of choice was vodka. I used to think all Scotsmen drank whisky, but a lot of them like their vodka, which I find a bit baffling because there's no taste to it. I've always found that to be a dangerous thing.

One of the first times I encountered him was at a TV tournament at the Seashore Holiday Village in Great Yarmouth in the late seventies. Lowey was there and all the top players including Jocky who was just starting to establish himself on the scene. The night before the tournament Jocky had hit the bottle in a big way and the following morning he came into the practice room and was bad, really bad. He couldn't focus, he had the shakes, everything was going wrong for him: 'I don't think I'm going to play,' he said to me.

He'd been to the toilet moments before and there were splashes of sick on his shirt. I told him not to be silly, took his shirt off him, washed it in the toilet basin, put it under the dryer and said, 'I'll sort you out, no problem. You come with me.'

I took him to the bar and got him a port and brandy, which is two shots of port to one measure of brandy. Jocky looked at me and snarled, 'What sort of girl's drink is that?'

'It'll settle your stomach, Jocky,' I said. 'A couple of these and you'll be fine.'

I had to have one with him; otherwise he'd think I

was trying to poison him. That was the way he was, he didn't trust anybody – but he liked it so he had another one. I left him there and he was fine. An hour later he was practising away as if nothing had happened. Five hours later the final was on TV. I was playing him, and he ended up stuffing me. He'd been on the port and brandies all day and halfway through our match he winked at me and said, 'These are fucking great, they are absolutely fucking great.'

'You were only supposed to have two,' I said. He'd had about twelve of them.

When I told Dad about it he laughed and told me, 'That'll teach you, son. You look after your own game, don't worry about the others.'

Although Jocky was jovial and had a smile on his face 90 per cent of the time, you didn't go out with him at night. He'd embarrass you. For instance, one time I was at a casino in Denmark, playing blackjack. I was sitting next to a Japanese man and Jocky came and sat on the other side of him. Unfortunately this Japanese bloke couldn't play the game and he was doing some crazy things like twisting on eighteen and getting a ten or a picture card. Jocky, sitting next to him, was getting more and more frustrated because he'd be holding eleven or ten and be watching this bloke on seventeen or eighteen twisting, drawing a picture card and going bust when it could have been him getting that card and sticking on twenty or twenty-one. This happened three or four times and Jocky was getting more and more irate. Suddenly, on the next occasion this happened. Jocky snapped. He grabbed hold of the poor bloke by the throat and wrestled him to the floor where he pinned him down and screamed, 'You're taking all my fucking cards. Stop taking my fucking cards, pal.'

This Japanese guy couldn't speak a word of English and didn't know what was going on. His eyes looked as if they were about to pop their sockets and he was jabbering to Jocky in panic. I had to wrench Jocky off him.

That was Jocky through and through. He was a danger to himself and in the end he just pushed the self-destruct button once too often. If we were in places like Denmark, Sweden or Finland, he'd come downstairs in the hotel for breakfast and apologise to everybody. We'd say to him, 'What are you apologising for, Jocky? You didn't do anything.' But the thing was he didn't know whether he'd done something or not because he'd been too out of it.

Despite his drink problem he had a great sense of humour. He was going to play an exhibition match at a Roman Catholic club in Ireland, and as usual had proved to be a top draw – tickets had sold out within hours, as they would today if he ever made a comeback – but just before the big day someone ran off with all the money. When Jocky arrived he was confronted by embarrassed organisers who weren't able to pay him.

'Go ahead and play,' they said to him. 'We'll get your money by tomorrow.'

'OK,' said Jocky. 'No problem.'

The exhibition was going well and the crowd loved him. After the interval, and one or two large vodkas, Jocky came back on stage in high spirits and noticed a large effigy in the hall of Christ crucified.

'Ah,' he said at the top of his voice and with a wave of his hand, 'I see they caught the bastard who stole my money.'

Jocky got me during a World Cup game. He was playing for Scotland and I was representing England in the final of the singles up in Glasgow. We were both standing at the back of the stage waiting to go on, the TV cameras were running and everything was set. Then the announcer said, 'Representing England we have Eric Bristow.'

Just as I was about to bounce on stage and give the booing crowd some gyp Jocky took a run at me and kicked me as hard as he could in the shin. He took about two inches of skin off as his shoe scraped up my leg. Christ it hurt, so I grabbed him by the throat and I was going to kill him, but five officials managed to prise me off, and shoved me on-stage into the bedlam of lights, television cameras and baying crowd – they were Scots, what do you expect? I could feel the blood dribbling down my leg as I stood on stage, and all I could think was that I'd have to shake this tosser's hand in a minute. As Jocky came up he looked at me with beady, squinting eyes, fearful that I might go for him again, but we shook hands and I proceeded to thrash him. I had to after what he did to me. I was fuming all the way through the game. When it was all over he put his arm around me, pulled me close to him, and with a smile on his face said, 'I've got to try to beat you somehow.'

I couldn't do anything but laugh. One minute I wanted to tear him apart, the next we were at the bar having a drink. It was a good job I had red trousers on and not white because my leg was bleeding badly. But that was Jocky. He loved practical jokes, but not if they were on him. If they were on him he'd take it the wrong way and would more than likely stick the nut on you.

When we played at the Seashore Holiday Camp everybody stayed in caravans. I used to find out which one Leighton Rees was staying in and when it was dark I lobbed half a loaf of bread onto his roof. The next day, at about four in the morning, as the sun was coming up, the seagulls would attack this bread on top of his caravan and all he could hear inside was bang, bang, bang on the roof. The first time it happened he nearly filled his pants; he didn't know what was happening and rushed out of the caravan in panic holding a tool because he thought his caravan was under attack. Then I'd turn the water off outside other people's caravans so they couldn't flush the toilet. I did loads of things like that, but only for fun. You couldn't do it to Jocky though. Jocky would've got the hump and would want a fight with you.

Even though you couldn't play pranks on him, he could always be relied upon to get into scrapes that would have you wetting yourself with laughter. Bobby George was in the States with him in 1981 during one such scrape. They'd both finished an exhibition at a bar in San Bernardino and the two of them had collected their money, but as they were preparing to leave one or two of the locals challenged Jocky to stay on and play them for a few dollars more. Jocky could never resist the chance to win money but Bobby was tired and wanted to go back. 'If you won't come I'll have to leave you,' he said, reminding Jocky that he would be taking the car.

Jocky wouldn't leave, so Bobby set off alone across the Nevada Desert, one of the hottest places on earth, and headed back to Las Vegas. When he arrived at the hotel after a couple of hours driving he began to worry about how Jocky would get back, especially as he had to cross one the most inhospitable places on the planet.

Two days later Jocky still hadn't appeared and Bobby was frantic with worry and on the verge of calling out a search party. Then there was a knock on his hotel room door and he opened it to see Jocky, exhausted and as red as a beetroot. The silly Scot had hitch-hiked his way across the desert, and it had taken him forty-eight hours.

'It's fucking hot out there,' he told Bobby. 'I'll nah fucking do that again.'

How he managed to get across such barren terrain like that I will never know, but there's one thing for sure, he was a fighter. He'd have battled his way across with gritted teeth, cursing the elements as he walked. He was a tough nut, Jocky; you didn't mess with him. He was quite handy in a punch-up and was never more aggressive than when he'd had one too many. I'd sometimes look after him when he was like that, but a lot of other darts players gave him a wide berth. They were quite happy to leave him in a stupor. Often I'd be the one that put him to bed if he'd had one too many. He listened to me. Deep down I think he liked me, and I had a soft spot for him.

While I persuaded him to go to bed he'd have other so-called friends with him – I'd prefer to call them hangers-on – who just wanted him to have another drink, then another and then another. They basically exploited him and were out for a good time on his money. Throughout his life he seemed to attract the wrong people, when all he needed was looking after properly. Their excuse would probably be: Well *you* try looking after him. It's a shame. If I had one wish it'd be for him to have his boat again because he didn't want a lot in life, just a small boat, that was all. He deserves that for all that he's done for the sport.

*

Back in 1980 Jocky was a far cry from the living ghost he is now. Then he was the fiery Scot climbing up the world rankings. I knew I was in for a tough quarter-final against him, but I was also playing well, far better than I'd played in 1978 and 1979. I crushed him three sets to nil to set up a semi-final clash with Tony Brown.

Tony is a good player, a great player, but he was never going to be a legendary player because of one thing: he had no confidence in himself. Every time he played someone, he would always back his opponent and have a bet on them. That is too negative. Back yourself and kill them; it's an even better feeling then. But give him credit, he backed a winner in me because he lost four sets to three and I was in the final against Bobby George.

This was the final that changed the game of darts for ever. Before that the audiences were always quite subdued, there was never really a buzz around the place, but when Bobby and I played in that final every member of the audience got involved. Everybody quite simply was going mad. It was a pit of noise. He had his fans, I had mine and both wanted to out-shout each other.

Bobby came on carrying his trademark candelabra; it was pure theatre. He was the Liberace of darts, the showman. He brought a showbiz feel to the game. Then I made my appearance, taunting his supporters and geeing up mine. Darts was taking off and it needed showmen like me and Bobby to push it forward. If all players were like Lowey it would be boring and probably wouldn't have exploded into life like it did.

So there I was, it was my moment and I was revelling in it, I loved it. In the practice room beforehand Bobby had come up to me and said, 'I've written a poem about you. It's about how I beat you in the Embassy World Final,' and he started laughing and walked off.

I said nothing and carried on practising. There was no point me trying to wind Bobby up. Bobby played darts and that was it. Anything any player did to try and put Bobby off his game Bobby would just laugh at them – but he had tried to get to me with his little poem quip. I wanted to make sure those words would come back to haunt him.

No player has ever got to me, but I've got to a lot of them. I've beaten half of them in the practice room. If they didn't like me they tended to try too hard and stopped playing their normal game. Then I won and won easy. Bobby was different. I knew there was no point saying anything, so I just made sure I was fully prepared for the final. I had a nice breakfast in the morning and then ate loads of pasta during the day, which helped to soak up the alcohol. I also made sure I limited myself to no more than five pints of lager before the game. I knew I just had to keep playing the way I'd played all week, and I had to do what I'd done day in and day out – walk into the exhibition centre the same way, do the same routine, not do anything different

– then on the day I'd be ready and would win. Trouble was, Bobby was also up for it.

The game proved to be a classic. The first six sets all went to a deciding leg until I won the seventh three legs to one, to establish a four sets to three lead. The next sets went to the deciding leg and Bobby had a glorious chance to level the match and take it to a decider. He wanted double nine but hit nine. So he went for one, to leave double four, but missed and busted out on twenty. I couldn't believe it. He'd missed a single number. No good dart player ever misses a single number, especially one playing in the World Final. The pressure had got to him. He put his darts back in his top pocket before I'd even checked out, a signal that he knew it was over.

I checked out and I had won the title. I was World Champion. My ambition had been realised.

As I went over to shake Bobby's hand I said to him, 'Where's your fucking poem now, pal?'

His head was in bits. He went, 'Uh, uh, uh,' and blustered as he tried to search for something to say.

Then I was interviewed for TV, still on stage, and they asked me if I had any words for Bobby. With the poem still fresh in my mind I said, 'I suppose that's why I'm rated number one in the world and he's not.'

The interviewer told me Bobby was a legendary player like myself and I responded with, 'He's going to be the number two of the future.'

Harsh looking back, and perhaps a little bit out of order but it was good stuff because in the background you could hear my boys cheering and his lot booing. I reignited the crowd after that interview – I'm surprised there wasn't a riot – but underneath all the bravado I knew it had been a real fight to get over the winning line. I went up there mentally expecting a battle and I got one. Who knows what would have happened if he'd made it four sets all.

Poor old Bobby wasn't the same player after that. When he had that chance at double nine and missed he never really seemed to recover. That World Championship final finished him; it knocked the stuffing out of him. This sort of thing happens. It's happened since to other players. For instance, Mike Gregory got to a final and had four darts at double top to beat Phil Taylor. He couldn't do it, and he never had a run in the World Championship again.

You should never dwell on a loss. You should always look forward. Mike and Bobby dwelled too much on their defeats and it finished them. Bobby got a World Final years later, but that was when all the top players had broken away to form a separate World Championship in the form of the PDC (the Professional Darts Corporation). It was a phoney World Final.

As soon as I won my first World Championship I was everybody's biggest nightmare. It was the worst thing that could have happened to the players because they were now getting it in the ear from me at every tournament. I'd won all of them apart from the *News of the World*. One of my ambitions was to win a tournament in every country, which I had done, but I'd never won that one. What made it worse was my dad telling me shortly after I'd won the World title, 'You're not a proper World Champion until you've won the *News of the World*.'

He'd been brought up on this tournament, one of the first in darts, which began in 1927. There were around a thousand entries for that inaugural tournament, and by 1939 there were in excess of 280,000 competing, with a record crowd of nearly fifteen thousand spectators filling London's Royal Agricultural Hall to see Marmaduke Brecon beat Jim Pike by two games to one. In 1970 it became the first nationally televised darts event on ITV's *World of Sport*, and in my dad's eyes this was the true World Championship.

It was hard to win because every round was best of three at 501. It was quick, and if you were only slightly off your game you were out. I just couldn't seem to win it; I'd not even got to the final. Then in 1983 I finally made it and beat Ralph Flatt two games to nil to lift the trophy. I won it again the following year beating Ian Robertson by the same score. That made Dad very happy. '*Now* you're a World Champion,' he said to me. '*Now* you can call yourself a proper darts player.' It was typical of my dad. I'd won more than eighty tournaments all over the world, but he wanted me to win just one, the *News of the World*.

After that I'd done them all. None of the players really minded me winning these other tournaments, but all of them hated me winning the World Championship because even before a dart had been thrown I was telling them I was better than them. When I won it, they'd had it, they were doomed.

I went back to Mum and Dad's house the night I won the championship with the trophy under my arm. When I got up the next morning, Mum was going to work – she was working as a switchboard operator – and had put the trophy in a huge plastic bag which she was carrying.

'What are you doing with that?' I said to her.

'I have to take this to work to show everyone. They've been watching you all week and I promised them they could see the trophy if you won it.'

Mum was about to walk half a mile to the bus stop with it, so I said to her, 'Don't get on the bus with that thing, it's too heavy. Get a cab instead. I'll pay for it, I've got thousands of pounds.'

'I always get a bus to work in the morning.'

'But you've got the World Championship trophy there.'

'It doesn't matter,' she said. 'Nothing will happen to it.' And off she went with it on the bus.

She showed all her workmates and at the end of the day brought it back with her on the bus.

It was typical of mum. If she was a multi-millionaire she wouldn't waste money on a taxi. I remember thinking: Well, if the trophy gets lost or stolen the BDO will just have to find another one. Anyway, I'd won it so it was mine to do what I liked with.

From that moment on my world was changing all the time. I was never off TV, there was tournament after tournament, exhibition after exhibition and the money was rolling in. I could see the game I loved was growing on TV and spreading worldwide. There were opportunities to travel and I wasn't going to waste them. After the World Masters win when I was eighteen I had gone completely off the rails and hit the bottle. Now it was different. I was with Maureen who didn't drink and we moved up to Leek, well away from the temptations of London.

Then there was my new found fame to contend with. I was more in demand than ever. I remember the first time I watched myself on TV, it was weird, especially when I heard myself talk. I sounded odd. That's something you get used to.

By 1980 I was lapping up all the attention and signing autographs wherever I went – but only for people who said 'please'. If they said, 'Oi, sign this,' as some did they'd get my standard response which was, 'Say "please" or you get fuck all from me.' And I didn't like signing beer mats. Why would anyone want to take a wet beer mat home either for themselves or for their dad with my signature on it? Get a picture, buy a picture! I'd sign these wet beer mats to their dad or whoever they were for and say, 'You think a lot of them, don't you?'

When the 1981 World Championship came around there was a bit more pressure on me because nobody had ever won it as reigning champion and my ambition was to be the first to retain the title. Now that I'd done everything in darts I had to put different pressures on myself to keep motivated, so I started chasing records. It was hard to lose focus during this time because, thanks to the sheer theatre and melodrama of the 1980 final, darts was becoming more and more popular on television and attracting ever increasing viewing figures. It was a good spectacle. A game of 501 with two good players is over in about two or three minutes and it makes for exciting telly. If you compare it to snooker, which has lost out to darts in recent years, snooker's boring by comparison, especially if you had someone like Terry Griffiths playing Cliff Thorburn, two of the most yawn-inducing players ever to grace the green baize. I wanted darts to take off and I wanted to be at the centre of this. I wanted the popularity of the sport to be down to me and the fact that I never lost.

I did lose tournaments, though, going into the 1981 championship. I failed to retain the World Masters, but I won others so I wasn't rusty. In fact I was looking forward to it. Where other players got nervous the closer the big day came, I couldn't wait to get up there. I was counting down the days until the start.

As I was driven to the venue at Jollees Cabaret Club in Stoke, I listened to 'Dreadlock Holiday' by Bob Marley on the tape; I went in the same entrance that I used the year before; and I practised in the same part of the practice room as I had twelve months earlier.

The hardest part for me was the first round because I had been caught out in the past. This was the only time during the whole tournament when I had doubts. All the players knew I was vulnerable in this round and were desperate for me to lose to give them a chance of winning it.

It proved to be wishful thinking on their part. I breezed through the first round, beating Terry O'Dea two sets to nil, before overcoming Dave Whitcombe two–nil, Nicky Virachkul four–nil and Cliff Lazarenko four–one to set up a classic final with number two seed John Lowe.

I was out to get Lowey that year. He'd annoyed me. In the semi-final he'd beaten Tony Brown convincingly by four sets to nil, but towards the end had started playing exhibition darts, by which I mean if he needed seventy-six he would go double thirteen, bull, which is showing total disrespect for your opponent because it's harder to hit the bull than go for a double checkout. After he won his match I met him in the practice room and said, 'You won't be taking the piss out of me tomorrow, pal.' I didn't like how he played against Tony; it was wrong.

That was the last thing I said to him before meeting him on stage for the final the next day. I knew it was going to be tough, because Lowey has the perfect throw and he is a steady rather than spectacular player, but all I had to do was play my normal game and I'd beat him every time because he can't go up a gear. He couldn't raise his game like I could, or Jocky for that matter. However, I also knew that if I was off my game he'd grind me down and win by simply hitting ton, ton, ton, ton and just being consistent with his throwing. This is why I could never believe he became the first player to hit a televised nine-darter. He was never a 180 man, and yet he did it, which was a remarkable feat.

In the final I lost the first two sets without winning a leg and Lowey was as steady and as consistent as ever. However, I managed to pull myself together and edge ahead four sets to three. As in 1980, Lowey then had darts to take the match into a deciding set, but he missed three darts at double ten leaving me to hit double four and take the title for the second year in succession.

I had only one thing on my mind after that, the hat-trick, and I had a good run up to the 1982 Championship.

I'd won the World Masters and practised all over Christmas, including Christmas Day. I never have a day off over Christmas. Christmas is for amateur drinkers. They come out of the woodwork, get drunk, fall all over the place and make a right prat of themselves. I can get drunk any time I want, so why would I want to go out and get drunk over Christmas?

'It's Christmas, have a drink,' people tell me.

'I do it all year round, pal,' is my stock reply. 'Christmas is when I have time off from drinking. Christmas Day is my day off.'

On Christmas Day I'd be quite happy to practise for three hours and then get an Indian takeaway before lazing in front of the telly. I don't like Christmas, never have done. It attracts too much trouble because too many people mix their drinks and don't know what they're doing.

In 1982 I also had a lovely draw; Lowey was in the bottom half so I didn't have to meet him until the final. On paper it looked great, but on paper doesn't count. I came up against Steve Brennan and I lost.

Steve was a civil engineer from Lewiston who began playing county darts for Suffolk in 1979. He was never good enough to play for England but was eligible to play for Northern Ireland because his dad Pat was born in Derry. This was his World Championship debut. On paper I should have murdered him, but the first round jitters struck yet again and I didn't play well at all. Even playing below par I should have beaten him, but he managed to raise his game and hardly missed a double to take the match two–nil and cause the greatest upset in darting history.

I was annoyed, and what riled me was that these players who cause these sorts of major upsets never go on to win the damn thing. This player wasn't good enough for England and shouldn't really have been there. He was picking up ranking points via Ireland, so that upset me a little bit. I was also annoyed with myself. I had prepared properly and everything felt right.

When I lost John Lowe and Jocky were ecstatic. They shook my hand in the practice room and said, 'Unlucky', but as they did so they had big beaming smiles on their faces. For twelve months I'd been telling everybody who'd listen I was going to win it three years on the bounce and all of a sudden I was out. I was faced with a long couple of weeks because I always took a week off after the tournament finished. Now I had two weeks without darts, so I settled back and watched it on TV. Brennan played Whitcombe in the next round and beat him two sets to nil before going out four–nil to Swede Stefan Lord. Again this wound me up because I knew I could beat all these players. I'd have beaten Stefan with two darts never mind three. Brennan beat me again four years later in the MFI World Matchplay tournament, prompting me to tell a TV interviewer afterwards, 'I'm sick of getting beat by wallies.' Everybody called him Wally after that.

I have no excuses for being beaten by Steve, though.

I just remember playing and thinking that it didn't feel right. Everything was going in OK in the practice room, but sometimes you can play lovely in there and just not take it out with you onto the main stage. Other times you can play badly in practice and it suddenly all comes together when it's game on. I've never been able to understand that. That's why I've never worried about what people say in the practice room. I'd have people coming up to me telling me such and such a player who I was due to meet was hitting one-eighty after one-eighty after one-eighty and I'd say to them, 'I don't give a shit what he gets in here, it's what he gets out there that counts.'

Jocky won the 1982 World Championship. He beat Lowey five sets to three in the final. That was his first title, but he had a much easier ride with me not being there. He owes Brennan a drink for that one.

I just threw myself into the next tournament. The great thing about darts is that you haven't got time to dwell on anything because the next tournament comes round within weeks if not days. I took out my anger on the dart board and looked to 1983. In the meantime I had other commitments in the form of additional TV appearances on game shows and the like. Suddenly darts players were in demand as celebrities and I was right in the thick of it.

EIGHT

You Can't Beat a Bit of Bully

TV catapulted darts into the mainstream just as I was beginning to make my mark. As I've said before, it couldn't have come at a better time. The inspiration for darts becoming huge on the box, the bridge to success as it were, had to be *Indoor League*, which was first televised in 1972. It was hosted by England cricket legend Fred Trueman who wore a cardigan whilst smoking a pipe during his links! The show featured indoor games such as shove ha'penny, bar billiards, pool, skittles, arm wrestling and darts, and Trueman always ended the show with the phrase 'Ah'll see thee.'

The show was the brainchild of Sid Waddell, who'd later go on to become the voice of darts when the World Championship began. Sid, a Geordie and Cambridge graduate, is completely mad and has established himself as darts' number one commentator when in fact he knows very little about the maths of the sport, which I think is important if you want to be a good commentator. He couldn't tell you how to go out on something like eighty-six or sixty-seven, and I've always thought that if it's your job you should learn how to do it.

He's enthusiastic, however – a little too much so at some points. At one tournament, when he first started in the 1970s, he became so excited he actually threw up over his microphone. This sums him up really, he loves the game with a passion – but he doesn't know the check-outs. If truth be told he doesn't care, because he'll always have someone with him in the commentary box to whisper in his ear. It's normally me or Keith Deller now.

He does tend to polarise opinion. People either love or hate him. I know people who have to turn the sound down when he comes on, but he has said some brilliant things, especially about me, from 'Bristow reasons . . . Bristow quickens . . . Aaahhhhh, Bristow' to 'When Alexander of Macedonia was thirty-three he cried salt tears because there were no more worlds to conquer . . . Bristow is only twenty-seven.'

Indoor League, which was filmed in Leeds, was Sid's baby and it was fun. Within a couple of years of it first being shown viewing figures were going through the roof and it made celebrities out of people like Clive Myers, who was the arm wrestling champion. I remember watching it when I was sixteen and they had these eight professionals playing in the darts part of the programme, two of whom I'd absolutely destroyed in the pub for money, so I was desperate to get on it because they were earning upwards of £3,000. However, I had to go through the rigmarole of local league, Super League, county and international darts before I'd even be considered for the *Indoor League*, even though the guys who won it, players like Colin Minton, Tommy O'Regan and Conrad Daniels, I could beat easily.

I made it onto the show when I was eighteen and got knocked out in the semi-final. So much for my frustration at not getting on the show ... when I did I couldn't win it.

Not every aspect of *Indoor League* ran as smoothly as the darts, which proved to be the main draw. One year, only seven professional arm wrestlers turned up, and so the organisers asked if an audience member would like to make up the eighth slot. Whoever volunteered would get £125, a lot of money back then. A big burly bloke volunteered, but snapped his arm during the wrestle. His screams could be heard outside as well as inside the building. Nobody had taught him that when you're arm wrestling and you're losing, you are supposed to let your arm go and accept defeat, otherwise your arm breaks like a twig. Nowadays it would never have been allowed to happen, but if it did the victim could have sued the TV company for thousands of pounds. Back then, nobody gave a toss.

I also played on one of the last *Indoor Leagues* in the late 1970s which was a pro/celebrity tournament. I was paired with Nicholas Parsons who back then hosted

Sale of the Century. I was still trying to make a name for myself and just before we were due to go out and play he said to me: 'How does my hair look?'

'Forget your hair, you silly sod,' I said. 'Just get up there and throw darts.'

He looked at me wide-eyed. 'What's going on here then?' he said, 'You're a bit aggressive aren't you?'

'Get up there and throw those darts,' I said, 'and less of the "how's my hair", you fucking plonker.'

It was perhaps a bit over-the-top and maybe I shouldn't have said it, but that's TV people for you. They are all so vain. We did win, but he was awful, a really poor player.

There were some decent ones though. Robert Powell liked his darts, and so did Dennis Waterman. They were regular players at charity events and often played with or against me in matches that were just as competitive as a World Championship final. Telly or no telly, I played everything to win, and the celebrities were just as hungry too – well, maybe not Nicholas Parsons – and as soon as they stepped up to the oche these showbiz types became deadly serious. They wanted to get one over on their mates. Charity didn't come into it.

The biggest showbiz darts nut I ever met was the singer Engelbert Humperdinck who embarrassed the arse off me in Vegas. I was playing at the Tropicana in the nineties when I got a message on my mobile saying it was Engelbert Humperdinck's son and would I please call him. I refused to ring at first because I thought it was a wind-up, but when I did this voice on the other end said, 'How are you, mate? My dad wants you to come and watch him.'

He was playing at Caesar's Palace. I still thought it was a wind-up, right until the moment I collected the complimentary tickets and we were put in the front row.

Everybody in the place was allowed to take two drinks into the auditorium, but Engelbert had organised it so I had my own personal waiter and I was ordering White Russian after White Russian after White Russian, oblivious to the fact that the rest of the audience was looking at me in envy. Halfway through the show, which got better the more I drank, Engelbert stopped the music and a hush went about the place. Then he said, 'I'd like to make a special mention . . . we have five times World Darts Champion Eric Bristow with us tonight.'

I didn't need that. Half the audience didn't have a clue who I was because they didn't follow darts, but I stood up to the applause, much to my embarrassment, and as I did I turned to my waiter and said, 'Two more White Russians.'

After the show I was invited backstage where Engelbert had a dart board set up in his dressing room. We had a couple of games and I said to him, 'Where's the ashtray then?'

Engelbert said to his son, 'Get Eric an ashtray.'

So I had a smoke and a drink of his wine, which was top quality claret, and we played a few legs of darts.

Afterwards his son said to me, 'I don't believe it. No one is allowed to smoke in his dressing room. We can't smoke and you're even drinking his wine. He won't let us near that either.'

He was a good player. I murdered him but he was good. He could've played for a league team easily.

The next day he invited us to have a round of golf with him and we played for five dollars a hole. Engelbert was desperate to win, even though he had enough money to last him two lifetimes, never mind one, but that is how it should be. When he gave us our balls to play with they had EH on them. I was with a friend called Dick who lost his in a pond on the seventeenth. He hitched his trousers up, took his shoes and socks off and waded in looking for it.

'What are you doing?' I said. 'I've got some spare balls.'

But Dick found it, wiped it clean and said, 'I want him to sign it later. It's the only ball I've got left with his initials on it.'

Engelbert really was darts mad and invited all the players up to his Vegas gaff for a few drinks. Jamie Harvey was there and Engelbert had a karaoke machine. Jamie has a thing where every time he sees a karaoke he insists on having a sing on it. So he sang for Engelbert and at the end of it said, 'I bet not many people have sung for you have they, mate?'

I played at Engelbert's house for two hours in Leicester once and the TV cameras were there to film it. We played and he won one leg. Guess which leg they kept showing on TV. But he was great, very down to earth and would have enjoyed appearing as a celebrity on *Indoor League*.

Eventually *Indoor League* dropped the bar games and concentrated solely on darts as the top players battled it out in Leeds. For people like Nicky Virachkul and Stefan Lord filming always proved to be a big temptation because they loved gambling – if they were in a pub together and spotted two flies they'd bet on which one flew off the wall first – and there was a casino straight across the road from the studio. As soon as they collected their prize money they'd be straight into the casino and a few hours later they'd come out with nothing. It didn't mean anything to Nicky because he came from a rich family. When he was younger and living in Thailand, he'd always go down town to a certain pub because it had a dart board. His dad said to him, 'What do you do when you go down town?' And when Nicky told him he played darts, his dad simply bought him the pub so he could live there and practise whenever he liked. Nicky was into the darts scene in general, rather than just trophy hunting, and his big enjoyment was travelling around the world with us, having a laugh. Money couldn't buy that.

*

The biggest TV game show connected to darts had to be *Bullseye*, which began its run in 1981 and in its prime was watched by fifteen million viewers on a Sunday evening. Teams of two competed, but one member of each team had to be a non-darts player who answered questions to allow his partner to throw the darts. There was also a charity interlude in which a top player would be invited on to throw nine darts at the board. The aim was to get as high a score as possible which was then converted to pounds and donated to a charity of the player's choice. If you got a score of 301 or over the money was doubled. That was nerve-racking.

The first time I went on I supported two Welsh lads who got through to the final. They had six darts between them to score 101 or over to win the star prize. The non-darts player stepped up to the oche first and his first dart missed the board completely. His second went in treble twenty and his third landed in double top. That meant his mate needed one with three darts. I think they won a speedboat, which is handy when you live in a high-rise block of flats.

I made about seventeen appearances on *Bullseye*. I loved it, and I hit 301 or over in about six of them. You'd be there for about four hours during filming and in those four hours they'd play the theme tune about thirty times. Afterwards you just couldn't get it out of your head.

Jim Bowen, the presenter, was great. When he wasn't

doing *Bullseye* he had a jazz band. He played on the *QE2* when I was doing exhibitions on it with Maureen. Everything was paid for; the whole thing was all-inclusive – except for the bar bill. I was only there for a week's stint, but on my first trip the bar bill came to £1,800 and the second time I went it was £2,200. I ended up out of pocket. Jim would play with his band until about half past eleven at night then join me at the bar with his wife until three in the morning.

Going on *Bullseye* was worse than appearing in any World Championship. I remember when I first went on, I was wondering what would happen if I had a repeat of my 1980 match where I went bounce out, bounce out, one. It would be utter humiliation. Fortunately I did OK. The best ones were the Christmas shows. In 1983 it was Keith Deller, Jocky Wilson and me as special guests and we all appeared in fancy dress. I was a Pearly King, Jocky was a Scotsman all togged up in full kilt regalia complete with a *sgian-dubh*, which is a small dagger, and Keith was the Milky Bar Kid.

We were all in the green room before filming started when Rod Hull came into the bar. He was the surprise celebrity guest who came on at the end of the show. I wasn't keen on him; I'd seen what he did with other people. He basically used the puppet to feel up women and stick his hand between people's legs. It was out of order. We'd all had a drink, perhaps one or two more than we should because the Christmas special did attract a kind of party atmosphere. I turned to Jocky and Keith and said: 'I'm going to sort this out right now.'

I walked up to him and Jocky followed close behind. He always followed me in these sorts of situations. I went straight up Rod Hull's face, eyeball to eyeball, and said, 'Now listen, pal. When you come on set later on with that fucking silly bird of yours, if you come anywhere near me with that fucking thing I will knock you out straight, on telly, whether it's fucking live or not. I will bop you.'

I kept looking him straight in the eyes and he knew I meant it. I added, 'I will fucking put you down, mate,' and turned to walk back to my pint.

As I did that Jocky came up to him, pulled his *sgian-dubh* out of his sock, and brandishing it said, 'Aye, pal, and I'll fucking kill the bastard bird!'

When Hull came on later on he was pulling Jim Bowen all over the place with his stupid Emu, but he didn't come anywhere near us; he daren't. Then the silly sod went and fell off his roof and died some years later. What a plonker. When I heard about it I thought, well it's a pity that bird can't fly or it could've saved him. I didn't like Rod Hull. He was a pervert who was getting away with something that wasn't right. That's why if he'd touched me inappropriately with his hand I would've sparked him. His bottle went when I threatened him. He'd only come down to have a quiet drink before the show, but I had to nip it in the bud. I didn't want another situation developing as happened on Michael Parkinson's show a few years earlier where he assaulted Michael so much that he fell backwards off his chair. That was well out of order.

Fortunately there was no repeat of this on *Bullseye* and it ended up being a great show. They filmed the Christmas shows in August and it was very strange to see everyone in the audience dressed up all Christmassy. There was Christmas music and at the end we were all lined up waving to the camera and wishing everyone Merry Christmas. Then you stepped out of the studio and outside it was boiling hot. Bizarre! The prizes on the show always used to make me laugh too. They were rubbish: a set of Charles Dickens's books, a Teasmade, canteens of cutlery and the boats you could win if you got the star prize. What is the point of speedboat if you live in Sheffield or Birmingham? Where's the nearest water? But the programme makers always offered a cash alternative instead of the prize once the cameras were turned off. Jim Bowen, the presenter, was nervous as hell throughout the filming. He made that many mistakes all you heard was 'Cut, Cut, Cut'. While I was there he asked one contestant, 'And what do you do?'

'I'm unemployed, Jim,' came the reply.

'Great, super, lovely,' Jim said, and then you'd hear laughter from the audience and the producer going 'Cut, right, let's start again.'

He may have been a nervous wreck but Jim made *Bullseye* the ratings puller that it was, and he was absolutely devastated when it was axed in 1995. It was still attracting huge viewing figures. Somebody at the top made a big boo boo getting rid of it. It was a working-class tradition: go down the pub on a Sunday, come home, watch *Bullseye*, have a nap, then have your Sunday dinner. What could be better than that? It was also great for up and coming darts players. With upwards of thirty shows a year you couldn't just have the top players on all the time, so it gave lesser-known ones the chance to put themselves in the limelight – and it was quite a prestigious thing to own a Bronze Bully for the highest nine-darter. No darts player ever refused to go on that show.

They filmed three-a-day and the whole series was filmed over ten days. When the curtain came down on it I felt so sorry for Jim. He said to me shortly afterwards, 'I can't understand it, Eric. I told them I only wanted another two or three more years. It was still doing well.' There were tears in his eyes as he said this. It was like a bereavement to him. Even today the decision to axe it still doesn't make sense. Jim used to go round all the colleges and universities taking *Bullseye* on tour and there were loads of Jim Bowen Fan Clubs. It had a cult following among students.

If Jim was the face of *Bullseye*, Tony Green was the voice. He was a good darts player in his time. When

I won my first World Championship in 1980 Tony was a very good Lancashire County player. During those championships we all stayed at the same hotel for about eight days and we'd practise there. Tony loved playing for money. He'd play 1001 for a tenner a game, and one night he took all Jocky's cash because Jocky saw him as a commentator and had no idea he could play darts as well. Jocky had already had far too much to drink and Tony threw ton, ton, ton, eighty, one-forty.

It made me laugh on *Bullseye* when the finalists came up to the oche to try and hit 101 in six darts and win the star prize, and Tony would be saying to them, 'Take your time, take your time, don't rush, nice and easy now, nice and easy.' I'd be at the side if I was the special guest, watching this and thinking: Tony, will you shut up and let them get on with it? And as they were about to throw you could see him start to lean towards the dart board, almost willing them to hit treble twenty. Then the dart would hit the board, miss twenty, and he would say, 'That's five.' You could almost read the mind of the player thinking: I know it's a frigging five, pal. Now will you shut up and just let me throw? And then he'd be off again: 'Take your time, take your time, easy does it, take your time, there's no rush.'

They brought the programme back on Challenge TV with Dave Spikey as host, but it wasn't the same. Phil Taylor was one of the guests for the nine-darter and he threw a bad score. Dave interviewed him afterwards and Phil said, 'I threw shit there.' The producer yelled 'Cut' and they refilmed it, allowing him to have his nine darts again. He got a good score second time around. But what was that all about? That's cheating, in my opinion.

I only did one show. It was only the second one Spikey filmed and he seemed more nervous than Jim. I couldn't get into it – it just wasn't as enjoyable. I wanted to see Jim there. He *is* Mr Bullseye.

TV was great because it brought darts into millions of people's living rooms. With quiz shows like *A Question of Sport* I played to win, just as I would a World Championship darts final. I played with Emlyn Hughes, Bill Beaumont, Willie Carson and Ian Botham, to name but a few. When I was with Botham we'd won it halfway through the show, we were so far in front. We knew all the answers because we were experts on all sorts of sport. I was on there twelve times and won about half of them. I was good on my own sport and very strong on things like snooker, cricket and football. Your worst nightmare on there is to get your own sport question wrong, but I also had an embarrassing moment when trying to spot the mystery sportsman. I was convinced it was Paul Daniels but my team mates were saying to me, 'It can't be Paul Daniels, what sport does he do?'

I was having none of it and said, 'I don't give a damn what you say, it's Paul Daniels. I'll bet you anything you like it's Paul Daniels.' I'd met him a couple of days earlier so I was recognising all his features in the little glimpses I was getting. It turned out not be Paul Daniels but Pat Pocock. I felt a right idiot. They even put it on the *Best of* . . . video for Christmas.

I enjoyed appearing on *A Question of Sport*, but these days it's got far too skilful. Everyone is swatting up too much before they go on. When they recognise a synchronised swimmer just by their toe it takes the fun out of the game for me. You like to see these sportsmen getting it wrong as much as they get the questions right. The whole idea was to watch sportsmen and women making fools of themselves. If something can make you laugh on telly it's worth watching, and the programme has just got a bit too technical for me. I like to go straight into these things without any priming and without seeing the questions beforehand.

There was another similar programme called *Sporting Triangles* which ran on rival channel ITV from 1987 until its welcome demise in 1990. It was captained by Jimmy Greaves, Tessa Sanderson and Emlyn Hughes, and was billed as an ITV *Question of Sport*. It was far from it. Whereas *A Question of Sport* worked on a simple points-for-getting-questions-right basis, you needed a degree in logic to work out how to play *Sporting Triangles*. It was based on the game Trivial Pursuit and had an electronic board with three teams of two round it. Teams would roll an electronic dice to decide how many squares they moved. They'd then get a question depending on what colour they landed on. There were four colours: three of them represented the teams, in which case they'd get a question on one of that team's sports. If they landed on white they could get anything. Are you still following this? That's the simple part. In later series they added other rounds to the game like 'Who Am I'. There was also a rule that let teams change squares into their own colour if they answered a question on an opponent's square. It was all utterly, utterly baffling.

I did a few of them and one of the guests was Nigel Mansell. He did one show and got everything wrong. He was useless. It got scrapped shortly afterwards which I was glad about, because it was crap.

I didn't need that show because I was doing loads of others all the way through the eighties. Christopher Biggins did a good one called *Jungle Safari*. I was with this little girl and we had to scramble across ladders, climb ropes and do all sorts of things. Again my win at all costs attitude kicked in and we were easy victors. She did what she was told though. I was saying to her, 'Now get on this rope, swing over to that one, give that back to me and get over there.' I was focused on winning and I wasn't there for anything else.

It was the same sort of mentality that I took to the *Leo Sayer Variety Show*. They wanted me to play the drums to the Bob Marley classic 'I Shot the Sheriff' and I had a drum kit in my house for five months practising for that show because I didn't want to make a fool of myself. I made sure I could play those drums, otherwise what was the point of going on there? It was Dick, my manager, who lent me the kit. The funny thing was, every guest I had round to my house always ended up having a go on them. Everybody had to have a go on these bloody drums. I used to have bets with Maureen as to who would have a go and for how long they'd be bashing away on them. Leo Sayer's show was good, as were others like *Punchlines* with Lenny Bennett and *Celebrity Squares* with Bob Monkhouse.

I actually fronted a programme myself as well, called *The Cockney Classic*. I was the darts presenter and Steve Davies presented the snooker. It was a straight knockout tournament and then I'd interview the players afterwards and get their thoughts on the game they'd just played. I'd get them the minute they'd stepped down from the oche.

I got one bloke who had won his match, shoved the microphone in his face and said, 'How are you, mate? Bet you're glad you're through to the next round?'

He went, 'Yep.'

I said, 'How many darts teams do you play for?'

'Three.'

'Oh right.' I said, getting desperate. 'And who do you fancy playing in the next round?'

'Not bothered really.'

'Who do you think will win then?'

'Dunno.'

I'd asked him four questions and got three one-word answers and a three-word one.

I turned to the camera and said, 'I'm not interviewing this fucking idiot any more. He is a fucking prick.'

Then I turned to him and said, 'Fuck off, pal, just fuck off,' before throwing the mic at him.

That moment probably spelt the end for any presenting ambitions I had. It must be hard for inter-viewers when their subjects are freezing in front of them, but he did it on purpose, this tosser, I'm sure.

Despite this the actual *Cockney Classic* concept was good. There were tournaments all over the Home Counties and the last eight got on TV. The winner won £2,000 and played me. If they beat me their prize money was doubled to four thousand. It was the same for the snooker part. I actually lost a couple of matches as well. One was to a guy called Rod Harrington who turned pro shortly after he beat me and is now a Sky Sports pundit.

Back then, during the late seventies and throughout the eighties, I was always being asked to appear on TV shows, and if I liked the programme I'd appear on it, it was as simple as that. Now I still get invited to go on television, but not as frequently as in my heyday. Recently I was asked by ITV if I'd go on *I'm a Celebrity Get Me Out of Here*. I said no, but looking back I wish I'd done it now. I would've eaten those bugs no problem. I'll eat anything. I was invited again a couple of years ago, but they didn't seem to have the same standard of celebrity as they did when it first started, so again I said no. I also had an interview for *Hell's Kitchen* when that first began. Gordon Ramsey wouldn't have spoken to me like he spoke to those other celebrities. All my mates were willing me to go on because they knew what could've happened if he'd had a go at me – he would've been wearing the pans on his head.

I've always enjoyed being in the limelight. I was lucky because fame came to me at an early age. I feel sorry for darts players who suddenly become famous in their mid-thirties; it's a bit of a shock to their system at first when people recognise them in the street. With me I never really knew any different so it was easy to handle. Some of them are pressured into playing up for the cameras, like Terry 'The Bull' Jenkins. Terry is a quiet, quite reserved and quite shy man, but Sky were adamant he had to make his entrance on stage a bit better. They got him doing all these bull impressions and it's just not him. I admire his bravery in doing it. He would rather go on a dart board, rip someone to pieces, then walk home and not bother telling anyone about it. Now he has to give it all this bully, bully.

NINE
The Milky Bar Kid

In the run up to the 1983 World Championship I was making good money, not only from darts but from all the TV appearances and exhibitions I was doing. The next big question was what to do with all this cash? I was living in Stoke with Maureen and we got together with Dick Allix and decided the best investment was in property. That's when I discovered that a local working men's club just down the road from where we lived was up for sale. To me it was a no-brainer: we had to buy it and turn it into a pub with darts as the main pulling point. I knew it'd succeed and it'd give Maureen and me somewhere to practise. The place was brilliant. It held 350 people and had a big snooker room as well.

The Coal Board sold it to me, but not without a few hiccups. Neighbours were opposed to me buying it on the grounds that the car park wasn't big enough. We had to go to court to do battle. On the one side was Maureen and me and on the other the objectors. When the judge asked if anyone was opposed to the car park all these objectors stood up. 'It's not the national anthem,' I shouted and then got bollocked from the judge for disrupting proceedings which was typical: I've never been one for getting on the right side of authority.

I was determined I was not going to be beaten by these nimbys, so to get round the problem I bought half the allotments that were bordering the club and made my car park out of them. When this was revealed to the court I won because the car park would now be big enough. I remember saying to one objector as I left the court with a big beaming smile on my face, 'Revenge is sweet.' They tried to stop me having my dream pub so I took their allotments off them. It's nice to win.

The place was a shell when I got it but by the time I'd finished it looked beautiful. It cost £21,000 just to carpet the place. I called it the Crafty Cockney, and as well as the snooker room it had all the trophies that I'd won on display and forty members had their own room. The pièce de résistance was the bar where I had over a dozen dart boards with pop-up oches. It was a massive success. Fridays, Saturdays and Sundays were hammered, and as people left I had security on the door letting other people in for fifty pence. It was the most popular place in Stoke. If you couldn't pull a woman in there you were gay, it was as simple as that.

All the local rogues came in, and the gangs, but there was never any trouble because I made sure I had it nipped in the bud before it even started. There was one gang I didn't recognise and they'd been coming into the place in twos and threes one evening until eventually there were about thirty of them standing at the bar. I didn't want any problems so I went over to them and said, 'Who's the boss round here?'

This young lad stepped forward and said, 'I suppose I am.'

'Right,' I replied, pointing at his gang and addressing him, 'well, if any of your boys start any trouble in here, *you* are barred.'

People didn't want to get barred from my place because it was the life and soul of the town, so by saying that I knew he was going to look after his boys and not cause any trouble. They were as good as gold all night. The best thing about my place was it closed at eleven so the gangs would use it to have a drink and then go down town to do their fighting. They'd come in the next day with black eyes, burst lips, all sorts of things. One bloke, a boss man, even came in with a metal brace round his face and there were sharp spikes sticking out from it. He looked like an extra from a Wes Craven horror movie. I said, 'You can't come in here with that thing on your head. You've only to turn round and one of those spikes will have someone's eye out.' So I took him into a small room, the wine room, and got a load of corks and stuck them on the end of the spikes. He looked a right plonker.

On another occasion this idiot – I'd never seen him in the place before – got annoyed and took his anger out on one of several great big lamps I had dotted about the place. They looked plastic, but they weren't; they were made out of reinforced glass and marble. He soon found this out when he nutted one of them. It split his head all the way down the middle. Fortunately for him there was a doctor present who was there to oversee one of the boxing matches which I occasionally put on at the Cockney. He began examining this plonker, who was out cold in a pool of blood. 'Don't worry about his head,' I said, 'I want that light paying for.' Then I saw that blood was shooting everywhere because the bloke must have hit an artery and was in a bit of trouble. He was losing pints of the stuff. I don't like the sight of blood so I just said, 'Right, bye, bye,' and was off.

I loved the Cockney. They were fun times. We had a dance floor in the middle of the bar which is where I'd put a boxing ring and organise Army and Navy nights. They were brilliant. I also had a darts team, but the rule was if you didn't drink ten pints in a night you didn't make the team. It was great for the pub, but not so great for their league results. I got them all Crafty Cockney shirts and they looked the part, but unfortunately they came bottom of the league. But it was all a bit of fun. There was nothing serious ever went on.

The only real bit of trouble I had in all the years I was there was when these punks came in one night. They had spiky pink hair, piercings through their lips, noses, you name it there was a piercing there, so I told them to leave. It wasn't the sort of image I wanted for my pub. They left threatening to do me in, which didn't scare me. In the bar every night used to be this old man in his seventies who'd sit and have four Double Diamonds before leaving to go home to his wife and he was no trouble to anyone. He was just a pleasant old man who liked his routine. Unbeknown to me or this bloke these punks had gone outside and picked up a paving slab. They threw it through the window. It went straight across the top of this old guy's head, taking the curtain with it, and landed in the middle of the dance floor. If it had been an inch lower it would have taken this old fella's head off and more than likely killed him. The pub emptied and the punks scarpered, all except one, who we caught. I left the boys to sort him out. They pummelled him, and when they'd finished I got one of the bar staff to go outside and pick his bits of teeth from the pavement. I put them in a glass and kept them on show behind the bar: 'Next time he comes in,' I said, 'he can have his teeth back.' I used them as a warning to others as to what would happen if they misbehaved in my boozer. I never saw those punks again.

On a more positive note the Cockney was good for my darts and good for my health. By 1983 I had been knackered. I'd been travelling all over the place and hardly had time to breathe. My manager didn't tell me to slow down. He wanted me to work ten days a week because it was more money in his pocket. He also wanted me to have financial security in case anything went wrong, which it nearly did years later! But I knew I had to take the foot off the pedal a bit or I'd burn out and my game would suffer. This is where the Cockney came in. It was good because it became my home where I could practise every night and didn't need to travel. This is what kills most of the players, even today, the constant travelling up and down the country, especially if they're the ones who are driving. Keith Deller for example has always got from A to B on his own and if he's playing an exhibition he'll drive there, not have a drink, then drive back, sometimes hundreds of miles in a day. That becomes tiring if you're doing it four or five times a week. If the money had been there years ago, like it is now, a lot of the players back then wouldn't have had to go on the road, constantly doing exhibitions to earn a living but tiring themselves out. The current number one in the world Phil Taylor doesn't have to do exhibitions any more. All he has to do is win one of the big ones at least once a year and that's £100,000 in his pocket. It takes the pressure to earn money off for the rest of the year if you win one of these big events.

Perhaps a new breed of player will emerge because of this, one that doesn't need to go on the road to earn a living. The trouble with this is that darts could go the way of snooker in that snooker players, when the game really took off in the mid- to late 1980s, suddenly started asking for silly money to play exhibitions and many pubs and clubs couldn't afford them. It's killed the game because the top players suddenly become inaccessible to the younger wannabes. Why get a snooker player for five grand when you can fill a pub with a darts player for five hundred pounds? Money kills sport in the end and if darts gets too money orientated the same thing will happen.

Look at football. In the seventies and eighties footballers used to love playing the game; now they don't mind sitting on the bench for a full season because they're on seventy grand a week. It's wrong, and it's also wrong that they get paid for playing for their country. Why should you want to get paid for having the honour of playing for your country? That money should be used to develop the grassroots game. Footballers have lost the plot. They've become greedy. You can only earn so much and then money becomes meaningless. Take David Beckham for example. I had a telephone call a couple of years ago, asking if I would go to his house and teach his son Brooklyn how to play darts because he's a big darts fan and he'd told his dad he wanted to play me for his birthday. It fizzled out because all the American stuff took over with him moving to LA which took priority, but it got me thinking: How meaningless is money to them? They're into a sport so they pay whatever it takes to get the most famous sportsman to play the game at their house. It wasn't my cup of tea really. I hope that darts won't go the same way, and that players will stay in touch with their grassroots.

In 1983 darts was very much a working-class sport with only the very best players able to earn a decent living out of it. The Crafty Cockney was a godsend to me because it meant I had somewhere to practise *and* I had somewhere to rest. It was the perfect training ground for the '83 World Championship and I went into that competition fresher than I'd ever been.

It was a tough slog to the final, however. My first round vulnerability manifested itself again when I scraped through, beating Peter Masson two sets to one. Then I beat Dave Lee in the second round three sets to two and Dave Whitcombe in the quarters four sets to three, before hitting my stride in the semis and murdering Tony Brown five sets to one.

It was in the other half of the draw, though, that things were really happening because a new player had come on the scene and he was beating everyone in sight. When people talk about Keith Deller they call him a one-hit wonder, but we all knew him because he'd been on the scene two or three years before that, winning smaller tournaments and doing quite well for himself. He was no pushover and the 1983 Embassy World Darts Championship was where it all came together for him.

He was 66–1 rank outsider coming into that tournament, and when he drew Nicky Virachkul in the first round everybody expected him to go out, but he beat Nicky two sets to one to face another good player, Les Capewell. He beat him three sets to one. Then he played Lowey, who was the world number two, in the quarters and beat him four sets to three to set up a semi-final clash with world number three Jocky.

Jocky looked in control of that game until he missed double eighteen for a nine-darter. This was what cost Jocky the match. His head went down when he missed that double because he would've been the first one ever to have hit a nine-darter on television, and the prize money for doing that was astronomical. It was preying on his mind for the rest of the game and he lost it five sets to three. Keith had knocked out the world number two and number three. Now only me, the world number one, stood in his way.

The other winner in his surge to the final was my dad. He was there all week and before Keith played Nicky in the first round he said to him, 'How do you feel, son?'

Keith is a bit lippy like yours truly and said to my dad, 'I'm going to win this tournament.'

So Dad put money on him every round he played, and as Keith was always the underdog my dad won a pot load of cash, at least forty pounds every round.

The day before the final he bumped into Keith again and said, 'How do you feel, Keith?'

'I'm going to beat your son tomorrow, George.'

I knew I had a fight on my hands because Keith had hardly got to the final through the back door. He'd beaten the world's greatest players. Dad didn't bet on him in the final, but I bet he wished he had because Keith won six sets to five. It was a sensation, a huge shock, especially to me. It hurt me more than it had twelve months previously when I went out in the first round. Usually, by the time I got to the finals of these big events I was in my stride, I was unbeatable. I didn't lose finals; my time to go out was earlier on in the tournament, so this was a new feeling for me and I didn't like it. I didn't play badly either. We were both taking our doubles and it was always a tight game. Both of us were cleaning up so there was no room for error, but I was always chasing the game. I was never in front, so I never felt I had control of the match.

In the last set he had a chance to win, but missed three darts at double ten. Basically his bottle went. In the next leg he had a 138 checkout to win, and because of what had happened earlier I thought there was no way he was going to get that. I could've checked out myself, but would have had to hit bullseye with the last dart, which was a big ask. So I left myself double sixteen, my favourite double, and then watched as he went dink, treble twenty, dink, treble eighteen and dink, double twelve, to take the world title. I was left standing there, smiling like a wally and thinking I should've gone for bull after all. I shook his hand and congratulated him when all I wanted to do was punch his lights out.

He was in my book after that checkout. I wanted my revenge. I had my chance a few months afterwards, and again I left him a 138 checkout, knowing that the odds of him doing it for a second time were heavily stacked against him – and the tosser went dink, dink, dink and did me again. I couldn't believe it. You couldn't have scripted it any better. I just cracked up with laughter. I was speechless.

Looking back on it, I'm glad he won the world title because it would've only meant one more title for me, but he's still earning money from that win today. What's the difference between winning five titles and winning six? It is nothing really.

He was like me, he was a young freak. And like me he was gobby. I don't think it ever really sank in he was World Champion. Only eighteen months earlier he had been at work putting jam in doughnuts, which didn't have the greatest career prospects to say the least, so to go from that to being top of the world was a bit of a head-mash for him. He was young in age and mentally young also. He's still like that now. He has never really grown up. But he's a fighter.

A couple of years after the World Championship I played him in the final of the World Masters. He'd had a tough year and wasn't playing well, so much so that he had to get to the last eight to keep his top-sixteen world ranking. There was loads of pressure on him before it started, because if you dropped out of the last sixteen you kissed goodbye to TV tournaments. You weren't eligible to play in them and lost quite a lot of income as a result. He played magnificently, raised his game and got all the way through to the final by playing some sublime darts. I drilled him in that final, however. I did him good and proper. Finally I had revenge, of sorts. I could scribble his name out of my little black book.

He's got balls, I'll give him that, though he is one of the biggest, if not *the* biggest plonker I've ever met in my life. You can always tell when he's been practising because he leaves chalk all over the board and over his face, hands and clothes. I've never met anyone as untidy as Keith. All the other darts players looked after him because he constantly got himself into trouble. How he has not been hammered I will never know – he's come very close though. There was a tournament in Wales at Prestatyn; it was a big tournament with about twelve hundred players. I was with my boys from Stoke; there were five of us, and a few other players who I knew. Suddenly Keith, who was practising on a nearby dart board, picked a fight with some geezer who then slapped him across the face and said, 'I'll see you outside.'

Keith, who had his wife Kim with him, ran over to me as white as a sheet and said, 'Eric, Eric, I'm in a bit of trouble here.'

I said, 'What's the matter this time?'

'This bloke's going to fill me in.' He really was worried.

I looked over and there were about five or six of them and eight of us. Turning to Keith I said, 'Right, where's your car? We'll walk you to your car.'

As we took him out of the place these blokes followed us, so I said, 'Don't bother, lads, it ain't worth it. Don't get involved because it's not going to happen.'

We walked him to his car and then I went back to where these blokes were standing and said, 'Look, *we* know he's out of order, *you* know he's out of order, but who gives a flying fuck because he's going home. He's got his missus with him anyway, lads.'

So Keith got in his car and tentatively drove past where these blokes were standing. They'd accepted what I had said and just watched him, but as he went by the stupid sod started flicking the V-sign at them. They all went potty again and started chasing after the car, but he sped off. I had to take them inside for a drink to calm them down because they wanted a go at me then. I would've loved it if his car had stalled. Then I would've left him to his fate because he'd made me look a right prat. I'm surprised it didn't stall because Keith is an idiot. How he ever passed his driving test is beyond me. He is impatient and always pranging cars.

The best one was when he phoned me to tell me that a car firm had agreed to sponsor him and given him a brand new motor. Dead chuffed he was. He got it and the next morning went out to drive it. It was cold and frosty on this day and the car had frozen up, so Keith put the windscreen wipers on, and the heaters on the front and back windows, but he was so desperate to drive this new car he couldn't wait for it to defrost so he opened the driver's door and stuck his head out to reverse. He slammed the car straight into a lamp post and that was the end of his sponsorship deal. Another time he parked in the middle of an empty field that stretched for miles. The only thing in this field was a concrete pillar. Keith managed to reverse straight into it and wrote the car off. It would have been easier to miss it, but not if you're Keith.

Even when he managed to get from A to B without crashing he still cocked it up. There was the time he drove to the airport to meet me and my driver Trevor when we were all going to a tournament together in America. We were in the airport bar having a drink when I said to Keith, 'Where are you parked?'

We'd all parked in one of the numerous long-stay car parks that were dotted around Heathrow.

'Oh fucking hell,' he said, 'I don't believe I've done that.'

'What are you on about?'

'I made sure I knew the level and number of the car park I was on by writing it in chalk in the car boot.'

This had me in creases. I'd written the car park details on a piece of paper and put it in my wallet. This idiot had written it inside his car.

'What was the number?' I said.

'I can't remember.'

'You're fucking joking! Nobody is that much of a wally. You're having me on aren't you?'

And he was looking at me all goggle-eyed saying, 'No, Eric, I have, I've written it in the boot, honest.'

So when we came back from nine days in America we all went to look for the car because I wanted to see this number written in the boot. I still couldn't believe someone could be so stupid. I had to see it with my own eyes.

When we found the car after a forty-minute search he opened the boot and inside, in chalk, he'd written the number fourteen.

Keith always, always does everything wrong. He was shouting at me on a plane once at the top of his voice, 'I've gone deaf, Eric, help me, I've gone deaf!'

He was sitting there with two white things sticking out of his ears: tissues or ear plugs or something, he'd put them in but forgotten about them during take-off. I had to shout to him, 'Shut up, you dick,' and point to the plugs.

And he's accident prone. I was close to an airport escalator when there was a kerfuffle with everybody standing around at the top of it looking down. I walked over and at the bottom was a heap of people. Somebody had fallen and taken everybody with him. There were writhing bodies, bags, everything. I said to an old woman standing at the side watching it with me, 'I bet Keith Deller is at the bottom of that.'

Security was helping get all the bags and people up, and the last one to be pulled clear was Keith. He stood up, came into the bar and said to me, 'Just my bloody luck. The person in front of me puts his bag right at my feet and the person behind falls on me.'

Even on something as innocuous as the London Underground, Keith can cause problems. One of the first times he ever went on the Tube, he spent the whole journey reading the world ranking lists in the BDO diary. He became so engrossed that he got off and forgot his bag. By the time he remembered, bomb squad officers had shut off part of the Tube line between Heathrow and London. People missed their flights because of him and he got a right bollocking when he tried to retrieve his bag.

Everything that can go wrong will go wrong for Keith and it's funny the way he does it. He doesn't kill or hurt anybody, it's just happenstance. In America, in the big tournaments, they would set up about thirty boards to practise on and Keith would always be one of the first in the practice room in the morning. All these boards had just been put up and he'd throw three darts at the board of his choice and on the third dart you could almost guarantee that the board would fall off the wall. If there was one loose board in the thirty Keith would find it. He didn't just do it once, he did it several times, yet it never happened to any other player. There was never anything wrong with the other dart boards, just Keith's.

America was a bit of a hot potato for Keith. Things tended to go wrong for him there. A year after he won the world title all the darts players went to LA for the three-week beano, and we were all in a bar where Keith was chatting up a beautiful blonde. She was stunning, and he was getting somewhere with her as well. There's no doubt he was only minutes away from getting her up to his hotel room and giving her one – that was until a player called Nick Miller sneaked up behind him and whipped Keith's trousers down, taking his underpants with them as well. He was left standing, drink in hand, with his pecker hanging out. Everybody saw it and they were all shouting, 'Hey, Keith, you OK, Keith?' as he struggled to pull his trousers and underpants back up, and that took him a while because he nearly fell over twice doing it.

The blonde went. Keith was begging her to stay but she was off like a shot. Then he turned on us and snarled, 'You bastards.'

Sometimes we do go a bit far in winding Keith up. He's a great bloke to be with, a lovely bloke, but the boys and I do like to rib him. In Denmark we were sitting in a restaurant eating, about eight of us round a table, and Keith had been to get his meal. He'd come back with this massive full-Monty kebab. It had every-thing on it.

After taking a bite he turned to me and said, 'Eric, try this, it's lovely.'

I tried it and it was good, I'll give him that. 'This is gorgeous,' I said.

The other players were saying, 'Give us a bite then, let's have a taste,' so it got passed round the table and all the players were giving it bite, bite, bite, bite, until there was hardly any left. Then it got to Big Cliff, and he just opened his tunnel of a mouth and down it went.

Everybody was licking their lips and saying, 'Mmm, you're right, Keith, that was really lovely.'

He flipped, he totally snapped and screamed, 'That was *not* fucking funny lads! You should never, *never* fuck about with someone's food.'

He wouldn't shut up about it. 'I don't need this shit,' he kept saying, until I said, 'Oh for fuck's sake,' got up and bought him two of these giant kebabs.

But Keith had spat his dummy out, and he threw these kebabs at a wall and we watched as they slowly slid down. 'I don't want them now,' he said, and stormed off.

He makes us laugh, though, and that is why every darts player loves him, and if he gets the hump it makes it even funnier. The poor lad is doomed in that respect.

When he gets the hump he gets it big time. I've been on the *QE2* with him twice. On the first occasion we stopped off in Bermuda for an exhibition where we played four singles matches each. I won my four and I did brilliantly; I played some really good darts. He lost three out of four of his games and started sulking.

'Don't worry about it,' I said. 'It's the same money whether we win or lose.' Then we played each other head to head and I absolutely slaughtered him. He got the hump even more then. He refused to speak to me on the way back to the ship.

The second time on the *QE2* was farcical, but it was typical Deller. I was with my wife Jane then and it was August 1997. Jane was in bed and I was in the casino playing blackjack. Suddenly people round me started crying. Then the croupier started crying and said it was the last three hands. It was weird.

I whispered to him, 'What's the problem? What's going on? Why is everybody in tears?'

'Princess Diana is dead.'

Minutes later the casino closed and that was the end of it for the night. I went back to my cabin and woke up Jane to tell her the news. She cried her eyes out. That was on the way to New York.

On the way back the ship's captain announced, 'We are going to slow down for a day or so to keep us in the footprint of the satellite so that we can all watch the funeral of Princess Diana.'

We were due to play darts between one o'clock and two o'clock in the afternoon in a conference room they were now using to show Di's funeral. They took the dart boards down and erected a giant screen. The place was packed. Almost the whole ship was in there watching this historic but sad moment.

Keith came into the hushed room at half past twelve and collared me.

'They can't watch this in here,' he said. 'We're due to play darts in here in half an hour. They'll have to watch it somewhere else.'

I whispered to him because people could hear Keith and said, 'Keith, you ain't fucking playing darts today, not on the day of her funeral.'

And the daft sod still kicked up a fuss. 'But we are booked to play. How are we going to get the games in?'

'Look, Keith,' I said, 'trust me. They won't want us playing darts today.'

But he had to ask a member of staff and turned to this officer and said, 'Are we playing darts this afternoon?'

This bloke just looked at him as if he was silly, nodded towards the funeral that was being played on the big screen and mouthed the word 'No!'

I couldn't believe him. Not only had he made himself look a prize prat, but he'd made me look a plonker by association – but that's what he's like and darts would be a less happy and less funny place without him.

In 1982 and 1983 there were serious manoeuvrings afoot. In 1978 the winner of the inaugural world championship, Leighton Rees, won £3,000, by 1980 the winner got

£4,500, and in 1982, when darts was really taking off, the champion took home £6,500. Despite the huge sums of money darts was bringing in, the *total* prize money pot for the 1982 world championship was a paltry £28,000, and it didn't look as if it would go up significantly in the forthcoming years. For other tournaments it was even less, so if you weren't one of the top players it was difficult to earn a living from darts.

John Lowe was one of the first to spot this, so he started sounding players out on the possibility of starting a Darts Players' Association. It would basically have taken the form of a union that would look after the players' wellbeing, because in the eyes of events organisers, and to a greater extent the BDO, darts players were nothing.

I was all for it, I thought it was a great idea, but most of the others were oohing and aahing and were just plain ignorant. When John and I talked to them about it, I began to realise half of them were brain dead. They couldn't see the future. They couldn't see that a Darts Players' Association would give them a voice. We were looking at pensions, insurance for players, retirement incentives, all sorts of things, but they were saying, 'No, we don't want to get involved with that,' and it fizzled out.

Lowey had the intelligence and the foresight to see that something had to be done, but the rest of them were more worried about themselves. They couldn't see that however brilliant the BDO was at bringing players through the amateur ranks via the pyramid structure they had put in place, it wasn't a professional organisation that looked after the top thirty-two players once they had reached the summit of that pyramid.

Although the money was good at first, it wasn't really going up at a rate that reflected the level of interest in darts that was being generated by greater television coverage. Lowey felt very strongly that players were being abused. When the TV ratings shot up after the 1980 final between Bobby George and me, so should the prize money have done, but it didn't. Darts players were seen as working-class filth by the powers that be, to be exploited by the businessmen in suits. It's the same businessmen that today talk about introducing darts into the Olympic Games, but darts doesn't need the Olympics; it's full of druggies. In saying that, at least we'd be guaranteed another gold medal for Great Britain.

In 1982, however, the Darts Players' Association wasn't to be. Despite the support of Lowey, Big Cliff and myself, nobody else wanted to be involved. There was no trust among the players. The meetings, when we did get the players together to discuss the proposal, were farcical. We proposed meetings every three months to discuss the state of the game and how we could improve it. Then a player would pipe up, 'Do we get expenses to travel to these meetings? Because we don't have the money.'

I'd say to them, 'But you will *have* the money, because we'll ensure that more money is in the pot for the players.'

'But we need the money now in order to travel to these meetings,' they'd say.

It never really got past that stage. It'd end with me throwing my arms into the air in resignation and telling them, 'Don't worry about it, lads, we're only trying to help you.'

They saw it as a conspiracy among the very top players to line their own pockets, which couldn't have been further from the truth. We were trying to bring all the players together for *their* benefit, but in some ways it only served to drive us apart.

The BDO were aware of this move; in darts circles you can't keep anything secret. What they should have done was taken it as a warning that the players wanted to be treated right and be seen as professionals on decent money. Instead they chose to ignore it, and ten years later they were to pay the price.

TEN

Back on Top

The following year, 1983, proved to be traumatic in more ways than one. I lost the World Championship final to Keith Deller, and shortly after that Dad keeled over in the kitchen at home. He had burst an ulcer and there was blood everywhere. He was rushed into hospital, put on a ward with other people who had burst ulcers, and in the days he was in there at least three of them died. Dad survived, but he knew it had been a close call, and it frightened him.

He left hospital a changed man. He had a totally different outlook on life and was basically someone my mum no longer recognised, so they split. That was horrible for me, but at least I was twenty-six. At least I was a grown man. It's different if you're a teenager.

When the marriage broke apart I helped to pick up the pieces. They sold the house in Stoke Newington and divided the money: eleven thousand pounds each. I told Mum I'd buy her a flat to help her out. We found one for £22,000 and Mum said to me, 'I'll put my eleven thousand in and you make up the rest.'

I said, 'And what are you going to fill the house up with, Mum? You'll have no money left. Or are you just going to sit on a box?'

So I gave her £15,000, which meant there was enough cash left over for her to have a telly, three piece suite, nice furnishings and that sort of thing.

My dad went to live on the Kent coast, at Sheerness, where he has lived ever since. He goes down to this bingo hall now where there are all these old dears whose husbands have died and he pulls them. He's still a good-looking bloke and a few years ago he had four going at once. He was seventy-one. It amazed me where he got his stamina from. He's had to slow down a bit now, though, and just has the one girlfriend who he won't let me see. Maybe he thinks I'll disapprove, but I couldn't care less. As long as she makes him happy, that's all that matters to me.

He moved down there because my nan was there and he went to look after her. Dad lived with her for years until she became ill and had to go in a home. He went down to that home every morning and pushed her along the sea front in her wheelchair.

After the split Mum and Dad both found happiness of sorts, but I always dreamed that they would get back together. Years after the split, my wife Jane and I would go off to America on darts tournaments and they would move in to look after our children while we were away. I'd come back hoping they'd greet me holding hands, but it wasn't to be. They were beyond that point, but it was always my little dream, my one wish.

My big dream going into 1984 was to get my World Championship title back. It hadn't been a bad twelve months for me because I knew Deller hadn't fluked it in 1983 – he deserved to beat me fair and square. However, I knew I had to put him to bed in '84 because he had been nagging, nagging, nagging at me, in fact at all of us, saying how he was the best in the world and all that rubbish.

Twelve months later he didn't last long. He was beaten in the first round by Virachkul, and the good thing about Keith is that once he loses he is gone. There was no bragging after that. He went off to lick his wounds. I said to Nicky afterwards, 'Cheers for that. Now we don't have to suffer that twat for another year. We can get on with the tournament now.'

I was lethal in the run-up to the final. I beat Finn Jensen, Rick Ney, Peter Locke and John Lowe without dropping a set, to play the new number three seed Dave Whitcombe in the final. He'd had a monumental battle with Jocky in the semis, scraping home by six sets to five.

I had no doubts going into that match that I'd win because I was playing the best darts of my life. I'd hit top form. Whitcombe on the other hand breezed through darts as though it was a meaningless sideshow. Sometimes he'd practise; a lot of the time he couldn't be bothered. Before our match he had a great interview for the BBC in which the interviewer asked him if he did any exercises and what his keep fit regime was. Quick as a flash Dave said, 'I play chess with the window open.' It was a brilliant response and left me in stitches.

On the day of the final I was downstairs on the practice board and he was up in his hotel room with two or three videos, watching them on telly. Just as he couldn't be bothered practising, he couldn't be bothered socialising. He was never a great talker, Dave. He still isn't now. I'll go, 'How are you, Dave?' and he'll reply, 'All right,' and that'll be the end of that.

I bumped into him recently and said, 'Hi Dave, have you been practising?'

'No, not really.'

He owns a pub now so I then asked him if he did any practice there.

'No, not really,' he said. 'Not any more than usual.'

I tried to have a bit of a laugh with him. 'I've heard you've been playing for four or five hours a day.'

And with a deadpan face he looked at me and said, 'No.'

That was it after that. I just gave up. It was like the interview I did with that tosser on the *Cockney Classic*.

Dave never came out and had a drink with us or anything like that. He just wasn't a party boy. I don't hold that against him – you need variety in darts. You need the lunatics like me, Jocky and Cliff, but then you need the counterbalance of players like Whitcombe and Lowey.

Anyway, on the day of the final I'd been practising and with an hour to go Dave came into the room, sat down and just chatted. With half an hour to go he still hadn't thrown a dart – and usually every player likes to get in at least an hour of practice before a match to get their aim sorted and get a feel for the darts. It began to play on my mind. I began to think he was up to something and I couldn't understand it.

My dad was there and I said to him, 'This bloke isn't throwing.'

Dad said, 'I know, I've been watching him.'

He was freaking me out. I've never been out-psyched by anyone before a game, but Whitcombe, by not practising, was inadvertently doing it to me. I used to practise longer than half an hour for exhibition games, and this was a world final! Then, with twenty minutes to go, he got up out of his chair and had a couple of throws. It was spooky.

Once we got on stage all that was forgotten, and to be honest, it wouldn't have mattered if he had practised all day because he would never have beaten me. I was on fire and won easily by seven sets to one. My ambition had been to get a hat trick of titles and now I had achieved it. I'd done it. But then I got greedy.

*

It was a case of wondering how long I could keep winning this thing, because with every new victory I was setting a new record. I set myself a target: to see how long I could retain my title. I'd retained it once, now I wanted to retain it twice. Also, I always had the memory of the 1983 defeat in my mind. I had had a year of hell off Deller, telling me he was better than me and constantly being introduced as the World Champion. It did my head in a bit. After 1984, however, it was me not Deller who was everybody's worst nightmare. I was winning everything, I was back doing exhibitions as the current World Champion, and I was back in everybody's front room.

By this time I had also become close friends with snooker player Steve Davis, and we had a bet to see who could win the most world titles. He won in 1981 and 1983; I'd won in 1980 and 1981 and then in '84 to go three–two up. He levelled it in '84 and won again in '87, '88 and '89 to go six–five up. I'll never catch him up now, he has beaten me, but from '84 onwards, instead of comparing myself with other darts players, I had my eye on Steve and how many titles he was winning. I didn't like losing at anything and this was another challenge I had to win. We both recognised back then that we were pioneers of our respective sports because snooker, like darts, had just made its TV breakthrough, and every year we were effectively making and breaking new world records.

So 1985 represented lots of different challenges for me. I wanted to be the first darts player to win four world darts titles, and I wanted to nudge ahead of Steve. For the second year running I was on fire, beating Ken Summers, Willy Logie, Alan Glazier and Whitcombe again to set up a final clash with Lowey. I was confident going into that match, because my average against Whitcombe in the previous game had been just short of one hundred, but, although I won that final by six sets to two, it was far from easy. Lowey is never easy to beat and never will be, even if he is still playing when he's ninety-five. He has a perfect throw and he doesn't bottle it.

These were the matches people wanted to see: me against him. This was what set the nation on fire, the good bloke against the bad boy, the great ambassador for the game against the firebrand. He would get suites whenever he stayed in hotels, whereas the owners wanted to put me in the cellar. On paper it looked as if I thrashed him, but in my mind I hadn't because I just couldn't relax while playing him, however far ahead I was in the game. I always had to be at my best. One slip and he'd be in there and back in it. But once I got three sets ahead I was certain he wasn't going to come back so I just concentrated on putting him to bed because I knew the only chance for him was if something went disastrously wrong with my darts, which never happened in those days. He wasn't like Jocky who could suddenly up his game to do a couple of eleven-dart finishes and a twelve-dart finish to drag himself back into the match.

Jocky was unique, however, because when I faced the other players I'd know if I'd got them rattled by their mannerisms. Lowey would sweat a little bit, and sometimes he'd throw his darts just that bit faster, which was his big giveaway. He was always very steady, but when he got behind he'd suddenly throw three quick ones to try something different, and then I'd know he was panicking a bit. I got to know all the players' flaws inside out as well, from the way they walked back after they'd thrown the darts to how many times they went to the table to have a drink. It was like a game of poker; sometimes they gave off huge giveaway signs – but with Jocky you could never tell because he'd just walk back to the table after he threw and take a blast on his fag. At the end of the game, though, whether he'd won or lost against me, Jocky would always try to walk off with his fags and mine, which he'd steal off the table.

I can't count the number of times I've played him and I'd have a fag in my hand, he'd have a fag in his hand, and when I went back to the table there'd be another fag burning in the ashtray. Whose fag was that then? Then I'd realise it was mine. I was always doing it: I'd forget I'd put my fag down and go to the packet and light another one up. I knew it was me because on the times I played Lowey, like in the 1985 final, there'd be a fag in my hand and one in the ashtray, and he didn't smoke. Apart from lighting fag after fag, I always tried to keep calm under pressure, and even if I was losing I tried not to change anything. I just carried on playing my game and didn't want to give anything away. And in the 1985 Final I gave nothing away. I'd retained the title again and I was four–three up on Davis.

Twelve months later I was on fire again. I beat Whitcombe six sets to nil in the final to claim a new record of three on the trot. He really did play at the top of his game in that match and it should never have been a whitewash, but I played magically. He didn't do anything wrong. As I threw my last dart to clinch the championship and turned to shake his hand, he threw his towel at me in a gesture of resignation and it hit me right in the mush. I said, 'That's the best throw you've done all night.' He threw it as if to say: I just can't beat you, however well I play.

He was like a boxer who had just been battered until he was black and blue. If he had left a double and I wanted a 129 checkout, I got it. There was nothing he could do. I didn't even have to think about it in that final: I just looked at the board and let the dart go. Whitcombe had just tried to hang on in there, hoping against hope that my game collapsed. He was very much in Lowey's mould in that respect, in that he was unflappable and gave nothing away in his facial expressions. He was unlike Lowey, though, in that I don't think I've ever met a more lethargic player. There was absolutely no get up and go about him. Don't get stuck in a lift with him; you'll end up hanging yourself.

Despite his lack of personality, and the fact that I kept walloping him, he did achieve some glory as part of an unbeatable England side of that time which included both myself and Lowey. He was a great player to have in that team because he was rock steady.

Our England team was dominating everything in the mid-eighties. Before each game the sides would sit around this big dinner table to see who would be playing who in the draw. Other teams knew they'd be in for a hell of a game whoever they drew, whereas we'd want to avoid only four or five of them. For our opposition, to be sitting at that table was like waiting on death row. If they drew me they knew they didn't have a chance because 1986 represented the pinnacle of my career. I was twenty-eight years old and I saw everything opening up for me. Things were going well and I just wanted to go on and on and on, winning title after title after title. There was no reason why I shouldn't. I was at an age where most normal darts players start getting good. I'd been good for over a decade. If you asked me back then how many titles I expected to win I'd have probably estimated another ten more World Championships to add to my tally of five already.

The next twelve months did nothing to disprove that. I continued my rich vein of form and in the 1987 World

Championship breezed through to the final, losing only one set along the way. I was up against Lowey who'd been equally as impressive in disposing of Jocky five sets to nil in the semi-final.

I lost that final six sets to four and it hurt. For some reason I had a lot of bounce outs, and you can put that down to simple bad luck, but I also didn't play like I had done in the previous three finals and if you're not on top of your game, as I have said before, Lowey will punish you. You have got to be consistent against him and this time I wasn't.

After the final the BBC in their analysis pointed to my throw as being one possible reason why I'd lost. They showed the World Championship finals from '84 onwards, and in each year my throwing action was getting slower and slower. I wasn't releasing the dart as quickly, and I was continuing to slow down. I didn't read anything into it. In many respects I dismissed it because I fully intended to bounce back and retain my title in 1988, and it certainly didn't catch the attention of my dad or he'd have told me.

Then, in the summer of 1987, playing in the Swedish Open, it all went wrong for me.

My game simply fell apart. I couldn't release the dart, and when I did it was going all over the place. It was purely a mental thing. In snooker some players can't play with the rest: they think they are going to miss with it and invariably do because they don't then go through with their shot. I wasn't going through with my throw. That Swedish Open was the beginning of the end for me. I knew if I couldn't sort out this problem, which is known as dartitis, I'd never dominate the game in the way that I had done throughout the 1980s.

I managed to get through to the last eight of that competition but it was a real struggle, so when I got back to Britain I went to see a hypnotist to see if he could cure me. I was desperate. This was the biggest crisis I had ever faced. The hypnotist sat next to me, giving me all this rubbish about opening pathways into my mind and unblocking this and that, and I was looking at him, thinking what a stupid job he had. Before I left he gave me tapes to listen to, which he said would help me overcome this problem. They're still in the box. I decided I had got myself in this mess and I alone would get myself out of it.

That was easier said than done. I knew I had a big problem because I just couldn't throw the dart. It got to a point where I honestly believed my career was over, that I was finished. Dartitis affects only a very small number of players, and of those, 99 per cent of them are fine in the practice room but only get it when the announcer says 'Game on.'

Not me. I had it in the practice room as well. When I get something, I get it properly. There are no half measures for me.

At that time I did a lot of exhibitions for the brewery group Bass, organised through their entertainments manager Malcolm Powell. I had one set for a date three months after returning from Sweden, but my dartitis had gone off the radar. My throws were all over the place – on some days I wasn't even hitting the board – so I phoned my manager to tell Malcolm that I couldn't do the exhibition, which was for a group of about five hundred people. Dick was horrified and pleaded with me to honour the commitment. 'I can't,' I said. 'I can't turn up to a place where there are decent darts players, knowing they will beat me. I can't do it, Dick.'

My game at this point was at the level of a very poor local league player. I was lucky if I hit the twenty in practice, never mind the treble, so I said to Dick, 'Just get Big Cliff or Deller as a replacement. Better still, see if the pair of them will do it, then Bass can have two for the price of one.'

But Malcolm didn't want them. He wanted me, and he told Dick, 'Tell Eric to come, and if he can't let his darts go we'll tell them he's injured but will do a question and answer session instead.'

I really was on the verge of packing in darts. I'd had enough; dartitis had wiped me out mentally. That was how far I had got down the road. I was ready to end it all. I couldn't play the game I loved any more because I didn't want to step up to the oche and make a fool of myself. I remember at the lowest point saying to

Maureen, 'What the hell am I going to be now, a postman or what?'

I was only in my late twenties and I knew I had nowhere near enough money to retire on. I was even contemplating going to college. Only eighteen months earlier I'd been celebrating three World Championships on the bounce; now I couldn't even throw a dart. To make matters worse it came and went. One night I'd be OK, the next awful. So I agreed to the Q&A session and turned up. I started practising and did round the board. Everything seemed OK, everything felt all right, so Malcolm said to me, 'We'll go out and do the first game and see how it goes.' So out I went, and I played brilliantly all night with not a yip in sight.

If it wasn't for Malcolm I wouldn't have done that exhibition, and I seriously believe I never would have thrown a dart again, my confidence was that shot, but I found the plot again and got some of my old cockiness back. I knew that despite the dartitis there were occasions when I could still play well. It gave me my belief back. However, the dartitis always came back, maybe for a week or two weeks. Then it would go again for a week or so, and then it would come back. I really didn't know if I was coming or going.

I could tell when it had come back because my arm would lock when I threw and the muscles in the back of my leg would tighten up while I was throwing. What was all that about? How can your leg muscles go when you're throwing a dart? It shouldn't have anything to do with your legs. It was weird. Who needs drugs when you can have something like this? The body is a strange tool.

I continued with the exhibitions and some nights I played well; other nights the dartitis hit and I was awful. It was a lottery I knew I was going to have to live with for possibly the rest of my darting career. I was desperate to conquer it. In some exhibitions I went on stage and threw a pretend dart first, just to get my throwing action right. It looked ridiculous, and I felt that people were paying to watch me throw air darts just so I could conquer the yips. Then I'd throw the actual darts. It helped for a while but I had to stop because I looked a wally. I was the only player who threw four darts: it was silly. It did work for a time. I had two months of perfect darts whilst I was throwing a pretend one, but then the yips came back for a week and I was back to square one.

I did notice that as time went on the gaps between the dartitis bouts were getting longer, and that is what kept me going and kept me motivated to continue playing. When it wasn't there, I could feel the dart in my hand going wherever I wanted it to. It almost became my sixth finger. When I had the yips I could hardly pick the thing up. It felt heavy and uncomfortable, too uncomfortable for my hand to release. So I lived for the feel-good nights, the ones where I could play darts and win, but it was hard keeping motivated.

That same year I went to Canada because I was chasing world ranking points and for the first time in my career I did find myself wondering why. I went nonetheless, and as I threw the darts my arm locked. Here we go again, I thought. I was locking, my legs were going, I was throwing forty-fives, sometimes eleven and in the end I was just letting them go and hitting the board. It didn't matter where the dart landed I just wanted game over so I could get knocked out and go and get drunk. It was depressing to watch.

From Canada we had to fly to Japan for another tournament. I knew I had to get past the first round of that one otherwise I'd have no money – I'd have travelled to Canada and Japan and come back with nothing, what a waste – but I wouldn't have bet on myself after the trauma of Canada. Even my mate Al, who had come over with me for the ten-day tour, had deserted me. He'd fallen in love with a hooker I'd got him and spent the whole time with her. He loved her so much she ended up giving him freebies.

Japan was a lovely place but very expensive. In the first round I got drawn against a local player who was a nonentity and expected me to slaughter him. Luckily he didn't know the torment I was going through. I had to beat him, though, to at least get four grand. If I lost it was a big fat zero. I said to Al before the game, 'Fuck me, Al, I'm going to lose to a Jap here. I can't even let my darts go. What am I going to do?'

We were all drawn against Japs first round: me, Lowey, Leighton Rees, Big Cliff, all of us. It was best of five sets, five legs to a set and for one of the very few times in my life I was nervous as hell. I shouldn't have been. We all played our first-round games simultaneously and I went three–nil, three–nil, three–nil. I never dropped a leg, played marvellously and was the first one to finish.

That was it then; with no sign of the yips I was strutting round the place thinking I was the dog's bollocks once more. I went over to where Leighton was playing his game because I'd drawn the winner of this game next round. I love Leighton but my head was telling me: I hope this Jap beats him. It was wrong but it was competitiveness: I wanted the easiest route to the final.

Leighton, however, won three sets to two and played me in the next round. I murdered him four–nil. Again no yips; I was playing proper darts now, the sort of darts that got me five world titles. Mike Gregory came next and I beat him, so my prize money had gone from four thousand to seven thousand to eleven. I couldn't believe that only two days earlier I'd been unable to throw a dart. In the semi-finals I played Bob Anderson and he didn't have a chance. In one set I threw an eleven-dart finish, followed by a twelve-darter, followed by another eleven-darter and ran out the easy winner by six sets to two.

I left the hall, because you couldn't drink or smoke in there, had a beer and a fag, and came back in to watch

Lowey playing an Australian called Russell Stewart who in my opinion couldn't throw a dart for toffee, so how he made the semis was beyond me. When I walked into the hall it was five sets all and two legs all. This was the decider. Lowey went ton, one-forty, ton; Stewart went one-forty, ton, ton. They were both on 161 and Lowey stepped up and went sixty, fifty-one and then chipped the twenty-five wire when he needed bull to win the match. Stewart walked up to the oche and threw sixty, fifty-one, bullseye to take it. What a game to witness. I shouted out 'Yeeeeessssssss' when he won because there was no way I wanted to face Lowey in the final, not if the yips came back. It would've been humiliating, and I knew that in normal circumstances a player like Russell Stewart wasn't going to beat me over thirteen sets.

The final was the following day, so on the morning of the game I went down to the hotel restaurant for my breakfast, had a couple of beers and started practising. Russell came down about an hour later looking a bit the worse for wear. He'd been out celebrating his semi-final win and the £27,000 pay cheque that came with it. It was a lot of money to him. He'd never come close to winning anything like that in his life, and he was talking about how it had paid off his mortgage and how he'd get a nice car out of it, all that sort of thing. It was all a bit too negative as far as I was concerned; it was as if he thought he wouldn't be going any further. I was enjoying it because I was playing this guy and not even considering the money I'd won or was going to win. I just wanted to win the final and that was all I was focused on – that and not getting the yips back.

Russell liked his Jack Daniels and he'd had a few in his room before he came down. As I looked at him practising I thought he was very, very close to the mark, so, because I needed some insurance against the yips coming back, I decided to go for it and walked up to him, put my arm around his shoulder and said, 'How are you, Russ, mate? Let's me and you have a drink to celebrate us being in the final.'

He was all beaming smiles and said, 'Yeah, thanks, Eric. I'll have a JD and Coke.'

I went up to the barman and whispered, 'JD and Coke. Make sure it's a large one.'

I gave it to Russell and he said, 'Cheers, mate, good on ya, sport.'

Five minutes later I was at the bar again. 'Can I have another large JD and Coke?'

Russell said, 'Aw, mate, let me buy a round.'

'No way,' I replied. 'We've won loads of money between us. What are a few drinks between friends?'

And I carried on buying him large Jack Daniels and Cokes until it was time to go on stage.

By this time he was totally wrecked, so I didn't need to worry about whether the yips came back or not. They didn't and I won the first five sets three–nil, three–nil, three–one, three–nil, three–one. He won just two legs, and that was only because I'd missed six darts at the double. At the break I led five–nil in sets and only needed one more to become World Grand Prix Champion.

Backstage I went straight to the bar and ordered him another large JD and Coke. With five minutes to go before the end of the break he was finished. He was all over the place. Checking his top pocket he slurred, 'Hey, fucking hell, where are my darts?'

That was all I needed. I wanted to get him up there and get him beaten while he was pissed and before my yips came back. Everybody was looking all over for this stupid sod's darts, including me; I was more desperate than anyone to find them. I felt like saying, 'Here, use mine.' Then one of the officials, after what seemed an eternity, announced on the mic that they had found his darts. He'd left them on stage!

So back we went and I won the last set by three legs to nil. It was brilliant, the easiest final I have ever won in my life because he was trolleyed. I got an extra £15,000 for winning and all it had cost me were about half a dozen large JD and Cokes. It's the best money I have ever spent in my life. Afterwards Russell was all over me and kept saying, 'We've done well here, me and you, haven't we?' He was still buzzing from his 161 finish in the semi-final. He just needed topping up, and I was the man to do it.

*

I will never know and still do not know to this day what caused the dartitis. Maybe trying to achieve perfection was what gave me the yips. I do put a bit of it down to that, a desire not just to beat my opponents but to crush them. I always wanted to get every single aspect of my game perfect, whereas, in hindsight, maybe I should have just thrown the darts the way I had been doing year in and year out. I always tried to get better and better, and maybe sometimes you can try too much. I see a lot of Nick Faldo in me. He changed his old swing and never won a thing afterwards. Before that he was always down the middle, then on the green and in the hole it went. He was beautiful to watch. Then he changed his swing and that was it. You can get too deep into what you're doing sometimes. If something comes naturally to you, then you should just go with the flow. I messed about with my technique when I should have just left it alone.

The worst thing was having all these people telling me what to do to beat it, when most of them had never played darts or won anything in their life. One guy, a builder, wrote to me and told me to stand with one leg in a bucket of water when I threw. Yeah, right, how much of a dick would I have looked then?

I soldiered on and carried on playing, and made my dough for the next ten or so years, but every now and again I was losing to people I should not have been losing to and that was what hurt me more than anything.

Players not good enough to even carry my darts case were sometimes beating me when I had the yips. I called it my bogeyman. It came and went, came and went. If it came during a tournament, that was it, I lost. If it came while I was playing a top boy I'd get battered and they'd shake my hand in embarrassment. They didn't know what to say. County players have had it, league players also, but I was the only professional to have it. Mark Walsh has had it and he's done well to get through it. I have a soft spot for him. I really do want him to do well because I know what he has gone through. He has won the battle, I haven't. But you name it and I've tried it, apart from standing in a bucket of water, that is. I've changed my throw, I've thrown faster and slower. I even gave up booze and fags for a couple of months because I thought it could be that. I took beta blockers instead – they're supposed to slow your heart down and make you less nervous. I got through to the last eight of a tournament in LA on these things. I never had a drink and never had a fag: it was the most boring day of my life.

I now felt that I had absolutely nothing to look forward to. I could've looked myself in the bathroom mirror every morning while shaving and cut my throat. These beta blockers are like aspirins, you're only supposed to have about three or four a day, but because I wasn't drinking or smoking I was taking them by the handful, and when I had my last-eight match I must have had about a dozen. I got up to play and thought: Why am I shaking like a leaf when these things are supposed to steady your nerves? I still won two sets to nil, but after the match I went straight to the toilets, threw the pills down the loo, went into the bar, told Big Cliff to get me a large beer and went outside for a fag. I came back in feeling all giddy because I hadn't smoked for months and proceeded to get monumentally pissed. It was a great day. I do feel for these teetotallers because not to be able to have a drink and a smoke must take some getting used to. I enjoy cigs, they are my heroin. Every morning I get up and have a cup of tea and a fag for breakfast. It's something to look forward to.

ELEVEN
The Beginning of the End

In many ways 1987 signalled the beginning of the end for me. My darts was suffering because of the yips and my relationship with Maureen was also floundering. We were growing apart. She was a great darts player but she was becoming disillusioned with the sport and the lifestyle in general, and we split up straight after the World Masters of that year.

We had been due to fly to New York the next day. The tickets had been booked and our bags had been packed when Maureen suddenly said to me, 'I'm not going.'

'What do you mean, you're not going?'

'I'm not coming to New York.'

This was after nine years of going everywhere together and she said, 'I'm not enjoying it. I'm not enjoying the lifestyle or any of it. There's too much travelling. I don't want to go.'

'Don't be silly,' I told her. 'If you don't come to New York, then where's the future for us?'

'Well I'm not going,' she said. We were in the car at the time and she drove back to the hotel in London, got her stuff together and went home to Stoke.

That was it. That was the end of the relationship.

When I flew without Maureen I went on a Monday but I wasn't playing until Thursday. We'd planned to have a few days sightseeing and shopping. I was a lonely Englishman in New York, wondering what the hell I was going to do on my own: I had only gone early for a bit of companionship with Maureen.

Across the road from my hotel was an Irish bar, so I popped in there and asked the barman if the pub had a darts team. They didn't, but he gave me the name of a pub that did. In that pub the landlord gave me a pen and paper and told me all the addresses, in street order, of the pubs that had teams and dart boards and I did a pub crawl of them.

The sixth one I hit was called The Recovery Rooms and as I walked in it was like opening the Pearly Gates. What a pub that was! It had four dart boards, and was full of sexy nurses from a nearby hospital – and they all loved darts. I really was in heaven.

On the first night I played these nurses then ended up pulling the barmaid. She was called Linda, had dark hair and was gorgeous. I knew it was over with Maureen, so there was no guilt when I took her back to my hotel room and gave her one.

When I got back home there was no going back. My

accountant sorted out who should have what and I gave Maureen the Crafty Cockney. That was the only thing I regret doing in hindsight. We should have kept it as a going concern because it was a licence to print money, but it's difficult to think straight when you split. People compare it to bereavement. I also had to say goodbye to her three sons, Mark, Craig and Wayne, from her previous marriage. That was hard because I'd helped to bring them up. I still see Mark and Wayne occasionally, but Craig never spoke to me again after the break-up. It was hard for them too, but it's not easy staying together.

Maureen and I had travelled the world together. We saw the sights and had a great time. Then she fell out of love with darts. She didn't want to play and she didn't want to see me play. If you're not enjoying something then why carry on? She wanted a life away from all the travelling and upheaval. It's also not easy living with me because I'm here, there and everywhere. I'm a bit like a whirling dervish at times. It was more tiring for her because she was doing all the driving. I still don't drive and have never taken my test. Also, because we worked together we didn't have much time to ourselves and I think you need that. You don't want to be constantly under each other's feet in any relationship.

There was also the fact that she was teetotal. This was a problem for her because I liked beer and sometimes needed a drink to wind down. If I was playing in an exhibition I'd be drinking all night, but as soon as it had finished and I'd signed all the autographs I fancied another pint. She'd say, 'You've been drinking all night.'

'Yes I know, but this is a proper pint now. This is where it's all finished. This is a winding down pint,' I'd say, but I don't think she understood that, being a non-drinker.

Then it would get a little heated and she'd say, 'Look, you've been drinking all night, for Christ's sake, what do you need more for?'

I could understand her point of view, but she could never understand where I was coming from because those couple of beers at the end were nice ones. My darts were in my pocket, there was no pressure, I was just chatting to people who I hadn't been able to talk to because I'd been on stage all night.

It was the same in the Cockney. I'd be there working behind the bar all day and playing the occasional county game for Staffordshire, and having a few beers as well, and then at eleven o'clock at night when everybody had left, about ten of us would stay behind for a lock-in. This would infuriate Maureen who'd say to me, 'You've been in here twelve hours, why do you need to have a lock-in?'

Again I'd say, 'I've been working for twelve hours. I've been behind the bar and I've been organising and playing darts.'

Maureen couldn't hack it, even though by about half past midnight we'd be done. She just didn't get it. I needed time to relax and when I relax I like to have a beer. It was just little things like this that added up to one big explosion, and when it came we split and Maureen gave up darts as well. Not many people last any more. Marriage and relationships are lethal, as I was to find to my cost years later.

When I split with Maureen I went to live with a bloke called Al. I called him Al Pal. He was an alcoholic, a Guinness drinker who never ate. I'd try and make him eat, but Guinness men never do. Every night we went to the pub together and afterwards we'd go to the local Indian for a meal, only he never had a curry. He just sat drinking Irish coffees. Then we would go to the casino. I lived with him for eighteen months. He's dead now. He went into hospital when he was bad and they put him on a bottle of Guinness a day for medication, to give him iron. He said to me, 'Fucking hell, Eric, I've even come in here and they're giving me Guinness. I can't escape the stuff.'

Those eighteen months were absolute mayhem. We'd have all sorts of people back, mainly women, and I was living the life of a mad teenager, sowing my wild oats and doing all the boozy things I'd missed out on because of darts. What made matters worse was that I needed a driver when Maureen left so I employed a mate called Trevor Band.

The trouble was, Trevor was as loopy as Al Pal, if not loopier. He was a good darts player and played to County B level. On his day he could beat anyone. This was a dream job for him. He was a single lad travelling the world and getting paid for it, and what made it better for him was that he really loved darts. His nickname was Two Hit Trevor, because he'd hit you and you'd hit the floor, that was it.

We were a bad influence on each other and we did get into trouble. Shortly after I employed him we went on the lash to Stringfellows in London and got absolutely smashed in there. Coming out we were both stumbling about when a copper decided to have a go at Trev, telling him he'd had one too many and warning him to behave. Trevor wasn't doing anything wrong, so he got the hump and started having a go at the copper, fronting him up and getting a bit stroppy with him. This policeman took one look at all six foot four inches of Trev, and called for back-up. When it came they tried to arrest him. That got me riled, so I said to them, 'If you do one, you have to do the pair of us.'

They nicked us both, but what could I do? I couldn't walk off and leave him.

The next day in the newspapers it was all 'Eric Bristow Arrested!' The articles mentioned Trevor, but only in the context of 'Eric and a friend'. I just couldn't win.

I had some good times with Trevor and we travelled the world together, but he died a few years after I employed him, and when the end came it was shocking. It was his night off and he was in his local pub, the Park Inn in Stoke, with another of my pals, Dave Bould. At the end of the night Dave asked him if he fancied an Indian, but Trevor didn't have any money. Dave said he'd stand him one. In the restaurant Trevor went to the toilet; it was one that didn't have stand-up urinals. Trevor went in and ten minutes went by. No Trevor. Twenty minutes passed, then twenty-five minutes, and still there was no Trevor, so Dave went to look for him.

The door wasn't locked so Dave pushed it and Trevor was behind it, lying on the floor and out cold. He hadn't drunk a lot so it wasn't as if he'd passed out through alcohol. He was wedged between the toilet itself and the door, so they had to call the fire brigade to take the door off. When they finally got in there Trevor was dead. He'd slipped on the carpet going in, and as he fell his chin had smashed against the edge of the toilet bowl which snapped his neck and killed him instantly. It was a stupid way to die for somebody who had so much to live for and such massive energy for life.

Dave went into shock when they pulled Trevor from the toilet. He walked from the restaurant to my house, which was five miles away, and knocked on my door at three in the morning. I came down all blurry-eyed and said, 'Dave, what the hell do you want at this time?'

'Trev's dead.'

I couldn't comprehend what he was saying. 'What are

you on about? Come in for a cup of tea and tell me what you want to tell me inside.'

He said, 'No, I don't want anything. I have come to tell you that Trevor's dead.'

And with that he walked off and I have never seen him since. I lost two mates that night. He felt guilty because he was the one who took him for a meal, but that's got nothing to do with it. What happened, happened. I was devastated. We'd had four absolutely mad years together, Trevor and me. It was a silly and a senseless way to go.

My next driver, Phil Dacasto, has also gone. He was sensible and didn't drink. The deal was he'd drive me home from the pub at eleven-fifteen, because I was married by the time I employed him, so, unlike Trevor, he kept me out of trouble rather than got me into it. His only vice was he liked a smoke every now and again, which could account for him getting cancer.

He had to go into hospital to be operated on and before he went in he was convinced he was not going to get out of there alive. It was a big job. They cut him open from both sides of his chest, all the way down to the bottom of his torso, and the surgeon had to go in either side with his hands to let his lungs down, then they cut out all his cancer.

Phil went through hell and back in there and when he was released from hospital he had to start going on daily walks to build his lungs back up again. He did that and walked for longer and longer distances each day and eventually got over it and was fine. Then, months later, he woke up with pains in his chest, went back to hospital and got them to check him out. Initially they couldn't find anything and told him he was OK, but then a senior consultant decided he wanted a more thorough check and took him for a full body scan. Afterwards this consultant told him the cancer had come back and basically he had ten days to live. He had gone through that initial operation, all the pain of it and the discomfort, only to be told that it was all worthless in the end and he was doomed. The poor bloke didn't deserve to die, he deserved another three or four years, but once you get cancer you are never really over it. Even when the doctors tell you it's all clear it often comes back.

Phil died a couple of years ago. I lost a driver, a mate and a brilliant MC. He could have made it as a stand-up comedian if he'd wanted to. Once you got him on stage the quips just came out one after the other. Away from the stage he was as quiet as a mouse. I suppose you could call his on-stage persona his alter-ego.

I've got a third driver now, called Barry. He used to be my doorman at the Cockney and is another one who doesn't drink. These non-drinking types really suit me now. I couldn't do with another Trevor type, however good it was back then. I'm on the wrong side of fifty and I don't need it any more: an Indian and a few beers will do me. If I did now what I did back then with Trevor, I'd be a goner. My body wouldn't cope with it. I have my odd little bender watching the football in the local, but whereas years ago I'd be in there at noon and out at midnight, now I turn up from three in the afternoon until midnight instead and have a sensible drink. Losing people like that has taught me one thing: that life is for living and you have to enjoy yourself.

That applies now as much as it did back in the mid-eighties when dartitis served to bring a premature end to my glory years and rob me of a few more world titles. The 1988 World Championship was the first one I'd gone into with that condition. I started well, beating Ray Farrell three sets to one in the first round, Richie Gardner three–nil in the second, Jocky four–two in the quarter-final and then, yet again, John Lowe stood in my way in the semis. My game failed me. I didn't play well and lost five sets to two. Whether it was the yips or not I'm not sure, but I was totally and utterly gutted because I just didn't play well at all. Bob Anderson was the other finalist and he had raced there, dropping only one set on the way.

I was sick of Lowey beating me so I went to a bookie and told him I wanted to have a bet. I opened an account with him and Anderson was four to six on to win the final. I had eighteen hundred pounds on him, the biggest bet I've ever had on a darts match. He won the final six sets to four, and I won twelve hundred pounds. That went some way to easing the pain, but he made me sweat for my money.

Anderson was the new kid on the block and he had an impressive CV. He threw his first maximum aged seven, and as a teenager he was a champion athlete who was picked as a javelin thrower in the British Olympic team of 1968. However, he broke his arm before they left for Mexico, an injury that ended his athletic career. He turned to football next and played for Lincoln United, Guildford, Woking and Farnborough Town. Then, when a broken leg ended his footballing ambitions in 1970, he turned to darts. Injury seemed to follow him, and two years after his World Championship success he underwent surgery to fix a back problem. When he returned to the game he was never the same player and failed to match the success he enjoyed in the late eighties.

Back then he was a little bit crazy. Whenever we toured abroad and he stepped off the plane, he adopted the accent of whichever country he was in. So if he was in America, he'd become a Yank. If we were off to somewhere like Quebec I'd say to him, 'What are you going to be today, Bob, an Englishman or a Canadian?'

They loved him abroad, especially in Canada. Because he could speak a bit of French they made him an honorary member of the Quebec Darts Association. He was a very consistent and very dangerous player who watched and took in everything during his rise up the ladder. He used to follow my game all the time. In my first World Championship he sat at the front, and you can see him if you watch it on YouTube. Years later he won it.

By then, things had changed for me; my whole outlook was different. In 1988 I was hoping to win the championship, whereas prior to that, in fact only twelve months previously, I *expected* to win it. I still got to finals, which surprised me, and my averages were still up there, but it just didn't feel right in my body. Whereas before I'd put the dart wherever I wanted to put it in the dart board, now I had to work to put it there. Before, when the dart left my hand, I knew where it was going. Now I felt as if I had to push it towards the board and I was never sure exactly where it would land. Sometimes I'd hit treble twenty and think, Bloody hell, that was going above it, and when I was on for a double I just hoped to get it instead of expecting to get it first dart. Things were definitely changing. Prior to 1988 if I'd had three darts at double sixteen anybody I played put their darts away in their top pocket because they knew it was over. Now they kept them out. They knew I was there to be had.

However, I wasn't going out of tournaments in the first round and that's what kept me going. From '88 onwards, if I had started going out first round in every tournament I would have packed it all in, but I was still there or thereabouts. I got to four World finals with this condition. I loved the game and I didn't want to turn my back on it, so I kept going.

I won the WDF World Cup Singles in 1989 so it wasn't as though I was constantly losing, but all the fun had gone out of it. It had become hard work: instead of looking forward to a tournament I became worried in the run-up to it, wondering how I was going to play. All the other top players knew I was struggling, but a lot of them thought it was a good thing: it meant I was no longer winning everything and there was chance for them to dip their fingers in the money pot. My dartitis opened the doors for other players to win things. In sport one man's loss is another man's gain and that's life. I just carried on. I've never managed to get rid of the yips, and I've never been the same player since I got them, but we are what we are and you can never look back.

In 1988 I was looking forward, to the next World Championship. I'd had a decent run up to it, and if I'd lost games I wasn't losing to idiots.

In that championship there was no sign of the yips. I beat the Canadian John Fallowfield three sets to one in the first round, Steve Gittens three–nil in the second, Peter Evison four–three in the quarters and Lowey five–one in the semi-final. That was particularly satisfying after what happened twelve months earlier.

I was up against Jocky in the final. He had hit his

career height, although after the final it was all down-hill from there for him. I was already on my way down, but despite this still contrived to produce one of the greatest sporting spectacles darts has ever seen.

At the break in that final I went in five sets to nil down. He was absolutely walloping me. I went back-stage and my sponsors from Harrows were all doom and gloom. Many of them couldn't even look me in the face, they were that embarrassed for me. I just went to the bar, ordered a pint of lager, turned to them and said, 'Right, we better start playing now then. I've given him a start.'

It was more wishful thinking than anything which made me say that, because even I would've been loath to predict what happened next – I managed to claw it back to five sets to four, by which time the whole place was on fire. It was a monumental struggle, akin to a darting version of Ali versus Frazier.

In the first leg of the next set I had eight darts at double eight. I had him by the bollocks and could tell that he'd gone. Jocky is all right when he's winning, but as soon as he starts losing, his head goes down – and it was almost on the floor at this point.

But I couldn't sink it. Two years earlier it would've taken me two darts at most. Now I couldn't do it with eight, and Jocky won the leg. Then, when he was leading two legs to one and needed just one more leg to clinch the title, he wanted 156. He went sixty, sixty, and missed the double eighteen for the match. I needed one-thirty and nailed it, going out on the bull.

In the final leg of the set he hung on for dear life and managed to clinch it, and as soon as his dart landed and he knew he'd won he sank to his knees in relief and kissed my hand. He was so pleased it was over he just became overwhelmed by the whole situation. I'm glad he won. He deserved another championship.

Things were changing, though. On telly the beer and fags image of darts was constantly getting slated, mainly through comedy shows taking the piss. *Alas Smith and Jones* had a sketch where Mel Smith and Griff Rhys Jones were two overweight darts players, only they didn't play darts but downed alcohol one glass after another as the commentator said things like 'And he's gone for the double – double vodka.'

OK it was funny, but it didn't do the sport any favours, especially with the media luvvies who ruled the BBC and the other channels. They were becoming increasingly disillusioned with what they saw as our boozy working-class image. All we were doing as darts players was going all over the world and having a great life, but we were getting knocked for it. A lot of the other players got upset by all the negative coverage darts got, but I didn't care. I stuck two fingers up at the knockers and would say to them, 'See you later, boys, I'm off to Canada for three weeks.' The people who knocked us and ridiculed our sport went on holiday twice a year if they were lucky. Darts players went all over the world a dozen times a year and got paid for it. So who are the idiots here?

It rattled the BDO, however. In the 1989 World Championship they banned alcohol on stage. Only water was allowed. A couple of years later smoking was also banned. They'd fallen into the trap of thinking the game needed to be cleaned up, but it didn't. The game didn't need cleaning up at all. There was nothing wrong with it. Darts as a spectator sport is perfect for television. What needed addressing were the BBC cameras and the dickheads behind them. With Sky nowadays, everybody works as a team. If they see somebody downing a full pint in the audience they don't zoom in on it, or on somebody else fast asleep because they've had too many, or on a big mountain of empty pint glasses, but the BBC did. They portrayed the audience as a bunch of idiots and confirmed non-darts fans' perception of the game as being not a proper sport. Sky on the other hand recognised they were promoting a game that was in their interests to show in the best light possible so as to get the highest viewing figures achievable. They made sure negative images, which can happen in any sport where an audience is involved, didn't get shown. The BBC didn't give a toss, and still don't, because they get all their money from the licence fee and aren't really accountable.

By the time Sky came on the scene, however, the BDO had already put in place their no booze, no fags on stage rule, and for some players it was a nightmare. Jocky didn't like it at all. He loved his fags and would chainsmoke his way through a match. When they banned smoking on planes he'd sit through the flight munching on nicotine tablets, and when the cig ban came he munched tablets on stage. It definitely affected his game – he had his mind on cigarettes when his mind should've been on darts. My mind never wandered; it was always on the game.

It was only a sign of things to come. The national cigarette ban that was introduced years later in pubs, restaurants and public places is completely out of hand. Why should a politician have the right to tell me I can't smoke in a pub, especially when the House of Commons was exempt when they first brought the law into effect? It's a dictatorship and it's costing the publicans their living. The smoking ban is OK in restaurants and food pubs, but in normal pubs it's wrong. It is killing the trade and destroying the British way of life. I know it's a silly, dirty habit and kills people, but I also know it's better than sticking a needle in your arm.

I blame Roy Castle for the smoking ban. He blamed passive smoking for the cancer that got him, but he wasn't complaining when he was playing the trumpet in those smoke-filled clubs and taking the money. I did a few charity events in aid of the Roy Castle Foundation and the one thing that got me was how all the smokers there were frightened to light up. I just went dink at the first opportunity and puffed away. Then I'd hear the dink, dink, dink of other people's lighters as they followed suit. What a bunch of idiots. There are far worse things than fags. Junk food is just as big a killer. What about the big fat idiots who live off fast-food takeaways? What is a diet of deep-fried chicken nuggets, burgers and chips doing to their health?

Times were changing. Lowey, Jocky, Big Cliff and myself – the old school – were the wrong side of the mountain. We were seen as antiquated dinosaurs, part of the beer and fags school of darts that had died out. A new breed was emerging, and I had the best player under my wing. His name was Phil Taylor.

TWELVE

The Power

In 1988 Phil Taylor, a local Stoke lad, was playing darts for Staffordshire and occasionally came into the Cockney for a drink. Despite my condition, I'd still practise as I always did, four hours in the morning and four hours at night. In many respects I'd upped my training regime in a bid to rid myself of the dartitis which I was determined to conquer. Players who joined me at the oche would have a throw and then drift away. Hardly anybody had the stamina to play with me for that long, and if they did, they generally had a job to go to and couldn't put in the commitment. Even my driver Trevor would say to me, 'I don't want to play darts for eight hours a day, every day. I want to go and pull birds and have a good time.' He loved the game, but he loved the life that came with it even more. That's probably why he never made it as a top darts player.

Phil was different. He came in one morning and we practised for four hours. Then he asked me what time

I practised in the evening, and I said about seven. So he was back there at night for another four-hour practice session. Then he said, 'What time tomorrow?' And so on and so on. The kid was keen and he was like a sponge. He was absorbing everything I was saying, and asking me question after question. I've seen thousands of players come and go, but Phil wanted to learn and get out of what he was doing.

He'd come up from the gutter. The house he had grown up in had no proper electricity – his dad tapped it from next door – and the stairs were condemned; they all had to sleep downstairs. He left school with nothing and got a job making toilet handles. He was still making them when we started practising together and was desperate to get out of his dead-end life, as you would expect.

My theory is that if you find someone who is hungry for success but has nothing, then you can train them because they'll have the commitment; they'll be that desperate to get out of whatever rut they're stuck in. This was Phil's predicament when he first came to me. If he'd had money, or come from a well-to-do family, I wouldn't have bothered with him. I would've been wasting my time. Anyone with money, ninety-nine times out of a hundred, is not going to make it. They've never had to scrimp and save and as a result they wouldn't have had the hunger that Phil had. They just haven't been brought up in the right way to make them World Champions.

That's why we struggle to produce a World Champion tennis player because tennis people have money and therefore they don't have the hunger. If this country wants a World Champion tennis player, set up a tennis school for children who live in Hackney, or Moss Side, or Liverpool and give the kids free equipment. Then you'll get a World Champion. That's the trouble with many sports in this country, there's snobbery involved. If you don't talk right and your face doesn't fit, it doesn't matter how good you are at the sport, you won't get on.

Phil was a nice family bloke who was a little bit naive. He'd not seen the world and the only holidays he and his family had been on were to holiday camps. A young bloke in a low-paid job and with four kids isn't going to go to Mauritius, is he? He was skint, totally flat broke. To earn some money he used to come round to my house and do odd jobs for me. When my garage door came off he put it back on. He put it on the wrong way, but he put it back on. Everything he did for me, I had to get somebody else in to put it right. He told me he was a handyman. Is he hell as like. Everything I paid him cash for was a complete balls-up. He got on well with my wife Jane though. They both liked their food. Phil is not a big drinker, it's food with him.

One morning he called at my house to do a job and Jane answered the door. There was a van parked about a mile down the road selling bacon and egg sandwiches, and as soon as she opened the door they were off in her car to this van to fill their bellies with bacon butties. He was supposed to be working for me! It's a good job his darts wasn't as bad as his handyman skills or he would never have made it onto a league team, never mind become World Champion.

I put up with his DIY disasters because he was a challenge for me. I was a bit lost at that time. What could I do? Did I sit at home and sulk and feel sorry for myself, get depressed and hit the bottle? No, I wasn't going to find salvation down that route. I needed a young up and coming player to channel my energy through. I needed a buzz through something else and Phil was the solution.

We'd practise for hours, days, weeks, mainly practising finishing and doing the maths to work out every possible checkout. He had a different way of finishing from me, so he changed to my way because he understood the reason I went double sixteen. He was a double top man before. Now he goes for double sixteen. That way, if you hit sixteen you've got double eight, then double four, then double two, then double one, and if you bust after that you're no good anyway – whereas with double top, if you hit twenty then you have double ten, but if you miss that you have a pressure double: double five. Miss that and you have to waste a dart to get back on a double.

He was good. So I sponsored him and took him and

Trevor to the mayhem that was the North American Open. I played darts and pulled, Trevor pulled and drank, and Phil was the wide-eyed Bambi, taking it all in.

At first nobody could understand why I spent money on him, especially Trevor, who would say on numerous occasions, 'Eric, why have you sponsored him? He's crap.'

In many respects, when I first saw him play he was nothing special, he was just a normal player, but it was simply a case of getting his head right and as the hours of practice went on he got better and better and better, until he was ready to enter tournaments. When I took him to his earliest tournaments there was the added factor of pressure and fear to contend with. One of the first ones he played in was at Vegas and he got beaten in the first round. He came backstage and just sat with his head in his hands, absolutely stunned – but it was good for him; it was all part of the learning process. I put him and Trevor together for the pairs and they made it through to the last eight. They could have made it to the semi-final, but Trevor missed three darts at double top to win. Phil never forgave him for that. He wanted to win so badly, and still does. Every time Phil loses at anything he hurts.

We went over to the Canadian Open next, and he got beaten first round in that, which was another head in hands and tears in his eyes moment. The boys were really having a go at me then. Even Lowey said, 'Why are you sponsoring him? He's useless. You need to have a rethink and sponsor somebody else.'

'He'll be all right in the end,' I told him. 'He'll be OK, trust me.'

If truth be told, I was enjoying the challenge he gave me. My philosophy was that if you're not doing something well yourself, then you have to put yourself into something else, something to get you up in the morning, something that gives you a reason for living. Phil Taylor gave me that motivation. I was determined to get him into the top thirty-two in the world. If I could do that I had, in my mind, succeeded.

It took about a year to turn him round. I offered him a £9,000 sponsorship on the condition he quit his job and concentrate on the darts, so he took voluntary redundancy and signed on. At first he played in minor tournaments, nothing big. He would set off from home on the morning of the tournament with three pounds in his pocket, a loaf of bread and a slab of boiled ham. If he won any tournament money a large percentage of it went back to me until the sponsorship money was paid off.

His first big win was in the Canadian Open. It was a great feeling for him and for me to know he was going to be a success. That night we celebrated by way of a monumental booze-up and his rise up the world ranking ladder began. By the end of 1989 he'd picked up enough ranking points to be invited to play in the 1990 World Championship.

I'd achieved my aim of getting him into the top thirty-two in the world, but, me being me, that wasn't enough. I then wanted to turn him into a World Champion. Doing so, and excuse my French, turned out to be the biggest fucking nightmare of my life. I was afraid I would draw him in my half, and what would've been worse was playing him in the first round. Because it was his debut, I wanted him to get a run at it. I didn't want to knock him out at the first hurdle.

Fortunately that didn't happen. My route to the final was fairly straightforward. I beat Leighton Rees, Steve Gittens, Magnus Caris and Mike Gregory. Phil, who was the wild card, was at the opposite end of the draw, so we were never going to meet unless we both got to the final, which was highly unlikely because he was a 25–1 rank outsider who still had a lot to learn.

He eased past Russell Stewart by three sets to one in the first round, and then beat Denis Hickling three–nil in the second, before disposing of Ronnie Sharp four sets to two in the quarter-final. He had total belief in himself throughout that World Championship and that surprised me. I hadn't realised how quickly he had matured as a player.

The other darts players were getting wary of him now. No one took the mickey out of him any more like they did twelve months earlier. He was gaining respect. They suddenly realised during that championship that he could play darts and he could play well.

Despite this, I still thought there was no way in a million years both of us would get through to the final. One of us was going to get popped, if not both of us. I won my semi-final against Mike Gregory quite comfortably and Phil was on next to play his semi against Big Cliff. All of a sudden I went from wanting Phil to win, from wanting me to train him up to be World Champion and bask in the glory of his success, to needing him to lose. When he won five sets to nil I was stunned.

I didn't enjoy that final, not because I lost it, but because I was up there playing him. I wanted to be backstage watching it, and laughing afterwards at the player he'd beaten and saying, 'That'll teach you to say "Why did you sponsor him?"' It took all the fun out of it for me.

He played well to beat me six sets to one in that final, but his being there definitely affected my game. Whether the result would have been different if it hadn't affected me so much we will never know. What I do know is that I didn't enjoy it one bit. I didn't even enjoy the set I won, I just wanted to get off zero. It was a weird feeling, the strangest I've ever had playing darts, because it just wasn't right. There was no rivalry there. I *wanted* him to be World Champion because that is what I'd trained him to be, but in that 1990 final I was the only person stopping him from achieving his and my dream.

It was a stupid situation. When we both won our semi-finals I would rather have shaken hands, stuck two fingers up at the rest of them and gone home without ever playing the final. Every player had laughed at us twelve months earlier; we could've had the last laugh. That would've done me. It would've been a fitting way to silence our critics. But we played and Phil won. He was the vampire who had sucked all the knowledge out of me and would use it to win world title after world title after world title.

I didn't mind him winning everything, as long as it wasn't against me. I was never going to be as good as I was during the early to mid-eighties so he became kind of my Mini Me, winning the titles I would've won if I hadn't been affected by the yips. The only reason I trained him, the only reason I created this monster of darts, was because he was a working-class lad like me – and years later he's still got the hunger. He'll still dominate darts for the rest of this decade because he remembers where he came from, he remembers the poor times and the Christmases when he would've liked to have bought the kids better presents. Remembering that makes you harder.

I always knew he was going to be good. I wouldn't have wasted my time otherwise. In the early days he went to a tournament and rang me up, absolutely ecstatic, and said, 'I made it to the final – I lost, but I made it to the final. Brilliant.'

I told him, 'Phil, don't phone me up to tell me you got beaten in the final. Next time you ring me up, tell me you won,' and I put the phone down on him.

All of a sudden, from being over the moon, he was gutted – but why would I want to listen to him telling me he was runner-up? That wasn't why I was training him. That hurt him. The next time he saw me he said, 'You bastard, I only rang you up.'

'Look,' I said, 'don't ring me up unless you have won, understood? I don't want to listen to losing shit.'

It riles him even now that I said that, but I'd spent hours of practice with him to get his counting right and to get his head right. For him to be happy to be second wasn't the idea. It would've been a complete waste of thousands of hours of practice.

I beat him in the British Open one year and I didn't like that. That was as bad as the World Championship final, and I gave him some gyp in his face afterwards. It was all part of his training. *Coming second is no good*: I was brought up to believe that by my father. *Nobody remembers the runner-up* was what he constantly drummed into me. The only time people do remember the loser is if an outsider beats them. They remember me in '83 because Deller beat me. If it had been Lowey they wouldn't remember.

Despite losing that final in 1990 and despite my condition, I still believed I was the best in the world. Phil just played very well in that tournament. He didn't really come on until two years after that final, but winning it was the stepping stone for him. What I always wonder was how much *I* brought his game on in that final. Would he have played that well against someone he didn't know? I doubt it. He knew he could beat me because we had played each other thousands of times, and he knew that if he lost that final I would've never let him forget. So he played my game. He finished the way I finished and he hit his doubles. It was a clinical job and one that wouldn't happen in any other sport.

I used to say to all the players back then that if it wasn't for my condition I would've killed them. I was still winning tournaments, still at the top of the rankings, and I'd hung in there for years, but then 1990 came and went and I really did start losing to dumb-dumbs.

After that nightmare final, Phil had made it. He'd paid off the money I'd put up to sponsor him and there was nothing more left for me to do. So we shook hands, I gave him a cuddle and we remained friends. That final was one career ending and another starting. Now he has thirteen World Championships under his belt and he's changed from the raw person he was back then. He handles fame very well indeed, but one thing I couldn't do was make him a personality. I could make him a good darts player but I could never make him laugh and joke and give it the bigmouth and the histrionics on stage like I used to do. In that we differ. That's simply not his way.

Yee haw! My girlfriend Maureen Flowers and I give it the Yankee Doodle Dandy look.

My mum Pam who always seemed to have a smile on her face.

The Brits are coming: On our way to America in 1978 we all posed for this shot. Then we went over there and gave the Yanks a spanking.

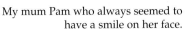

Poised for the kill – I was at the height of my career when this picture was taken in the mid-1980s.

In 1989 little was I to know that my marriage to Jane would end so acrimoniously. Our parents joined us for this picture. My mum and dad are on the left.

I'm not surprised Jane had to sit down. That dress was heavy.

Time for a few beers after receiving my MBE in 1989. Ollie Croft joined me for the party held on a boat on the River Thames.

My proud mum and dad join me on the boat following my investiture at Buckingham Palace.

Jane and I did a lot of work for charity. Here we are feeding the animals at a home for the mentally ill in 1993.

Jane takes the weight off her feet at our home in Leek.

Even at the turn of the millennium I was still playing in tournament after tournament. Here's me at one in Chesterfield, still winding up the crowd. No wonder Lowey's nickname is Old Stoneface!

(*Facing page*) Legends of darts together at a charity bash in 2006. From left - Me, Lowey, John Raby, Keith Deller and Cliff Lazarenko.

Winners past and present come together at a 2006 charity bash at the Dorchester. From left – Lowey, Phil Taylor, Raymond Van Barneveld and me.

At 18-years-old the world was about to open up for me, and I couldn't wait to see it.

He does make me cringe, though, sometimes, because he's a perennial name-dropper par excellence and that really does my head in. He has never realised that he is a big star; it just doesn't register with him. He rang me up after the 2008 Las Vegas Desert Classic and said he was in LA staying at Robbie Williams's house. He was almost breathless as he said, 'Robbie's been singing to me all night. He's been singing the new songs from his next album and asking me if I like them.'

I said, 'Yeah, so what? What the fuck do I care?' and that was the end of the conversation.

Since then he's mentioned Robbie on telly on numerous occasions. He's given it 'my mate Robbie' this, and 'my mate Robbie' that, never realising that he is a star in his own right. As soon as he gets in with anybody he keeps mentioning them on TV. The one before Robbie was Ronnie O'Sullivan, and the time before that it was Ricky Hatton. Me and the boys at Sky took bets on how long it would be before he mentioned Ricky Hatton after he met him, or how many times he'd say his name. We'd all throw a couple of quid in and the one who guessed correctly took the pot.

One time he said, 'I would like to thank Elton John's mum.' What was that all about? People watching the darts at home must have been scratching their heads over that one. He doesn't realise who he is and that annoys me because all these other stars are only the same as us. They've got two arms and two legs as well, but he still looks up to them. Why? To me Phil has still got that small-town Burslem mentality, which in a way isn't bad because it's meant he's kept his feet on the ground and hasn't adopted a starry persona, but he's a brilliant darts player and he needs to recognise that fact. He's a machine, a robot, the like of which darts will never again witness. I changed the world of darts with Phil Taylor. I gave the sport a phenomenon.

However, the thing with Phil is that he doesn't have the love for the game that other players, including myself, have. He won't miss it when he's gone. He's enjoying himself now, but in another few years he'll leave the sport and probably get a nice place abroad and go and live there. He'll put his arrows in his top pocket and never throw them again. I don't even think he'll watch darts on telly.

He used to hate playing exhibitions and would ring me up and say, 'What are you doing tonight?'

'I'm not doing anything,' I'd reply.

'Well, I'll pick you up at six. I'm in Nottingham playing an exhibition at nine. Bring your darts and your shirt and play the first half. I'll play the second half, we'll split the money and then go home.'

He really didn't enjoy doing those sorts of things, but now he earns over £300,000 a year in prize money and has a good agent, so he doesn't need to do the exhibition matches any more. He hasn't squandered his money, either. He's not a waster like me. When he finally retires some time in the next decade, he'll probably ride off into the sunset with Elton John's mum and be remembered not only as the best player darts has ever seen, but as a nice bloke to boot. He's got a good heart, but despite this a lot of other players don't like him because they're jealous of his success. He's a bloke who had nothing, who had to answer yes sir, no sir, three bags full sir, and now he rules the darts world.

He has seen the end coming, however. He got a glimpse of it when he broke down after winning the 2008 World Masters against James Wade. That tournament took a hell of a lot out of him, and it's not like him to show emotion as he did immediately after that win. I believe he saw in Wade a player who is going to usurp him in a couple of years' time and steal his crown, and that's why he cried.

For years commentators like Sid Waddell have predicted World Champions of the future, but if you had listened to Sid there would have been about sixteen over the course of Phil's domination. Kevin Painter was going to be one, Colin Osbourne another, but where does it end? At the moment there is only going to be one person who wins the next two World Championships and that's Phil Taylor. After that James Wade's time will come. James is another quiet lad in the mould of Taylor, but he likes a drink, though he's calmed down a lot now and keeps away from the booze until after the tournament finishes, which is why his darts has improved. I used to have a go at him for getting pissed during a tournament. 'Get pissed when you've won the fifty grand first prize, not before,' I said to him. When you mix with proper drinkers like James used to do it's hard because you feel you have to go at their pace. James has learned from his mistakes and will benefit in the future.

He's probably at the stage now that Phil was in 1990. Back then he was good but I still believed that despite the yips there was one more World Championship win in it for me. I kept getting pipped at the post. If I'd played Big Cliff, who Phil beat, I would probably have won that championship, and it was that thought that kept me going. I'd lose to a player in the final one year, then beat them in the quarter- or semi-final the next. I just needed a bit of luck: I needed to play certain players at the right time to beat them. If the jigsaw fell into place, then I felt certain I could win my title back in 1991.

Phil went out in the 1991 World Championship which was something of a relief to me. He got beaten four sets to three in the quarter-final. Why couldn't he have gone early twelve months previously? I'd played well to get to yet another final, beating Kexi Heinaharju three sets to nil, Mike Gregory three–nil, Dave Whitcombe four–three and Kevin Kenny five–two. The quarter-final against Whitcombe was my greatest ever comeback. I was three sets to nil down and it was effectively all over, but I managed to raise my game somehow and poor Dave didn't know what had hit him. He was distraught. He'd already lost to me in two previous finals; this had been his big chance for revenge, but it wasn't to be.

I was to face the then unknown Dennis Priestley in the final. This time the crowd, rather than being against me like they were in my prime, were all for me. They didn't want me to lose because they knew how much I'd been struggling. That's the English for you: when anyone wins they don't like them; as soon as they struggle they become the nation's favourite. In America it's different. They don't like losers. Second is no good.

I expected to beat Dennis. I knew I could and I knew I still had it in me to do it. Dennis had been a good county player for years, but nothing special. Then, all of a sudden, it all came together for him. He simply turned the corner. Something clicked and he never looked back. This happens with sportsmen sometimes. I wish it had clicked twelve months later because he kicked the living daylights out of me in the final. I lost six sets to nil. Again he was a slow player and again it did my head in a bit. I thought I had learned from my first World Championship, but obviously not enough. The problem here was that he was slow but also very good, unlike Conrad Daniels in the first one who was rubbish. Dennis was going ton, ton, one-forty, one-eighty, ton, ton. I was playing catch-up from the beginning and the way I was playing, which was well below his standard, meant I never had a chance. I don't even look back on that as one I should've won.

Days after the final it hit me, the thought that I hadn't put up much of a fight, and it knocked the stuffing out of me. I had always been a fighter, but in that final, when I needed to dig deep there was nothing there. There were good players coming through, like Dennis and Phil, and others, and deep down I knew any chance of another world title had gone. From not losing finals I was now losing them year after year.

To look at it positively, Dennis was a good bloke to lose to because he is a very lovely and warm guy. He wasn't a party boy though, mainly because he is a Yorkshireman i.e. a tight bastard – all Yorkshiremen are tight, it's not a fallacy because I've met them. Every time he walked through the door I shouted, ''*Ow* much?'' That was his catchphrase. If he bought a drink he'd cry ''*Ow* much?'' and if anybody mentioned the cost of anything he'd say it again.

He's clever, like Lowey. Those two are the cleverest of them all. Once Dennis got in the groove he would play a few exhibitions then go off to Tenerife with his wife for two weeks, come back, do exhibitions, and a month later he'd be off again. Lowey tries to do exactly the same. The Premier League didn't do Dennis any favours, though, when he entered it in 2007. It messed his lifestyle up because he couldn't have a holiday. He was playing every week for seventeen weeks. I told him he shouldn't have gone in for it, but once he'd committed that was it, there was no backing out.

After the 1991 final defeat I went away to lick my wounds, knowing that without the yips I would've beaten both Dennis that year and Phil the year before. Then, twelve months later, in the 1992 Championship I got knocked out in the second round, beaten three sets to two by Welshman Martin Phillips. I shouldn't have lost to him. He wasn't a good player. My game had gone and with it the fun. I would have quit, but things were changing – for better and for worse.

THIRTEEN

The Marriage and the Split

When I split with Maureen in 1988 it was party time again, but the party didn't last long because only a few months later I met Jane. I was at a tournament in Middlesbrough and had gone clubbing with two other darts players, Alan Warriner and Chris Johns, as well as my driver Trevor. They were my new party gang. We went to a club in the town centre called The Mall which had a big disco upstairs, and downstairs a place where you could sit and have a drink. Jane was with her pregnant mate. I asked her for a date and added, 'I don't want to pull you now. Let's have a date tomorrow night.' I didn't want to go with her half cut; it would've been messy. I wanted to do it properly when I was sober.

We hit it off straight away and within weeks she had moved down to Stoke to live with me. She then came to tournaments abroad, much to Trevor's despair, but, unlike with Maureen, we cherry-picked the best ones to go to as a couple such as New Orleans, 'Frisco, LA and

Vegas. Then, a few months after we'd met, I proposed to her in Canada.

We were in the back of a mate's car. I'd been thinking about kids, and how nice it'd be to have a couple, and Jane seemed the right person to have them with because she was a nice girl who was very religious. She even went to Lourdes every year. I didn't want to wait until I was in my forties or later to have children because it's not fair on them. They can't play football with their dad if he's stumbling about with a Zimmer frame, can they? So I proposed and we got married in September 1989. All the big names from darts were there, people like Ollie and Lorna Croft, Tony Green, Bobby George and Mike Gregory to name but a few.

A couple of nights before that a dozen of us got a mini-bus and went to a nightclub in Birmingham for my stag night. It was a big club that held about three thousand people and we had our own VIP section called the Piano Bar. We stayed there until about three in the morning and on our way back we stopped off at some services for breakfast. When one of the lads went to the toilet we did his fry up; egg, bacon, sausage, it was all gone when he came back. Then, when he went to get his fags, he found black puddings stuffed in all his pockets. He wasn't very happy about it. He had what I'd call a Keith Deller sulk on him. We got back to Stoke about six in the morning, had no sleep and just started boozing again. For our breakfast Trevor and I had two large vodkas and grapefruit juice. It went on, drink after drink after drink, until midday; we'd been boozing then for twenty-four hours. That's when everyone started falling asleep and that was the end of it, but what a session it was.

Two days later I was married. It made papers like the *Mirror* and the *Sun*, but there was no way I'd do what other celebrities do now and sell my big day to a magazine. The idiots that do that just want money for nothing because most of them have millions anyway. They sign away control of their wedding to a magazine, yet it's their wedding, nobody else's. They must be barmy. I could understand if someone was short of a few bob, but then the magazines wouldn't want their wedding anyway.

We didn't have a honeymoon. There was no point because I'd taken her everywhere she wanted to go by then.

That wedding capped what was a great year for me, not in darting terms, but personally, because I was awarded an MBE in the April. I was playing in the British Open at the Rainbow Suite in Kensington when I found out. I knew something was up because suddenly there was a buzz about the place. One of the BDO officials came up to me and said, 'Have you heard, Eric? You've got an MBE.'

'What are you on about?' I said. 'Stop winding me up.'

I'd been nominated by Ollie and Lorna Croft and it

was accepted. Ollie couldn't believe it; neither could I. Finally darts had been recognised for something: it had been recognised as a sport and had gained credibility. It was great for everybody really, but more so for me because you can win tournaments all your life but you can't win gongs.

I was put in a predicament because you are only allowed to take two people with you to the Palace and there was Jane, who was then my fiancée, and Mum and Dad who I also wanted to take. I had to choose. I decided that it had to be Mum and Dad who went, after everything they'd done for me throughout my life, and Jane understood.

We all went down together and Mum and Dad went into the Palace to watch – and I messed it right up. All those who were to be honoured were taken into a room, just off where the ceremony was due to take place. In there a posh lad took us through the procedure and protocol involved. We had to line up, then at the right moment walk up to where the Queen was standing on a podium, because she is only little. We had to face her, she would pin a medal on our coat, and she would say what she had to say, then we had to reverse walk to another door, making sure we never turned our back on her. It was about twenty feet to this door which led outside to where the press were waiting to take pictures. I remembered everything, I wasn't nervous and I was really looking forward to it.

When it was my turn I walked up to the Queen and she said, 'You're a darts player.'

'Yes ma'am,' I replied, and she said a few more words then pinned the medal on.

I stood up and walked towards the door leading to the waiting press. Halfway there I realised I'd not walked backwards and had turned my back on the Queen, so I stopped, turned round and said to her, 'Sorry, darling,' and started walking backwards. I was thinking: What the hell have I just called the Queen? She cracked up with laughter and I couldn't believe it. The next thing I knew I was outside with this press pack screaming at me, 'What did you say to her, Eric? Eric, what did you say?' And there I was, as red as a beetroot, saying to them, 'Oh nothing. I didn't say anything to her.'

Later that evening I went to a party that Malcolm Powell from Bass had put on for me in celebration on a boat on the Thames. Jane was there, and Trevor, Ollie Croft, Dickie Davies and quite a few other celebrities. It was great. There was a photographer, and I spent half the night posing for photographs – which didn't flaming well turn out. He was taking pictures with a duff camera. It's typical of my life. Everything that can go wrong does go wrong.

I cocked up again in the presence of royalty at a dinner in honour of Mohammed Ali, who is the only bloke I have ever looked up to. I was at a table with Jane and all these other sportsmen, including quite a lot of boxers like Lennox Lewis, Audley Harrison and Naseem Hamed, and Ali came in and sat right behind me. He was within touching distance. I have never asked for anybody's autograph in my life, but I wanted his. I felt a bit uneasy about asking him, so I got the official programme and said to this good-looking woman who was sitting across from me, 'Excuse me, darling, will you ask Mohammed Ali for his autograph for me? Cheers, love.'

Her look nearly killed me. 'You ask him,' she snapped.

I just put it down to her having an attitude problem and thought nothing more of it, so I turned round myself and got him to sign my programme.

The next night we were at the Royal Albert Hall for the European Footballer of the Year Awards, and Ali was there again to present an award. He came down the steepest stairs I have ever seen and he was quite wobbly because the Parkinsons had taken hold. As he walked down there was silence as everybody, including me, held their breath until he got to the bottom. Right on cue you could hear the sighs of relief fill the place from an audience relieved that he'd made it down in one piece. Then they introduced the next person to give out an award. It was Princess Caroline of Monaco and as she came down the stairs Jane said, 'Do you see who that is?'

I looked at her, turned to Jane and said, 'Oh shit, I've done it again.' What is it with me and royalty?

Around the same time I was invited to a garden party

at the Palace to celebrate the Queen's Golden Jubilee. That nearly turned into yet another disaster. There were thousands of us there, all invited because we were World Champions of one sport or another over the period of the Queen's reign. It ranged from top sportsmen like Frank Bruno, Stirling Moss, Henry Cooper, Roger Bannister, Virginia Wade and members of England football's World Cup winning side of '66, to others from lesser-known sports such as the World Champion tug-o-war team, who were from Stoke funnily enough. We had pictures taken together, and then we all sat down for lunch.

As we were eating, one of the Queen's aides came up to me and said, 'When you all line up to meet the Queen after lunch, she will stop and speak to nine celebrities. You have been chosen as one of the nine.'

I looked round at those that were being left out, people like Daley Thomson and Roger Bannister, and thought: Bloody hell she must hold darts in high regard to want to speak to me.

When this posh bloke was giving me the rundown on what to do when meeting Her Majesty, Jane started shaking. He said, 'As she comes along, you and your wife have to step forward from the line, your wife has to curtsey and you have to bow.'

Then he left, and Jane in a complete panic said to me, 'What, what, I have to do what, what do I have to do. I can't do this, I really can't do this.'

'Of course you can,' I said, trying to reassure her.

At the end of the meal all the top celebrities lined up, and as the Queen started walking along I linked Jane and we stepped out. As the Queen approached all eyes were on us. She spoke to me and then she turned to Jane. I now had my arm around Jane because her legs had gone, and as the Queen said something to her and moved along the line Jane's legs went from under her. She had passed out. I had to hold her up for the few seconds that it took her to come round and find her feet again. If I'd let go she would've been on the floor, out cold.

That was one problem sorted. Then another one arose of even bigger proportions: nobody was smoking. It was a huge garden, out in the fresh air, and no one was lighting up. I decided to find a good smoking spot where nobody could see me, so I sneaked around this huge bush next to a lovely pond, got a fag out and lit it. In less than ten minutes I had about eighty people around me, the sound of their lighters going dink, dink, dink, dink, dink. Half an hour later I went back for another fag and there were about three hundred people round there. From the garden party side it looked as if the bush was on fire. Everybody had been frightened of being the first one to light up and they were waiting for someone to take the lead.

Those royal events were one of the major highlights of my life, together with winning the World

Championships and the births of my children Louise and James. Louise was born in 1991.

I was with Jane's mum and dad in the pub across the road from the hospital after Jane had gone in. I was well-oiled, it was about three in the morning and they were due to induce her the next day. Suddenly I got a call on the pub telephone to say it had started. I had been about to leave to go home and get some kip ready for the next day and I panicked. If I went into the hospital in the state I was in, then the nurses would probably smell all the alcohol on me and throw me out. I shoved a load of Polo mints in my mouth to hide the smell and fortunately got away with it.

James was born two years later. The timing was brilliant because I was playing golf and I'd just got to the eighteenth hole and was putting out when the call came to go to hospital. I got driven straight there from the golf course after finishing my round.

Although I was at both births and people say it's a brilliant and wonderful thing to see, it's not. It's very, very messy and there's a lot of pain. With James it was also extremely traumatic because they hit the panic button and everybody, including me, had to go out. The umbilical cord had got wrapped around his neck. That was frightening. I was scared – possibly for the first time in my life I was *really* scared – but then everybody was told to come back in and there was Jane with my son. I'd gone through every emotion in the space of ten minutes, from fearing for my son's life to seeing him healthy and content in my wife's arms. It was knackering. I wouldn't want to video the birth like some people do. Why would you want to video that? What would you say to your kid? 'Don't watch *Dumbo*, son, watch the blood, sweat and tears of Mum having you instead.'

Jane's friend was also there when James was born. She sat at the end of the bed watching the gory stuff. I was at the other end trying out the gas and air; it was good.

It was great when James was born because we had the set then, a boy and a girl. I was never going to have more than two. Even if I'd had two girls I would've stopped. I know some people who are desperate to have one of each. Tony Brown has five girls. Imagine what his Christmases were like when they were opening the presents: dolls, dolls, more dolls, another doll.

I loved having babies around the house. I was fine with changing nappies and mopping up sick, and when I'd done an exhibition I'd come home and deal with the baby when it woke up, giving it a bottle and all that, so Jane could have some sleep. I was a New Man before the term had even been coined.

When Louise was born I did try to cut back on the darts. It felt as if I was coming to the end anyway, and I wanted to spend some time with my baby, but my timing couldn't have been any worse. Louise and James were born at possibly the most tumultuous and politically charged moments darts had ever seen. I wanted to spend time with my children, but I knew I couldn't turn my back on the game because it was about to be ripped apart by some vicious in-fighting.

Throughout the eighties there were about sixteen tournaments on terrestrial TV. By 1992 that number had gone down to one: the Embassy World Championship which was still shown on the BBC. Unfortunately, Ollie Croft had proven to be a poor negotiator in securing more televised tournaments. Either that or he had some bad advisors. The BBC weren't interested in darts any more, but they did want to keep the World Championship, mainly for kudos, and they didn't want to just hand it over to a rival. Ollie being Ollie just let them have it when they said they didn't want anything else. What he should have done was told them they couldn't have the big one unless they had four of the other tournaments as well. It was bad negotiating.

All of a sudden there was just one tournament a year and if any player went out of that tournament in the early rounds he'd get no exposure for another twelve months. It was no problem for me because I'd made my name by then, but for players like Phil Taylor and Dennis Priestley, who were just coming through, it represented a major problem. The TV money had gone and darts players were struggling financially. It was so bad that some top-ten players even got part-time jobs to make ends meet.

In the run-up to the 1993 Embassy World Championship sixteen of us, mainly the top seeds, decided enough was enough. Sky had expressed an interest in running a tournament with us, so it was time to confront the BDO and ask them what the hell was going on.

I went in to a meeting with Ollie only a day before the championship was due to start, and asked him three questions.

I said, 'Ollie, can you give us more than one tournament a year on TV?'

'No,' he said.

'OK,' I replied, 'would you mind if we ran our own tournaments on TV, because our livelihood is being affected here?'

'Yes, I would mind,' he said.

'OK, if we did run our own tournaments on television, what would happen?'

'You'll be banned.'

And that was it. I had to go back to the other fifteen players who were all waiting for me at the Lakeside Hotel and I told them what he'd said. They listened and then were all in agreement: they were going to pull out of the 1993 Embassy World Championship. Remember, this was only twenty-fours hours before it was due to start. I was stunned. I never expected that reaction.

'You can't all go home,' I said. 'How can you go home?' I could see a bit of fear in one or two players' eyes so

I added, 'You can't simply walk away from this. Embassy has never done us any harm. All they have done is look after us year after year. How can you let them down? How can you let Peter Dyke down? He has given us everything we asked.'

They'd said it in the heat of the moment, so when things had calmed down a little I added, 'Look, let's play this tournament. We are all on money and the winner will get £30,000. Even the ones who lose in the first round still get to bank a couple of thousand. It's stupid to just walk out. Embassy has sponsored us ever since the tournament started. It's not nice on them to just walk out.'

I managed to pull them round to my way of thinking, but the tournament itself was a dud because you could feel the players' animosity towards the BDO. The tournament officials knew exactly what was going on, so it became an us against them situation. Actually, they *wanted* us out because they thought we couldn't survive on our own and therefore wanted to teach us a lesson.

I didn't play well in that tournament at all – I got hammered in the second round by Bob Anderson three sets to nil – but for the first time in darts I was glad to be out of it. I nearly didn't make it to the second round at all. I was within a centimetre of being banned. I played the Dane Per Skau in round one and in the first set I lost three legs to nil and in the second I was two–nil down and heading for yet another early exit. Then

I won a leg. I don't know what possessed me to do this, but I just turned round, punched my fists in the air, shouted 'Yeeessss' and pretended to headbutt him. I only did it for a laugh, but then I saw it replayed on TV later that night and I went cold. I was within millimetres of landing him one right on his nose. I would've been finished as a player if I'd connected. No wonder I beat him after that; he'd gone. He probably thought if he knocked me out of the World Championship I'd knock him out. It was a good thing I did it, though, looking back, because it got me through the game, but it still makes the hair on my back rise watching it now. I was warned by the BDO for improper conduct. I hadn't meant it, but they had to give me a warning because it looked bad. That's me. I always get things wrong. That's not the way to get sponsors for the breakaway boys is it?

Lowey won that one, his third title in three different decades by beating Alan Warriner six sets to three in the final. Afterwards we announced the breakaway from the BDO and in retaliation Ollie banned us so we couldn't play darts for our country, our county or in the Super League. We couldn't play in exhibition matches either, because he then announced that any Super League players who played with us in exhibition games would also be banned. It got very, very nasty.

Our argument was that the BDO should just run the amateur game because they were no longer left with a credible World Championship once all the top players had gone. However, their pyramid structure is brilliant, and even their retaining a weakened World Championship wasn't necessarily bad for the game because with us going it gave thirty-two other players a chance to play on TV and get some experience, something they never would have got if we'd hung around.

The breakaway split darts. I didn't speak to Ollie, who had been like a second father to me in the early days, and he refused to have anything to do with me. I'd travelled the world with this guy, and he was my England manager, so it was a sad loss for both of us.

It had to be done though. For the love of the game there was no choice. All the big names came with us, apart from Bobby George, but in my opinion he made exactly the right decision in sticking with the BDO because whereas in the PDC all the players who joined were fully committed to the game in that it was their life and their be all and end all, Bobby, on the other hand, had other commitments. Darts was never the sole focus of his existence. He made his money through the building trade. That was his main profession and one that made him a lot more dosh than the darts. So Bobby had no real reason to rock the boat and leave the BDO. He's a great showman Bobby and has brought a lot of razzamatazz to the game and for that he should be applauded but when he looks back at his achievements he'll probably be slightly disappointed he didn't win more titles. He won the *News of the World* and North American Open, which are hard tournaments to win and he beat me in the final of the European Cup singles. But if you look at his career it never really took off like Lowey, Jocky or mine did. He made one more world final when all the big boys had defected but got hammered by John Part. So it was the right decision him staying, and it has proven to be so over time. Now he's doing well as a darts frontman for the BBC and is getting a lot of exposure. He made the right decision. But then he has always been shrewd in all his dealings. That's why he has been so successful financially. But then the BDO started to try and get players back off us and that was a much more serious matter. They promised Welshman Chris Johns he'd play for his country if he came back to the BDO, and being a proud Welshman that appealed to him greatly, and they also guaranteed him a steady income playing exhibition matches.

Next, Mike Gregory announced he was going back to the BDO. He'd been my room partner for four years and we were good buddies. We'd had some great times together. He was a practical joker like me. One time in Canada we were asleep and I woke up in the middle of the night to use the toilet. I didn't turn any lights on because I didn't want to wake Mike. As I was standing there having a wee all I could hear was what sounded like drums beating, and my legs and feet were getting soaked. The tosser had put clingfilm over the toilet seat. I had to mop the mess up with towels, it was everywhere. Then I jumped in the shower to clean myself. I'd only gone in for a wee and had to spend about an hour in there. The next night I borrowed Jamie Harvey's Deep Heat spray and sprayed Mike's pillow with it. Mike came in that night, a bit worse for wear, flopped in bed, went to sleep and the next morning when he got up his face was red raw.

We were always playing pranks on each other and we were close mates. When he went I couldn't believe it. He didn't even have the courtesy to discuss it with me beforehand. I could at least have talked to him about it and discussed the pros and cons, but there was nothing. He just walked out on us. I've never spoken to him since and never will. If another ten players had done what he did, we would have been destroyed as an organisation, but the BDO had promised him this and that and he fell for it. I roomed with Jamie Harvey after that.

The first time we roomed together was in Denmark. I had a Crafty Cockney suit holder that had all my shirts and stuff in it. I just hung it up in the hotel wardrobe and that was me sorted: I didn't have to worry about ironing anything or worrying where anything was because it was all in there.

As we were leaving to return home Jamie, being

helpful, looked in my wardrobe and picked up my suit holder. I said, 'Oi, get your hands off my gear. Sort your own gear out.'

He just stared at me in bemusement and said, 'All right then, keep your hair on.'

We both finished packing, went downstairs and took a cab to the airport. When we got there I pulled my bag out and thought: Where is my suit carrier?

I turned to Jamie to ask him where it was. and he looked at me, gave me the finger, and said, 'Fuck you.'

I had left it behind and I had to take the cab all the way back to the hotel.

What a start to our room sharing – but we got on great after that. In Chicago we were playing in a $10,000-dollar tournament and I went to my room at about two in the morning and set the alarm for eight so I could wake up, have breakfast and put in some practice before the tournament started at eleven. Jamie stayed out all night, but when he eventually came in, absolutely bladdered, he woke me up and said, 'Wake me up at seven.' He then passed out on the single bed which was next to mine.

I looked at the clock and it said ten to seven. I couldn't believe it.

I was knackered but I wanted to see this, so I got out of bed and sat on the edge of it, facing Jamie who was snoring away. I lit a fag and watched the clock.

Ten minutes later, at seven o'clock exactly, I woke

him up and he went, 'Yep,' and went straight into the shower.

While he was showering I shouted, 'Give me a call at eight,' and went back to sleep.

'No problem,' he shouted back – and he did.

I went downstairs for breakfast, we practised together, and then I got beaten in the last thirty-two. Jamie, who had only ten minutes sleep the night before, made it through to the last eight. We were splitting the money so he gave me half of his $2,000-dollar winnings. 'You know you only had ten minutes sleep last night,' I said. 'Did you realise what time you came in?'

'I knew it was late,' he said.

Jamie's a good lad, not like Mike. Mike's decision to leave hurt us badly because he was a good player and the good players really did need to show solidarity. When he defected back to the BDO we were down to fourteen and panic was setting in. The only way to settle it was through the courts. The BDO decision to ban their players from playing against us in exhibitions was crippling us financially.

The court case dragged on and on and on and we had to fund it all ourselves, each player putting a couple of grand in. Some players couldn't even afford that. We were almost dead but we fought back. It went to the Old Bailey. A morning session there cost eight grand and it was all adjourned, adjourned, adjourned, eight grand, eight grand, eight grand, and we had three weeks of that – but we won the right to play in exhibitions and to co-exist with the BDO who had to recognise us as a bona-fide organisation.

The players had held their nerve, but even with them chipping in for court costs we would never have got through it if it wasn't for the generosity of John Raby, the founder and head of JD Darts. His promotions company staged ranked and non-ranked tournaments around the UK, and he believed players had a right to play their sport when and where they chose. When he discovered what the BDO were trying to do to us, he immediately put forward about sixty grand of his own money to help us through the court case, and he wasn't a wealthy man. Without him there wouldn't have been a PDC.

He battled motor neurone disease and cancer in later life, and died during the 2008 Las Vegas Desert Classic. They put his body on ice for the funeral which was held when all the players had come back from that tournament, but I was the only one out of the original breakaway group who turned up. I felt gutted for him. They should have all turned up out of respect for the man who saved the game and effectively put money in their pockets. Some players couldn't make it because they had commitments and that's understandable, but for the ones who simply stayed at home and couldn't be bothered turning up, shame on you.

Thanks to John the original fourteen who stuck with

the Professional Darts Corporation never looked back. The first PDC World Championship was held in 1994. Because there were now twenty-four of us we had eight group stages initially, with the winners of each group going through to the quarter-finals. Rod Harrington won the group I was in and Dennis Priestley beat Phil Taylor in the final by six sets to one. When the competition was over there was the feeling that we were over the worst, and Sky couldn't believe the viewing figures, which, although satellite TV was in its infancy then, were high by their standards. The only sport that beat us, and the only one that still does, was football, and then only for the big games.

A few other players saw the exposure we got and wanted to come over to us from the BDO. After about three years the prize money started going up and we were away, but there was still a lot of non-forgiving among the players. Some of our lot wouldn't have anything to do with the others whatsoever. I wasn't like that. I held no grudges with any of them, apart from Mike Gregory. But it was a close call. We nearly didn't make it. This time there could be no repeat of 1982, when there were still seventeen tournaments a year on telly and the money was good so people didn't want to upset the BDO. Nobody would come with Lowey and me back then. Fast forward ten years and when players were deserting the BDO I got them all together and told them in no uncertain terms, 'There's no going back from here. If this doesn't work none of us will ever play for the BDO again, so we have to stick together for the good of the game. If we stick together we'll succeed.'

And we did stick together and we did succeed. If we'd have gone back to the BDO with our tails between our legs they would have picked us off one by one, they would have found any excuse to ban us, but it didn't happen and our organisation succeeded. My only regret was that I was never able to play for my country, my county or my league again. I loved playing for England and played in eight world cups and eight European championships. My and Lowey's record in an England shirt is fantastic.

I missed the county darts too. I had played for Staffordshire County up until the split with Maureen and then I joined Merseyside because it was a good laugh up there. I couldn't play for Staffordshire any more because I'd given Maureen the Cockney and they still played in there, so it would've been too embarrassing for me. Instead, one of Merseyside's top players called Jimmy McGovern invited me to play for them when he heard I was leaving. He'd become a good friend of mine after winning a competition to have a meal with Maureen and me years before. After the meal I got him on port and brandies. It was vintage port and we had a good session. Then, when we left the dinner table, we went into the bar where we ordered more port and brandies, only this time it wasn't vintage port, it was something much cheaper. He took one swig, scrunched his face up and said, 'This isn't right.' He had suddenly become a connoisseur of port.

So I played for his team and Trevor played for the B team. I really got to love the Scousers, they're great. They don't have any money, but they somehow manage to find enough cash to play golf every day and go to the pub each night. They've got life sussed. They were a good team because they cared about each other and looked out for one another. In other teams you tended to get cliques, but not with them. We organised a charity night after the Hillsborough disaster and they brought on a couple who had lost their son. Everyone started singing 'You'll Never Walk Alone' and it was tear-jerking. Big grown-up guys were crying their eyes out. It took my breath away. But all darts teams are like that. They do lots for charity because they are all working-class people who'll dig deep in their pockets to help others less fortunate than themselves.

I lost them thanks to the stubbornness of the BDO and I lost a lot of friends as well. I'm on speaking terms with a lot of them now, but it's all polite. The cheekiness is not there any more.

When I see darts on Sky Sports now, and the number of tournaments they play plus the huge sums of money they're getting, it makes me proud to think I was one of the pioneers who made that happen. I didn't want to see darts die, especially after all the knocking it had had for its booze and fags image. They don't knock it any more, now it's a success. I could never understand why they kicked darts off terrestrial TV, just like I could never understand why *Bullseye* went. The whole idea behind the PDC was to keep darts on telly. It wasn't for loads of prize money. We had to keep the game alive because it was dying.

After a few years the prize money did start to go up, then Vegas came in with a tournament, Blackpool came in and the BDO became a distant memory, part of another moment in time. This was a new era. With the BDO Ollie did all the negotiating, but with the PDC it was Barry Hearn, the boxing promoter, and he is the ultimate mercenary, with a lifestyle that is beyond compare. I did a show with him in Monaco where I had to appear in a tournament played in a big marquee. It was a PR stunt to sell the game of darts to TV companies from all over the world. These TV bigwigs were desperate to secure the rights to his boxing matches, but he kept saying to every one of them, 'If you want boxing you'll have to take one hundred hours of darts as well.'

They didn't want darts but he was adamant. 'No darts, no boxing.'

He really was the main man. That night I joined them all for a meal, but there were too many of us to sit round this table so Barry said to me, 'Eric, would you mind sitting with these four Americans on this other table?'

'No problem,' I said.

So we had a laugh and I taught them how to play spoof with coins. As we played we started ordering bottles of vintage champagne. Bottle after bottle kept coming and I said, 'Put it on Barry's tab.'

These Yanks could hardly walk by the end of the night. One of them couldn't even get up out of his chair. When Barry saw the bill he just looked at me and laughed. 'I see you kept them entertained,' he said. He didn't mind. He'd just sold over two thousand hours worth of sport.

Years later the BDO offered me an olive branch. Ollie phoned me up to invite me to their 2006 World Championship final when Raymond van Barneveld was about to equal my record of five BDO championships.

I said to him, 'If you pay me to go, I'll be there.'

He said no, they couldn't pay me, so I told him I wasn't going, and I thought that would be the end of it. But then von Barneveld's wife Sylvia rang me up, pleading with me and saying, 'You must come, you have to come down. Barney wants you there for when he makes it five.'

So I went reluctantly, but when I walked into what was effectively enemy territory at the Lakeside I could sense there was still a big rift there. I strolled into a back room where the TV people were preparing the cameras and had a bit of a laugh with them, and then I went into the players' bar. It all went a bit quiet when I walked in. Hardly any of the players who had come to watch the final said hello to me.

Bobby George was in there and he did come over, but I shouted, 'Hey Bobby, this is the first time you've had a decent darts player in here in fifteen years!'

'You're off again, are you?' Bobby said. 'Nothing changes with you, does it?' But it helped to break the ice a bit and the mood in the room relaxed.

After a few beers I went out to watch the final with Barney's wife Sylvia and a few members of Dutch royalty who I reminded myself not to call 'darling'. During the break I got up to go into the players' room where they had a private bar. I'd been in there for a good two hours before this thing had started and I wanted a quick pint during the interval. I was met at the door by a BDO official who told me, 'You're not going in there.' There were two steps behind him, leading through this door to the bar, so I launched myself at him with my shoulder and he flew down those two steps and landed in a heap on the floor of the bar. Walking in I said to him, 'Now who is going to throw me out?' I was sick of all the BDO and PDC rubbish. I just wanted a drink.

Barney lost the final, seven sets to five, to Jelle Klaasen, meaning he didn't equal my record and the whole idea of inviting me had become a bit of a pointless exercise – and he played rubbish which didn't help matters. He ended up with a low nineties average which was Mickey Mouse darts.

I went to the presentation dinner with Barry Birch, who had become my driver after Phil died, and we both had to sit with Barney, his wife and all these people who had come over from Holland for a big celebration. It was more like a wake. I said to Barry, 'We're having fun here aren't we, mate? Go and have a look on the winner's table and see if there are two seats over there. I'd rather party with Klaasen and his boys.'

It got worse when I was asked in a BBC interview for my opinion of the final and I called it amateur darts. That caused the rift to widen no end, but I said it on purpose. If it had been good darts I would have acknowledged it, but it wasn't. It simply wasn't as strong as the darts played in the PDC championship. I became public enemy number one again with the BDO after that.

Darts had always been my motivation in life and I don't like to see it suffer. In the early years I wanted to win championship after championship, then, when I got the yips, I had Phil Taylor as my motivation. When he started winning everything and we parted company, darts was plunged into turmoil with the breakaway and that kept me going for a while, but after that I lost my way a bit. That's when the trouble started.

FOURTEEN

I Fought the Law and the Law Won

When I was a young lad there were hundreds of reasons why I should have been arrested. Whether it was burglary, petty theft or violence, you name it I did it, but I always got away with it. I always seemed to be one step ahead of the police.

In the 1990s it was payback time. Suddenly I was getting done for what seemed to be no reason at all. There was the incident I've told you about with Trevor outside Stringfellows and that served as a warning for other incidents to come. Two of the most notorious involved a six-foot fibreglass snowman and a kebab.

In 1995 I'd just asked my pal Dave McGuiness, who was a scrap metal merchant living in Stoke, to be god-father to my son. He said yes and we all went out to celebrate. There was me, Al Pal, a guy called Mickey Longsden, Barry my driver, and Dave. Back then our local was a pub called the Wheel, and at Christmas the landlord Jeff put a white plastic snowman outside. We'd had a good session, and about half past one in the morning Jeff said he was going to put the snowman away, otherwise it would've probably got nicked by a passing drunk. I was a bit merry and in a party mood so I said I'd go and get it.

The police were on a drink drive clampdown at that time and every night, without fail, Barry would take us home and get pulled. It was getting annoying. On this particular night they were on patrol and had parked round a corner, waiting for us to finish drinking and for Barry, who was stone cold sober, to drive us home. I didn't know this when I went outside.

I picked up the snowman and started dancing round the car park with it. Suddenly a police car screeched up beside me. Quick as a flash I put the snowman on the cop car's roof and said to the driver, 'You better take him home, officer, he's had far too much to drink.'

I could tell he didn't find it amusing. He gave me the sort of look Lowey used to give me when I'd just beaten him. Then these two coppers got out of the car, by which time my mates had come out of the pub to see what was going on.

One of the coppers looked at the snowman sitting there and said, 'You've scratched the roof of my car.'

Dave, who isn't short of a bob or two said, 'Look, how much is it? I'll pay for the damage.'

This copper looked at him all stony faced and said, 'Oh, so you're trying to bribe a police officer are you?'

I couldn't believe it. I said, 'For fuck's sake, boys, let's all just calm down.'

But that was it, they were on their radios calling for assistance. Within minutes more police cars came, meat wagons turned up, the dogs were brought in, everything arrived. All they needed was a helicopter to complete the set. There were five of us and we weren't causing any trouble; it was a ridiculous situation.

This young copper then tried to handcuff me. I said, 'You're not putting handcuffs on me, pal. You're not big enough to handcuff me,' which in hindsight was probably not the wisest thing to say.

I started mucking about as he tried to put the cuffs on, moving my hands away and shaking my wrists, but in doing this I accidentally smashed his wristwatch. The cops were already happy because they had me on a charge of resisting arrest. Now that I'd smashed his watch they were ecstatic because they could get me on an assault charge, which they did. I got banged up for the night and was eventually fined £1,800. Talk about an over-reaction. I felt like a hitman when all those coppers turned up.

When I went back to the Wheel after being fined the snowman was back outside, even though it wasn't Christmas, only it had ERIC painted on it in big letters. Then, for months afterwards, every time I walked into the pub all the regulars would break into a chorus of 'Frosty the Snowman'. I even got good-luck cards with snowmen stuck to them, posted to me in the run-up to the court case. It's not an easy job being a copper, but sometimes they just completely lose the plot.

That was only the start. Two years later I was in court again after being accused of inciting a riot at Blackpool's De Vere Hotel during the World Matchplay championship. I got done for threatening behaviour and fined £250. This time it involved a straight fight between two people – darts player Scott Cummings and Sky TV lighting expert Gary Nolan – over a woman. All I did was stop other people getting involved – there were people there who wanted to stop it, but I wouldn't let them because it was a straight one-on-one fight and I've always been brought up to believe that in a one-on-one fight you let them get on with it. Why I had to get involved I'll never know, but I did, and the next thing I knew I was getting done for allegedly kicking this Sky bloke in the head when he was down. That was a load of rubbish. I can state quite categorically that despite punching and kicking many people in my time I never laid a finger, or foot, on him.

Before I was due to go in court I asked my brief, 'What's the worst thing that can happen here?'

'You can get eighteen months to two years,' he said.

I readied myself for the worst and was determined to show no emotion in the dock if I did go down. Fortunately I escaped with a fine.

I gave up on Scott shortly after that. He was only

twenty-seven, but he drank too much. His drink of choice was Scotch and he liked large ones. I took him out for a couple of years as part of my gang, but I was wasting my time encouraging him in his darts career because he seemed more interested in having a Scotch or ten with the boys and me. He could drink all these large ones and you'd not notice any change in him at all. That was frightening for someone so young. We had some fun, though.

If you go out together you go home together, that was the way I was brought up. You never leave anyone on a night out. The problem was, I would be the one who hit the next day's headlines when it all went pear-shaped. They say you learn as you get older, but as *I* got older I started getting done for things that were never as bad as the newspapers made them out to be.

A typical example of this was again in 1997. This time I was in Belgium for the Primus Masters and there was a fight. Two guys went for me. I was practising with Merv King – a 42-year-old former World Matchplay Champion who had only recently defected from the BDO to the PDC – and these geezers started having a go at him. I told them to shut up and all hell broke loose. As one of these idiots came towards me I knew he wasn't coming to say hello, so I kicked him as hard as I could in the nuts. I must have pushed them up to his throat because he fell to the floor screaming like a pig. Suddenly I was surrounded by five of his mates, all trying to have a go at me. I escaped with nothing more than a ripped shirt and went to a bar upstairs where I knew a few of my mates would be. They were drinking by the side of an arty pane of glass, about six feet high.

My mates decided to keep me out of the way, so they made me sit and have a drink with them, but suddenly one of the gang appeared, and from the other side of the glass started threatening me and making throat-cutting gestures.

I said to him, 'Yeah, whatever, pal, now fuck off.'

As soon as I said it, he started trying to climb over this glass to get to me, but as he got his leg over, the whole thing shattered. He fell onto the shards below, cutting himself to pieces, and had to go to hospital. As he lay there bleeding I stood up, walked past him and said, 'You're just a silly fuck.'

Under normal circumstances I would've got arrested for that, but I didn't. Luckily I didn't wallop him as he lay on the floor, but I was sorely tempted. If I had, I would've been in big trouble.

It didn't stop the headlines screaming, 'Bristow in Hotel Riot' the next day. I'm like a dream for the tabloids, it's just one incident after another, but that's my life. It's exciting and people like being with me because they know that nine times out of ten things are going to happen. Whenever I go abroad the players say, 'Where's Brissy going tonight?' because they all know it's going to be good fun.

My gang in the nineties was Alan Warriner, Rod Harrington, Trevor, Chrissy Johns, Chris Mason and Jamie Harvey. They were proper drinkers, and when we went out we'd all come back together as a group. In America we went everywhere in stretch limos. The darts finished at twenty-past eight in the evening and forty minutes later we'd all be showered and ready to hit the town.

It's changed now because they're not the same lads. Jamie's not there any more and Chris Mason has calmed down a lot since he got jailed for battering a bloke with a hammer. That was stupid because he's a handy lad and he didn't need a tool. That incident has left a lot of people frightened of him, but he's all right, he just lost his way for a few years. He'll bounce back. He's not really a fighter, or that aggressive. Some people want to fight the world after a few beers but not him, he's not that way inclined. Even so, he is very much like me in that trouble seems to follow him around. I don't mind that because it gives me a bit of a break. It got to the point where I couldn't even walk into a kebab shop without hitting the headlines, and towards the end of the nineties came my most infamous moment, when I made Bravo TV's *Street Crime UK*.

What a joke that was. I'd been booked to play Phil Taylor for a business crowd at the Grand Hotel in Stoke. There were two hundred people having dinner and watching us play the best of eleven sets, five legs to a set. It was a proper game, a long game which I liked, and all my buddies turned up to watch me – only I never had a chance because Phil did one of his silly acts where he has a 115 average. It meant he ripped my head off and spat down the hole. He was awesome. I lost six sets to nil. I was playing well going ton, ton, ton, one-forty, ton, but I wasn't getting a shot at a double because Phil was hitting one-eighty after one-eighty. He made me look a fool.

After the game we both did a bit on the mic, but I was more concerned with getting round the back to the bar and having a few beers to ease the pain of my humiliation.

In the end it turned out to be a good booze-up and in the early hours of the morning it was time to go, so I left with my driver Phil.

We drove up to the car park barrier but, just my luck, you needed a token from the hotel to go through it. Phil got out of the car to go back to the reception and get one, and I spotted a kebab shop across the road. I got out too and staggered over. I'd had a few and was basically smashed.

Inside the shop I was just about to order when this spotty youth pushed in front of me. I grabbed him by the throat, frogmarched him to the door and threw him out. Then I went back in and ordered two kebabs – I always order two; one never seems to be enough because they're moreish.

Suddenly from outside I heard a hum and everything lit up. I knew it was a TV camera because I've been in television for most of my life. This particular camera belonged to Bravo who were filming *Street Crime UK*. Basically they went to a different town each night, tuned in to the police radio and followed them to any trouble. Someone must have reported me for throwing this lad out and they were there in a shot. Talk about bad luck. I shouldn't have been in there, I should've been in the car on my way home. Phil came across, and as we walked out this camera was on me. I could feel the heat from the light. In front of me stood a copper, who looked no older than about ten, with this star-struck look on his face because he was about to have his two minutes in the spotlight. I didn't know what was going on and could barely string a coherent sentence together. That's probably why I just kept saying to him, 'I haven't threatened nobody, I haven't threatened nobody,' which was a stupid thing to say, but I was pissed.

I was very thankful when he let me go. It would have been so easy to nick me – but how unlucky was that, to find the one cameraman who was travelling the whole of Britain looking for trouble? That clip is now one of the most downloaded on YouTube. In my defence I'd argue that nobody goes into a kebab shop at one in the morning sober. Who the hell eats a kebab when they're sober? It wasn't even a crime. That lad was out of order. You don't push in, it's rude.

I had another kebab shop incident in the Isle of Man, though fortunately the cameras weren't there to record that one. Again it was in the early hours of the morning, again I was pissed, and again I was ordering two kebabs.

The kebabs came and just as I was about to pay, this bloke picked one of them up and started to eat it.

I said, 'Oi, that's mine!' but he just carried on munching away so I got the other one and slapped it full in his face and said, 'Here, have that one an' all.'

It had lots of chilli on it and he fell to the floor, tearing at his eyes with his hands, screaming, 'I can't see! I can't see!'

I just walked out and said, 'Good night.'

Can you imagine what would've happened if the cameras had been there for that one?

The nineties were a bad time for me because I did tend to hit the headlines for all the wrong reasons. The worst moment came in 1994 when the *News of the World* was delivered. I picked it up and there across two pages was a picture of me with my arm round a lad who played Super League with me. Above it was the headline 'Eric Bristow's Pal is Child Killer'.

I needed that like I needed a dose, and I never saw it coming. Nobody had warned me it was going in. I just sat down, read every word in utter astonishment and thought: Why does this always happen to me?

The guy in question was Robert Black. He was a good darts player who played Super League with me for a pub called the Robin Hood, close to where I lived in London in the early seventies. He was a scruffy sod who had nicotine-stained fingers and dirty teeth. I'd see him every week, and he was just one of the boys. He hired two rooms off my pal Eddie Rayson and his wife Katherine in Stamford Hill.

Nobody was ever allowed in these rooms which had great big bolts on their door. Maybe that should've set the alarm bells ringing, but nobody batted an eyelid. They just saw him as a very private person. Then, all of a sudden, this person who we all knew as a darts player was arrested and done for murder. The papers were calling him the biggest child killer this country has ever had.

He got caught in Scotland. He had bundled a six-year-old girl into a van and sexually molested her, but he'd been spotted by a sharp-eyed retired shopkeeper who phoned the police. When they got to the van they found the little girl bound, gagged and trussed up inside a sleeping bag. Minutes later and she probably would've been dead.

When police raided his flat they discovered more than a hundred child pornography magazines and fifty videos in there. He was later charged with three more murders: eleven-year-old Susan Maxwell who was raped, strangled and her body dumped by the side of a road near Uttoxeter in central England; five-year-old Caroline Hogg whose naked remains were found in a

Leicestershire ditch; and ten-year-old Sarah Harper who Black kidnapped from Leeds, raped, murdered and then dumped in the River Trent.

The police, however, suspected him of the disappearance of dozens more. That's when they came calling for me. I had the CID boys round almost the minute the picture of us appeared because they were convinced he'd done children from my area as well. I had to tell them all the darts teams he played for and get the BDO diary of events out to show them where he was on particular nights. They wanted to cross-reference when these children went missing and if he was playing darts that night. It was a laborious process, but the police were brilliant. It did seem ironic though that when they weren't arresting me for the most trivial matters they were asking me for help in a mass murder investigation.

Robbie Black has made me question my faith in people. We played darts with this guy and I had nights out with him. Nobody would ever have guessed what he was really like. If we had found out what he had been doing he would never have got out of the pub alive; we would have killed him on the spot. When the newspapers found out I was helping the police out, they came knocking on my door and asking for a comment. I gave them a no comment: I've got two children – what if that pervert got out? He might come after my daughter. I just didn't want to get involved because eventually these scumbags get released. Knowing my luck, the minute I did make a comment and said, 'Hang the fucker,' he'd escape, so I wasn't taking any chances because I know how things happen in my life and they don't always turn out for the best.

It's made me distrust all but my closest friends. You don't know people when you just meet them in a pub. Back home they can have completely different personalities. There was a guy who used to come in the Cockney with his wife. They were a lovely couple, but she always wore revealing clothes. Even in the middle of winter she'd come in with a mini-skirt on.

Around this time a prostitute got murdered down Burslem way and the police pulled in this woman's hubby. He was called Freddie. He'd been with this hooker an hour before she died. That was an eye-opener. Nobody in the Cockney knew that Freddie went with prostitutes, but they soon found out when he was pulled in. Then the cops went to Freddie's house to have a look round and found a load of bondage gear that he and his missus had been using for their sex sessions. There were whips and everything. This nice bloke we knew in the pub was a bit of a Peter Pervert on the side. He didn't have anything to do with killing this hooker, but he hardly ever came into the pub after that because on the couple of occasions he did, as soon as he walked through the door we all said, 'All right, it's Freddie the Murderer. What are you having to drink?' He was branded for life. That happens to people who lead double lives and then get found out. There's nothing better than being honest – but if you're murdering little girls you're not going to be honest, are you?

All the drama of run-ins with the police and child murder investigations failed to disguise one important fact: in the 1990s I was a shadow of the player who had dominated darts throughout the previous decade. I barely caused a ripple playing in PDC tournaments, although very occasionally during this period I played darts like I could play back in my heyday. Things would click and the dart became my sixth finger again. Although the yips were ever present in my game I did feel that if I conquered them, if only for a short period of time, I could've given Phil Taylor a run for his money.

Then suddenly it was my Indian summer, as it were. When I went into the '97 World Championship the yips had gone. They'd been on and off in the run up to it – I'd have two weeks with them and two weeks without – but for the period of the championship there was no sign of them.

The old Bristow was back as I steamrollered the number three seed Bob Anderson by three sets to one in the group stages, and did enough against Canadian Gary Mawson to go through to the quarter-final where I beat the number six seed Alan Warriner five sets to three. That set up a semi-final clash with my protégé Phil Taylor which this time I was itching to win. I always used to see me and Phil as having that teacher/pupil relationship, but this time I had no reservations about playing him. He'd been on his own for years and hadn't needed my coaching since his 1990 win, so I wanted to go out on stage and enjoy myself. Above all I wanted to destroy him.

I was up for that game – and utterly down when I lost it. I should've beaten him. I missed three darts at double top which would have set me up for a historic victory, but then there was a delay as the board came down and my game went a bit when we got back on the oche. Before the match had even started all the talk in the hotel was of how I wouldn't win a set off Taylor – but there was no way in a million years I was not going to win a set. In the end I lost by five sets to three. It was a good game and I did play well, so it was good to have at least one decent game against him on stage.

Phil spent the whole of the match shaking and trying to combat double vision. He had the whole crowd against him, and that was a unique experience for him which he struggled to handle – plus I was winding him up at every opportunity. I hit a cracking 141 finish against him at one point and could see his head had gone. Then in the final set, needing sixty-six to take it to a decider, I went straight in the middle and missed two darts at double eight to take it all the way. Who knows what would have happened if I'd got that double.

I was pleased I'd played well, because my record from

'92 onwards seemed to be playing well in exhibitions and then badly on telly. Unfortunately, 1997 became my swansong because after that I played badly in all TV tournaments. In '98 I lost both my group games by three sets to nil and Phil won his sixth world title. I did try to stop him beating my world record in '97, but it would only have postponed the inevitable by a few more years because back then there wasn't the strength in depth within the PDC to stop him. If all the BDO players had come over to the PDC right from the start, he wouldn't have as many world titles as he has now. He would've beaten five, but most probably he wouldn't be in double figures yet.

A year later, 1999, I got beaten three sets to nil by Peter Manley and that was rubbish. It really was the worst darts I have ever played on TV and possibly the worst darts ever witnessed in a televised tournament. The yips had come back and my confidence had deserted me. I had no fight. I just wanted to get off the stage. When his final dart hit the board, I breathed a sigh of relief mixed with elation that it was all over. It was embarrassing. I had people who had travelled a long way to watch me and they'd brought their friends with them to cheer me on. They sat in the front row and witnessed a horror show. I just kept turning to them and shrugging after I lost leg after leg and mouthed 'Oh well.'

They didn't mind. They were the same people who

had cheered me on when I was good and they were determined to follow my career to the bitter end.

That '99 Championship should have been the end for me, but I found it hard to let go. I still dreamed of one more World Championship. In the 2000 Championship I had a titanic struggle against Steve Brown whose father Ken I had played with in the England team when I was a teenager. I came from two sets to nil down to level it, but lost the deciding set.

It was only prolonging the agony because when you are struggling to get past the first round stage that says it all, really. A lot of players who play in the World Championship could play for twenty years and never win it. I had joined that group by the turn of the millennium. In 2001 I failed to qualify. I missed six darts at the double in every leg and that hurt. It was a bit sad really because also in that qualifying hall were Deller, Lowey and Big Cliff. We'd become ghosts of the past.

I decided it was time to leave the stage for good and went into retirement.

Now it was a question of what to do next. I couldn't just sit at home because I would've got very, very bored. All I have ever done is play darts and I had had a busy life. I didn't know any different and found it hard to adjust. If I'm at home and there's no sport on TV I'm lost.

I decided to continue playing exhibitions and making

personal appearances as well as concentrating on my new-found focus which was golf.

It was Deller and Jamie Harvey who got me into golf during the mid-nineties. They started doing these pro/celebrity tournaments so I started practising with them. We played for money, a tenner for the front nine, ten for the back nine and ten for the game. It was two pounds off every player for a birdie and one hundred pounds for a hole in one. No one ever got a hole in one.

I enjoyed these little games and got to a standard where my handicap was eighteen. That was when I got an invite from Howard Keel to play in his tournament at Mere Golf Club in Cheshire. I accepted, having no idea how big this thing was going to be.

I arrived the day before and was put up at the Piccadilly Hotel in Manchester. On the same day I was told I could have a practice round at the club with two other celebs who would also be appearing. They turned out to be Francis Lee and Rodney Marsh. I did a round and it was a proper course, much better than the ones I had been playing on, with good bunkers and everything. I just thank God I had that practice because I was a novice compared with most of the other celebs who were appearing. In the bar afterwards I bumped into Eddie Large who invited me to come and watch his team Manchester City play Middlesbrough. So there I was, in his executive box at Maine Road watching his side lose one–nil. Eddie was gutted. Afterwards in the executive lounge Middlesbrough's manager Lennie Lawrence came in and we hit it off straight away. Eddie just sat in the corner growling to himself. He took his football very seriously.

The next day was beautiful, so I popped down to the course to take a look about an hour before I was due to tee-off. Other celebs had already started and my legs nearly buckled when I saw about fifteen hundred people gathered around the first tee. I didn't need that sort of attention, so I told Trevor to get the Bailey's out. He always carried miniature bottles of the stuff around with him. I drank them at breakfast before a darts tournament, usually no more than two or three, but now I downed about a dozen. I needed some Dutch courage.

I strolled to the first tee, slightly the worse for wear, to face the crowd which had now swelled even more. As I teed up the announcer said, 'Now don't go round in one hundred and eighty!'

I wasn't laughing. All these people were standing round and I thought that if I sliced the ball, which I was prone to do, one of them would get hit. Fortunately I hit it straight down the middle of the fairway.

I played a lot of pro/celebrity tournaments after that. Johnny Mathis was at the Howard Keel event and invited me to play in his Johnny Mathis Classic. He played off twelve at the Howard Keel and fifteen at his own. I went loopy when I found that out. I couldn't believe it – that was a bit naughty.

Golf is the reason I have a nasty scar across my nose. I had been playing in a TV tournament at the Royal Oxfordshire Golf Course, and my driver Phil, who I was sharing a room with, had gone to bed while I was on the lash in the hotel bar with other celebrities. I came to our room hammered. It was pitch black and I didn't want to wake Phil so I got undressed in the dark. Suddenly I lost my balance, toppled over and hit the jagged edge of a brick TV cabinet with my nose. The blood spurted out.

I just lay stunned, crying out, 'Phil! Phil!'

'Where are you?' he said.

'I'm down here in trouble.'

When he turned the light on there was blood everywhere. He had to get a load of towels from the bathroom and cover my face.

'What's it like?' I asked.

'It's not too bad,' he replied.

But it was bad. I should have gone to hospital. That's why I'm left with a scar now.

Golf has given me some marvellous memories, as well as some daft ones. True to form the daftest day on the golf course involved Keith Deller, when I was playing with him, Trevor and Phil Taylor in New Brunswick during a Canadian tour.

We'd hired buggies for the day. I was in one with Trev,

and Phil was with Keith in the other. These things can go about thirty miles an hour if you put your foot on the pedal and as Phil passed me and Trev, he winked at us, swung the buggy round sharply to the left and Keith just flew out. He was rolling around the fairway and got up covered in grass stains. That was it then, the red mist descended and he wouldn't let Phil drive any more.

Trouble was, Keith then parked the buggy on a hill that backed onto a pond and forgot to put the hand-brake on. Suddenly it started rolling down towards the pond. Trevor was the first to spot it and went in hot pursuit. He was desperately trying to grab hold of it to slow it down, so that he could put the brake on before it splashed into this pond. He stopped it with only yards to spare.

Then, on the same course, I hit my ball and it landed on a strip of what appeared to be white concrete – but it wasn't concrete, it was quicksand. I stepped onto it and went in down to my knee. I couldn't get out and it took all three of them, with all their strength, to pull me free. When they did get me out my golf shoe had disappeared. If I'd gone in there with both feet I would've been in big trouble.

At the end of the round we went back to the club house and it looked as if we'd been in the wars. Trevor was knackered because he'd been chasing after a golf buggy *and* pulling me out of quicksand, Keith was covered in grass stains, and I had mud up to my knee and only one shoe on. We looked a right set of prats.

If I thought retiring from competitive darts was going to lead to a quieter life with more time for the golf course, I was in for a rude awakening. The decade that followed the end of the nineties proved to be the most testing, stressful and surprising I had ever known. To get out of it in one piece was nothing short of a miracle, and darts had nothing to do with it.

FIFTEEN
Oh Brother!

As the new millennium dawned I looked forward to a new century away from the pressures of the dart board. Mum sold her house in London and bought a simple two up two down in Leek so she could be closer to her grandchildren, and every Monday night I took her for a drink with me and the lads. She never really drank, but Monday nights were her big one. All the lads bought her drinks and she would more often than not leave the pub at closing time a little the worse for wear, in which case I'd send her home in a cab or one of the boys would take her in his car.

On one of these Monday nights, as we were sitting at the end of the bar talking about family and stuff like that, Mum took me to one side and said to me, 'Eric, I just thought I better let you know that you have a brother.'

I was forty-five years old. For forty-five years I was led to believe I was an only child so it was a bit difficult to take in. 'I'm sorry,' I said to her. 'Can you run that by me again?' I was stunned to say the least.

I don't know if it was Dutch courage that made her tell me, or the fact that she wasn't feeling very well and knew something about her health that I didn't, but I've never got to the bottom of the reason why she chose to tell me at that moment. She had been seeing a doctor in London before moving to Leek, and after the move she got a new doctor and saw him regularly so something was afoot.

'Right,' I said to her, 'who is he then? You have to get hold of him.'

'Would you mind if I did?' she said.

'Of course I wouldn't. He's your son, just like I'm your son.'

Mum had been terrified I'd go mad at her wanting to meet him, but all I could do was tell her to go. I said, 'For Christ's sake, Mum, go and meet him,' but I had to keep repeating this to reassure her. I was worried, though, because if she did try to contact him and found out he'd died, it would've devastated her.

She got into contact with a group set up to bring long lost relatives together. He'd also been in touch with this group and had wanted to contact her for the past ten years. A liaison lady encouraged them both to write to each other and she passed the letters on. It was nice the way they did it because she couldn't just appear on his doorstep and say, 'Hello, I'm your mum.'

After a few months and quite a lot of letters the liaison lady said they were ready to meet. Mum was as nervous as hell, but at least the letters had allowed her to piece together something of his life. He lived in London, at Purfleet, very close to the Circus Tavern where I had played darts for years.

The meeting went well and she asked me to meet him.

'I don't want to, Mum,' I said. 'I'm forty-five and it's a bit late for me to start meeting long lost relatives.'

But she was persistent, and I wanted to make her happy, so I agreed to meet him. He'd seen my mum for a couple of months and they were getting along fine, but before I went I needed to know the history behind my long lost brother.

Mum told me he was called Kevin, he was two years older than me and he was the result of a brief fling with an Irish boy, nobody knows who he was, who disappeared shortly after getting mum pregnant.

In those days there was no such thing as abortions on the NHS, and illegitimacy was frowned on. So, rather than go to a back-street abortionist, she gave him up for adoption. Shortly after that she began dating my dad.

Kevin did well for himself and became quite a successful businessman, and when his stepmother died at the beginning of the nineties he decided he wanted to find his natural mother. He put the letter into the agency and over ten years later Mum got in touch. How surprised must he have been to get that call out of the blue after such a long time.

I arranged to meet Kevin at a hotel in Purfleet and took a mate with me called Michael Longsden for moral support. Mum had given me instructions to come back with a picture of Kevin and me together, so Michael could take some on his mobile phone.

I was as nervous as my mum had been but I shouldn't have worried. When we met we got on fine. He was a lovely bloke. It was hard, though. You can't just go back in time and be brothers in the natural sense. When we had that first meeting we just started asking each other silly questions. I wanted to know if he played darts, but he didn't even like the game. It would've been funny if he had been a darts player in a local league – there would've been every chance we'd have met before this, and neither of us would've known we were related.

That first meeting was a case of catching up and there was a lot of it to do, over four decades worth. I found out he had been married and divorced but then was remarried with two kids, and obviously he knew of me through darts. What most impressed me about him was that he never mentioned the adoption and he didn't resent what had happened at all. When I brought it up he said to me, 'Those were the times, that's what happened,' and shrugged it off.

What began as a simple reunion became much more

than that when, eighteen months after we met, Mum's illness manifested itself in the worst possible way. She had cancer, and worse than that she had a rare form of cancer that quickly spread. It started with pains in her back when she was still living in London. I discovered this after she died when I was sorting her things out and found a letter that she had never shown me. Maybe that was why she sold up and came to live in Leek for the last couple of years of her life.

When it hit she became seriously ill and was admitted to Christie's Hospital in Manchester where she lasted just over two months.

She had never actually told me she had cancer, I just guessed when she started seeing her doctor more often and began going to Christie's which specialises in cancer cases. I went with her on one of her hospital visits and got a doctor in a side room and made him tell me every-thing. He told me, but not in a brutal fashion, that she had no chance. My head was just spinning. It didn't feel real. There was nothing I could do. You try and protect your family from everything but you can't protect against cancer; it hits every family.

Devastation cannot adequately describe how I felt, but I felt sorrier for Kevin. He had already lost one mother, his stepmum, and now he was faced with the prospect of losing a second. That's when we really bonded as brothers. When she was facing her final weeks in Christie's he drove up the two hundred miles to the hospital and spent the weekend with her. We knew she was never coming out and we both wanted to make sure that in her final weeks she was never alone.

When I went I'd occasionally pop outside for a cigarette and join other smokers who were all waiting for their loved ones to die inside. All of us were there puffing away, but all of us were suffering, and we were all hoping the end would come quickly. I met an old bloke outside there. He was brilliant. I don't know his name and barring a miracle he'll be dead now, but I'll never forget him as long as I live. He was puffing away, but he was hoarse and could hardly speak. While I was stood there, contemplating all the horrible thoughts that take over your mind in these situations, he came up to me and said in a rattling voice, 'How are you, Eric?'

'I'm fine, mate,' I replied.

'You were a great darts player. I used to watch you all the time when you won all those World Championships.'

'What are you doing in here?' I asked him.

'I came in here for chemotherapy on my throat. I've had two hours of it, but I told them to stop so I could come out here for a fag.'

It was probably the only time I smiled while I was there, and I just shook his hand, gave him a cuddle and said, 'Can't fault you, mate.'

He was a star, a real star who wasn't prepared to compromise for anybody – he could've been a Bristow. I loved him for that.

That aside, the weeks I spent in there visiting Mum were weird. When you see people go into hospital they go in to be fixed and then go home. But here, in most cases, there was nothing to fix. The only way they were going to come out was in a coffin. Cancer is a horribly undignified way to go, and Mum's final few weeks were no exception. The only money my mum ever spent in her life was on her hair. Going down to the hairdresser's to get glammed up used to be her big thing, it was her treat. When she was in London Steve Davis used the same hairdresser's and occasionally he'd be in at the same time as her. He always made a point of acknowledging her and asking how she was and she loved that. The times when he was in she'd always ring me afterwards and say, 'I saw Steve today. He was really nice. We had a really good chat.'

I'd say to her, 'Yeah, great Mum, fantastic,' and be thinking: So what!

But then, when she began treatment for cancer, one of the first things was that she lost her hair, which was heartbreaking to see – but she couldn't have cared less. All she wanted was to be out of Christie's, hair or no hair. That was her only wish.

On one visit near Christmas she said, 'If only I could get out of this place . . .'

There was nothing wrong with the hospital. The doctors and nurses were fantastic in the way they went about their job and the patience and consideration they showed at all times. Mum just wanted her old life back.

'I'll get you out. I'll take you out,' I said, and I took her downstairs from her ward in a wheelchair and we went for a walk outside – but it was winter and a bit cold and after about ten minutes she asked to go back in.

She never went out again after that.

I'd visit and walk into her ward to see a family, some of whom I'd been having a fag with outside, in tears and think: Oh Christ, there's another one gone – but part of me would be pleased the person had died because they were never going to recover. The pity for these poor families was more out of relief than loss, relief that someone they loved had been spared any more agony. When you see these sorts of situations you realise there's something to be said for euthanasia. Those who are really suffering, who have lost all their dignity and have no quality of life whatsoever should be given that option. Cats and dogs are put down when they suffer, and some people love their pets more than they love their own children, so why can't humans have that option? I've told my son that if I ever end up that way, and on a life-support machine, to flick the switch and end it all. I don't want to live like that, there's nothing worse.

But Mum hung on and hung on; she didn't really want to go. That's when Kevin and I really felt we were brothers. He'd come in as I was leaving and we'd have a little chat and try to console each other. In the final few weeks I just wanted Mum to let go, but she wanted to hang on in there. Life meant too much to her to simply throw it all away.

Then they moved her into what I can only describe as a final room. Once people went in there it generally meant they had days to live, but Mum hung on for a couple of weeks, she was so stubborn. When the end came there were nine of us there. All the people who really loved her sat round her bed as she drifted away.

The cancer that killed her was so rare that the hospital asked if they could perform an autopsy. I put it to a vote, because I know some people don't like their loved ones to be messed with, but everyone was unanimous – if an autopsy went some way to helping others, then they should perform one. I know Mum would have wanted that.

As I left hospital the other families were still there, waiting for their loved ones to die. Some of them came up to me and we had a hug and they said, 'Well, at least it's over.'

There's nothing else you can say really. We'd all been wishing our loved ones dead to get them out of their pain and everyone had kind of bonded in a way. We all became very, very close for the short period of time we were there because we all had this horrible affinity that ended in the worst possible way. Now I can't put a face to any of them because at that time of deep personal grief and stress I'd entered a different world. My head, for the time I was visiting Mum, felt as if it was in a dream-like other world. It was unreal, everything became totally unreal. I didn't want to be there, Mum didn't want to be there, and yet there was nothing we could do about it.

At the funeral I was standing with my dad when he spotted Kevin and said to me, 'Who's he?' He didn't have a clue. I said, 'I'll tell you later, Dad.'

It turned out that he knew all about Mum's illegitimate son and he'd never told me, the sod. He could've easily told me when him and Mum were having all their arguments prior to the split, but he kept schtum because he knew deep down that it wouldn't have been right. It would've caused even more conflict. To keep a secret like that and keep your mouth shut takes some doing, especially when things go bad.

After the funeral we all went to a nearby pub and that's when I told him. He was stunned. 'When did you find out about that, then?' he said.

So I had to retell Kevin's life story to Dad because all he knew was that Mum had put him up for adoption. I recounted how he had lovely foster parents who brought him up well and treated him like their real son, how they lived in a respectable neighbourhood, how he had a nice job and a decent house, and how he was totally unlike me in that he was quiet, was not a huge drinker and shared the occasional bottle of wine with his wife at weekends. As Dad listened open-mouthed, I began to question myself whether we really were related because we are so, so different. But we are related, and the one thing I can look back on with pleasure is the fact that after so many years Mum and Kevin finally met, albeit for only a very short time. At least she put that void in her life right. It must have been a terrible, terrible thing for her to have a child and have to give him away. It must have preyed on her mind right up until the point she met him, so I was glad they finally reunited.

I will never know to my dying day if she knew there was something seriously wrong with her and that that was the last chance she had to meet her long lost son. I suspect she knew something because why else would she suddenly buy a house within walking distance of me and her grandkids? She came round all the time. I'd be sitting watching the football on telly and see Mum walk past the front window and knock on the door. I'd think: For Christ's sake, she's bloody well here again, as you do. All I wanted was to watch the match, but she'd come round for a couple of hours and when she went the game was over. Now, all of a sudden, I'd give anything to see her walk past my window again, football or no football.

When you go you go. All these do-gooders saying don't drink and don't smoke – it doesn't do them any favours. You don't get any bonus points in life, and by abstaining from the more pleasurable things what are you trying to achieve? A few more years added on at the end, what's the point of that if you're not enjoying life in the here and now? Everyone feels better after a drink, and a smoke is the perfect accompaniment. I feel sorry for teetotallers. If they wake up in the morning and that's the best they're going to feel all day, then what's the point of carrying on? I would've been gobsmacked if Kevin was a teetotaller. He's not, he's a sensible drinker. I still keep in touch with him and I phone every now and again, though probably not as often as I should.

Life threw me that curveball just when I thought nothing more could surprise me. Then there was Mum's illness, and just when I was over the shock of that came the biggest crisis of them all, the mother of all shocks – my marriage breakdown. This not only tore the family apart but also threatened to destroy me as a person. If the split from Maureen was amicable, the one from Jane was anything but. It became a living nightmare.

It began a few months after Mum died when Jane went with her friend to Gracelands, the home of Elvis Presley. I stayed in England and looked after the children; Elvis doesn't do much for me anyway. When they came home we just started rowing and it all seemed to go downhill from there.

We became distant, she began to resent me doing the dart exhibitions and said she deserved a life as well. This to a certain extent is understandable because being married to a darts player isn't easy, especially when they are always on the road. The rows came thick and fast.

It culminated in me facing an assault charge after being accused of hitting Jane at home. We'd had a row upstairs and it ended with me storming down and putting the telly on. Minutes later a police car pulled up outside the house. They came in and said they had reason to believe I'd assaulted my wife. I felt like laughing at them. It was ludicrous. But then, when I went upstairs there were blood smears on the ceiling and on the telephone. Despite the fact that I hadn't done anything, this didn't look good at all. My whole career was about to be tarnished by a charge of domestic violence.

The cops took me away and at the station I met my lawyer who told me to put in a plea bargain, but the plea would have to be guilty.

I said, 'I am not going to plead guilty to something I didn't do. I'd rather go down than do that. I didn't do it.'

He looked at my hands and said, 'You wear those sovereign rings.'

I do have quite a few chunky gold rings on my fingers, I was bling before the term had ever been invented, but I said to him, 'I wear those rings all the time, but there's not a mark on her.' It was true, she didn't have a mark on her body, not a bruise, not anything, apart from a tiny cut by her nose which wasn't big enough to justify all the blood over the ceiling and telephone.

My lawyer was adamant. 'You can get a much more lenient sentence if you plead guilty,' he told me.

'If I plead guilty I might as well go and hang myself,' I told him, 'because if my kids believe that I'm a wife beater then what's the point in carrying on living?'

So I told him I was going to fight the charge all the way to the courts, but all the time I couldn't help think that this could be the ultimate payback for all the bad things I did as a teenager.

To her credit, I understand Jane then wanted to drop all charges – I think she realised the whole farcical situation had got way out of hand – but the prosecution team said they were going to go ahead with it anyway.

In court she gave evidence from behind a screen, so she couldn't see me and I couldn't see her. Christ almighty! We had been married for fifteen years and the end result was her testifying against me from behind a screen.

My lawyer didn't help. All he could say was, 'You'll probably get done for this.' And then it was the same old rigmarole again, with me saying, 'But I didn't do it,' and him asking me to plea bargain. But then this was sensible advice from a legal viewpoint. He had my best interests at heart, it was just something I didn't want to hear.

I said to him again, 'If I plead guilty everybody I work with, and all my friends and family, will think I'm a wife beater and I don't want that. And anyway, if I get done for it, it's all over for me. My career will be over, I'll lose my family, that will be it, the end. Life won't be worth living any more. There will be no point carrying on. I'm not going to go through life continually being ostracised.'

All the TV cameras and photographers were there as usual; they could smell blood. As far as I was concerned, if I was found guilty they might as well have pronounced a death sentence on me because it would've meant my life was over. In the grand scheme of things the rest of my life really did hinge on this day.

Everyone stuck by me. The people who knew me well knew I would never do anything like that. Harrows, who had sponsored me in exhibitions and the like, didn't even flinch, whereas a lot of other companies would have pulled the plug on you for something as serious as what I was facing – guilty or not guilty, it wouldn't have mattered. The people at Harrows, who had known me since I was eighteen, backed me all the way. Their representative Colin Harris even phoned me to say, 'Don't worry about it. You just get to court, sort it out and we'll take it from there. Don't put any pressure on yourself, just get through this court case first.' That gave me heart, as did Sky's reaction. I was working for them at this time, and as far as they were concerned I was innocent until proven guilty, which is how it should be.

I was acquitted and as the verdict was read out I just said, 'Thank you very much,' and left the court.

As I walked up to the press afterwards one of them said, 'Congratulations, Mr Bristow, you have won the case.'

I said, 'I haven't won a thing. I have lost a wife,' and with that I walked off, feeling utterly crushed.

Everyone who knows me knows my views on wife beaters. I grew up in pubs from the age of fourteen and knew the drinkers who came in for a pint and later went home to beat up their wives. They were brave lads weren't they? I barred a bloke from the Cockney for beating up his missus. I lost faith in people from a very young age. I don't really trust anyone, apart from a couple of very close friends, so to be faced with a wife-beating rap was just ridiculous. It's just not me.

Following the case I didn't talk to Jane for months. I felt very bitter towards her. It was sad because I wanted to watch the children growing up with my wife at my side.

When the assault charge came up, I moved into Mum's old house while it was all going on.

I really didn't see it coming, though I admit I wasn't the best husband in the world. In the run-up to the court case I was told I had to have no contact with Jane and was not to see her or speak to her. It was another situation I found farcical, especially when she phoned me to ask for some money. I told her that because of the court order I couldn't drop it off at our house, but instead I'd leave it for her in an envelope at my local Ladbrokes, where they know me. So I drew three hundred pounds out of the cashpoint, went into the bookies and told them Jane was coming in to pick up some money, and left the cash with them. Then I texted Jane the words, 'This is the Leek Lifeguard, the coast is clear'.

That was a big mistake. As soon as Jane got that text I'd broken the restraining order and had been in touch. The police were round to arrest me in a shot. As I walked out of Mum's house, I gave my watch and wallet to a next-door neighbour and told her I'd collect them the next day when they released me.

I was put in a cell down at the cop shop. This time the police were sympathetic. The arresting officer said to me, 'Eric, I'm sorry. There's nothing I can do about this. We have to follow orders here. We know where you're coming from but we have no choice.'

They gave me a crossword puzzle book and a pen and paper and I settled down for the night. They really didn't want to take me, but they had no option. In their eyes and in the eyes of the law I had broken the restraining order.

I was up in court the following day and when the full facts of the matter were explained the judge just gave a sigh and said, 'What's this doing here?' I don't think he could believe the police and court time that was being wasted. He simply said, 'You must not get in contact with her any more. You must agree to no more contact.'

I just nodded my head and I was a free man again, but I just couldn't understand how it had ever got to be like it had.

The kids had initially stayed with Jane when I moved out. This was the house I'd worked for all my life, and all of a sudden I was never allowed there again. I haven't seen it since and I haven't even been allowed near it to this day. A few months after the court case, I got a call from my daughter, and she said, 'Can we come and live with you, Dad?'

I was touched and told her, 'Of course you can, you don't have to ask, you are family and I'm your dad. Of course I'll look after you.'

So they came to live with me at Mum's house and have been there ever since.

I was worried at first when they came because the darts meant I'd be away from them for certain periods of time. Fortunately, I had two sisters living either side of me who agreed to take the kids in and look after them while I was away working, and the rest of the neighbours also chipped in – but if Jane had wanted to, she could've got them back quite easily, by pointing out that darts took me away from home quite a lot. However, there was no fight for them, which I was pleased about.

In the first few months after the divorce we sent messages by text. I couldn't speak to Jane after what had happened. But I felt more sorry for the effect it had on our children. They went from having a mum and dad together all the time to having a father who was in jail and being threatened with assaulting his wife. Surely to God we could've sat round a table and worked everything out amicably, like I did with Maureen.

When I moved out of the family home I didn't go straight to Mum's house; I stayed in hotels for a month. If I was playing an exhibition in Blackburn I would stay in a hotel up there for three or four days and then move on. I hadn't been to Mum's house since she died, I couldn't face all those memories, but in the end it just got daft because it was costing me a fortune in hotel bills so I went and it wasn't as bad as I thought it would be.

I hadn't let anyone touch anything in there when she died, so at first going through the drawers wasn't very nice. I'd suddenly come across old photographs that I'd never seen before, hidden in little special places. That brought back the memories and one or two tears with it. But I stayed there, in that modest terrace, and I'm still there now. I don't need a big house with a big mortgage to go with it, just like I don't need a massive amount of money. I've got enough to live a comfortable lifestyle and recently bought my daughter a two-grand car for her birthday. She hasn't passed her test yet but she's itching to use it. Every weekend she's cleaning it and checking the tyres. She lives with her boyfriend now, so I rang her up and said, 'Have you moved the car?' I was only kidding but it frightened the life out of her. James will get one as well, when he's seventeen.

I've never thought about getting the big house back. It just doesn't bother me. If Jane drops dead tomorrow the children will get it. I'll just carry on working and making money. I've always been a licence to print money anyway because of the darts, so I'll make more than make what I've lost.

As for relationships, that's me done now. I will never settle down again. I don't want to, I just want to do what I want to do. The divorce hurt me, and I have made a vow to myself never to get hurt like that again. It really did knock the stuffing out of me. Now I don't miss waking up next to somebody every morning. I like doing my own thing. I know how to use a washing machine, I know how to use a dryer, I can iron and I'm a brilliant cook, especially when it comes to roast dinners. My father taught me how to cook from a young age. He drummed it into me that the best thing to be in life is independent, which is right.

The only thing I have to remember to do, which I didn't have to when I was living with someone, is eat. I have never eaten a lot. The trouble is I don't get hunger pangs. I can go two or three days without eating and not get any twinges, nothing. I have never had them and I have no idea what people are on about when they say they feel sick through lack of food. I make myself eat, though. If it's there I'll eat it. I don't do breakfast or lunch but I'll have a curry most nights or cook a roast lamb or roast chicken dinner for James and myself, then that's me done until the following day's dinnertime.

SIXTEEN

Legend

If the eighties were brilliant and the nineties were the decade of being second best, by the turn of the millennium it was quite clear to me that my darting career on the professional circuit had come to an end – though I could hardly call my retirement peaceful with a brother suddenly being revealed to me in all his glory, my mum dying, court cases to win and a divorce to contend with.

Through this turmoil one thing kept me going and that was my work with Sky Sports. They approached me to become a spotter for them, something Keith Deller had been employed to do. I said no at first, I didn't think I'd be suited for it or enjoy it, but they persuaded me to try it out.

I went into one of their big Sky vans during one of the premier darts events, and there were all these TVs lined up inside, all focused on different dart boards, and monitoring about eight games in progress. I had to tell the producer which game to focus on, advise on what players would go for to checkout, and basically keep the cameras moving from board to board. I loved it. I thought it was brilliant and basically it meant I was being paid to watch the game I love.

It wasn't quite enough for Keith, though. He still wanted to be part of the limelight and found it very hard when he was no longer on telly. Legends of Darts was his brainwave. He had the idea of getting all the top players of yesteryear together for an eight-week round robin tournament that would culminate in a final at the Circus Tavern in Purfleet. Player after player signed up. As well as Keith there were Lowey, Bobby George, Big Cliff, Dave Whitcombe, Bob Anderson who went on to win it, and Peter Evison.

When they approached me I said I didn't really want to do it. Setanta had promised coverage but I told them I really didn't want to appear if I wasn't playing well – if the yips came I really didn't want to make a fool of myself on TV. I could still remember the end of my career with the PDC: I'd practise or play an exhibition game on the Tuesday night and be brilliant, and then as soon as a televised tournament began on the Friday I'd play horribly.

In the end I got harassed into doing it because they said they couldn't have a Legends tour without me being there. I was basically told in no uncertain terms that if I didn't play it wouldn't go ahead and it would cost them all close to £20,000. So I relented. Whether it would've happened without me anyway I will never know, but I became part of the first Legends of Darts Tour 2008 which formed part of the old school's last hurrah.

I would've liked Jocky to be there. He is possibly the biggest name from that era apart from me. We had heard rumours that he was playing darts again, so Keith rang him up, but he said he hadn't thrown a dart for twelve years and couldn't throw now because of his arthritis. If we'd got Jocky in, we'd have had a leg of the Legends Tour in Scotland and that had the potential to be riotous. But it wasn't to be, and it was also sad that the very first World Champion Leighton Rees was missing. He had died in 2003, aged sixty-three.

I did a charity show with him two weeks before his death, picking him up at his local pub in Ynysybwl and taking him to the venue. He was complaining then of fluid on his chest and he was clearly not well, but we ended the night having a good booze-up before my driver Phil took him back to his Welsh village. As I wished him goodnight and gave him a hug, he said to me, 'I want to come to America with you again. Debbie and I want to come out to Vegas, we miss it.'

I said, 'Brilliant. Come to Vegas and we'll have a piss-up. It'll be just like old times.'

A fortnight later the fluid retention killed him. His heart just blew. He had a doctor's appointment set for ten days after he died. If he had just gone to him earlier and said, 'Look, doc, this isn't right. I don't feel right,' he would still be here today.

I miss Leighton, he would've been great for that Legends Tour because he was the original Legend, the very first one at that inaugural World Championship. We had some great times together, me as the young lunatic and him as the disbelieving older player who got his laughs watching what I got up to. He used to say to me, 'Why do you always keep on upsetting people?'

'Because they're all cunts.' I'd say back.

Shaking his head he'd say, 'Leave them alone, boyo, leave them alone,' and he'd take a pull on the huge cigar he liked to smoke while having a drink.

I didn't go to his funeral. I couldn't go because it clashed with the funeral of Lorna Croft, Ollie's wife, who helped set up the BDO. I didn't go to hers either. Lorna was like a second mum and Leighton was my best buddy of old, so I thought by not going to either funeral I wouldn't be showing any disrespect by just going to one. You would've thought the BDO and the Welsh BDO could've sorted that one out and had the funerals on different days. A lot of county teams sent half their side to one and half to the other. It was the only way really.

So Leighton wasn't there at Legends, which I think he would've enjoyed, because other players like Whitcombe and Anderson were chomping at the bit. They hadn't earned anything from darts for years, and suddenly they were back in the game again, as were Lowey and Bobby George. Getting Bobby involved helped to bridge the gap between the BDO and PDC, it healed some old wounds, but the good thing about Legends was that it wasn't BDO or PDC organised. It was an independent tournament where maybe a guy whose career as a professional darts player was finished could get two or three years extra money and a bit of publicity to keep the exhibition door open.

The press launch was at Manchester United's ground and it was good to see all the old faces together again. Me and Lowey get on brilliantly now. He's a changed person from the guy I knew back in the eighties when he was a bit too serious for me. Now he is more relaxed and has completely lost the edge that used to personify him. When I asked him his thoughts on Legends he said, 'Well, we have to carry on, mate. We have to earn a few more bob because we don't know how many more Christmases we have got left.'

I said, 'Behave yourself, John,' but I must confess he is getting on a bit.

He changed when he met his new wife Karen. She likes a good time and they're an ideal couple who should've met years ago. You never know, I might meet someone like that – but don't bet on it.

Big Cliff is still the same, apart from he has a heart murmur now and has had to curb his drinking so he can lose weight to have an operation. He'd not be alive today were it not for his wife Carol. She has kept an eye on him and makes sure he doesn't drink too much most of the time. He still has his benders, though not as many these days.

Dave Whitcombe is still the same, very deep and very hard to get to. He's got a good sense of humour but he's a loner. And he still doesn't practise.

Bob Anderson went into retirement to come into the Tour. It made more sense financially because he'd just dropped out of the top thirty-two in the world. Peter Evison came in because he had a lot of niggles with his arm and leg which meant he couldn't play on a pro-circuit to a consistent enough level to earn a living. People might laugh at darts players getting injured, but if you've got something wrong with your leg you've got a big problem because playing in a tournament could see you walk the equivalent of ten to twelve miles a day backwards and forwards from the oche. Evison is still a class player who has beaten Phil Taylor eight–one when Taylor was at the top of his game.

Then there's Keith who is clumsy, stupid, but brilliant on the telephone. He gets superb deals and also comes across well on television, but in the real world he is the Peter Pan of darts – he is still nine years old. There's no harm in him, though. He's more harm to himself because of all the accidents he has. I'm glad I've met him and I'm glad I lost to him in that world final, because if I hadn't I wouldn't have had all the laughs I've had with him over the years.

When Bet Fred got involved and offered to sponsor the tournament, things got a bit more serious. It began to be seen among some of the players as something to be won, something more than just a bit of fun, and that's when the nagging started. They were earning eighteen grand for eight days' work, which is not a bad pay day and it had been years since they had earned anything like that, so why they had to suddenly start bickering is beyond me. It made no sense.

The opening round was at the Circus Tavern where the press wanted a picture of all eight of us lined up before the games started in the players' lounge, but nobody could find Bobby George. Keith began to get impatient and shouted, 'Fucking hell, we shouldn't have to wait for Bobby George.'

I could see the whole BDO/PDC thing raising its ugly head again so I snapped and said, 'Look, he didn't know about this photo shoot because they only told us about five minutes ago.'

Then Big Cliff started nagging and saying, 'Why do we have to wait for him anyway?' The only reason he was getting wound up was because he wanted to be on the practice board, having a few throws.

The tournament finally got underway and Keith beat Cliff seven legs to five in the first match. Next up was Whitcombe against Lowey and Whitcombe won seven legs to three. Then Anderson and Evison drew six legs each to leave me and Bobby George to play the final match in what was effectively a repeat of the 1980 World Championship Final. It was as though life had gone full circle. I had begun my tournament career with Bobby and I was ending it with him, and he hasn't changed one bit. He's still a lovely fella and he still calls Keith Deller 'boy' which tickles me.

I remember my first tour of America when I was a penniless teenager and him coming up to me and slipping me ten dollars and saying, 'Go and get yourself a drink, son, but don't tell anyone I bought you one.' He never bought anyone a drink. That probably accounts for why he has done so well out of life. He built his own mansion when he made some money out of darts. It's worth about four million pounds now and has about eighteen bedrooms as well as a fully stocked bar. It's also got two fishing lakes which he hires out. He's a shrewd businessman, Bobby; he's done well.

Bet Fred made me a rank outsider to win the Legends Tour and didn't hold out much hope of me beating Bobby, but I wanted to play well because there were nine hundred people there and it was a great atmosphere. I played OK, but, like that final in 1980, Bobby bottled it. He was hot, sweaty and nervous. I was hitting my doubles, he was missing his, and I ran out the winner by seven legs to five. He had chances to beat me but missed at the vital point, whereas I had eighteen darts at the double and hit seven of them, which wasn't a bad ratio. I only hit a single one-eighty, but I did notice, watching it on telly afterwards, that I twisted my arm as I threw which may be one of the reasons I get the yips.

It was a good feeling to win again. The adrenaline rush came back and I enjoyed that night. It was like going back in time and money can't buy that, especially when you're faced with the last double to win and your heart is going bump, bump, bump, bump. Bobby was gutted afterwards because he'd brought about eighty people down to watch him.

I was five to one against winning with the bookies that night. One geezer had two grand on me and won ten thousand pounds. My bookmaker even rang me up and asked if it was worth him having a punt on me. I told him not to bother. He sent me a text afterwards that simply said 'You wanker'. A lot of people in that place were having twenty and forty pounds on me, so I paid for a lot of people's drinks that night. Bobby went two–nil up initially, and most people must have been ready to tear their betting slips up, but I came back and that was it, I was always in front after that. In the last leg he had no chance. I needed double sixteen to win and he had over two hundred still left on the board. When I got it and everybody cheered I remember thinking to myself: I remember this feeling from thirty years ago.

It didn't last. That match against Bobby was effectively my final hurrah. I didn't play well after that and didn't really enjoy it. There was a lot of moaning about the board not being right, or the TV monitors being too close to the oche, or the lights being too bright, or it being too hot on stage. It's the same for the other bloke, so why complain? I have never been one for excuses and I don't like moaners, and playing on the Legends Tour felt like being in a classroom full of sulky schoolkids at times.

My second game was against Big Cliff who beat me seven legs to three. I remember halfway through the match feeling sorry for him and wanting him to win because it would've meant more to him than it did to me. That is just not like me at all. I'm a mercenary at heart. Against Whitcombe in the third round, at the Hilton Hotel in Birmingham, I was six legs to one down and got annoyed with myself because I was playing so poorly, but I managed to claw two legs back. Even so, it was a case of too little too late and I lost that one seven legs to three. When Keith beat me seven legs to one at Batley, I was effectively out of the competition because my chances of reaching the top four and hence the finals were virtually non-existent.

I have signed a contract to do it again next year, but after that I'll probably retire. I don't get a buzz out of it and don't want to keep making a prat out of myself on stage. Somebody else will take my place when I go, and in that respect I think the format will work year after year after year as players drop out and other players come in. Steve Beaton is on the fringes of retiring. He'd be good to have and could take my place no problem. I'm not carrying on if I keep losing seven–one, seven–two and seven–three. It's no good having dead wood in there. It has to be competitive to work.

I can't help but play darts, it's all I've known since the age of eleven, but even so I'm going to plan a lot more non-darting holidays. My work load with spotting, exhibitions and Sky is getting ridiculous. I love it, but I want holidays now as well. I've earned them.

It doesn't always happen like that. I went away for fifteen days at Easter recently to Agia Napa hoping for a non-darting holiday, and ended up playing exhibitions at four army camps over there. But who knows where I'll be in a few years. I might not even be alive. I smoke and I drink, and it's not a healthy mix. I'll keep an eye on my brother Kevin. I know that when he goes I've got about two years left.

I can't even see myself being in this country in four or five years' time. I'll be sitting in the sun somewhere like Tenerife having a drink and that will be me sorted. You can buy a nice two-bedroom apartment over there for about £120,000 complete with balcony. I'll do a few months over there plus the odd spotting job for Sky. That will be my life.

Britain has regressed in my opinion. It's more like

Stoke Newington back when I was a lad, in that everybody is carrying a tool. They all used to carry one back in the sixties and they're all carrying one now, and the MPs who run the country didn't and don't have a clue what life is like on the streets. They've probably never visited Guinness Trust flats with four thousand families crammed into these high rises – families of every creed, colour and religion – with high walls round them so they resemble an H-Block rather than somewhere to live. If some young lad decides to carry a knife in these places, then everyone will carry one as well, for protection.

I've been in gangs, but they were not like the gangs of today. London is becoming like America where the only way somebody can join a gang is if they stab a rival member of another firm.

The politicians who run our country just don't understand this. Parachute them into a Guinness Trust housing estate in Hackney and they'd sit in a corner and cry. They'd be on their mobile phones pleading with the police to get them out of the place, and yet people have to live there. There are a lot more stabbings now. I had a claw hammer. Other members of my gang had knuckle dusters and coshes, things like that. Hit someone with them and you wouldn't kill them. Now they've been replaced by knives, which can kill people, and Britain has become a bit more frightening because of it.

If someone came at me with a tool I'd put him down

and make sure he never got up again. Take the knives off the streets, though, and the gangs will go back to guns and start popping people like they did in the early nineties in places like Manchester. If someone attacked me with a knife or gun, though, he'd be dead, or I would be if he got to me first. I'd have to take him out because if I didn't and he got up it'd be me that would be six feet under.

The kids today who live on run-down council estates have no future, and because they have no future they've got no fear. That is why there should be a drive to get them into sport. The ones with no fear are the sportsmen of the future. If you've got no fear of dying you've no fear of anything. That, I believe, is why I succeeded and if I had my life again I wouldn't change a thing, apart from one or two women I went out with – although Maureen did keep me on the straight and narrow when I was winning all those World Championships, and Jane gave me two lovely kids. That divorce is my one big regret in life because I could see us growing old together and enjoying ourselves when the kids grew up and left home. But she was bored. I should've seen that.

Now I'm left with the spotting and watching a new generation step up to the oche. Phil Taylor has a few years left in him, but I don't think there will be another eighteen-year-old coming through to win a big one like I did with the World Masters. Then, you had to come through and beat maybe a dozen really good players.

Now any eighteen-year-old coming through is going to have four or five hundred good players to beat. Back then a lot of players played the game for a bit of fun, then TV came in and created a buzz and now with the prize money about to go through the roof it'll be a sport for mercenaries in the not too distant future – though I doubt anybody will dominate the game the way Phil has done. I love it when he wins, I want him to win everything, but he is under pressure not only from James Wade but others like my tip for the top Jelle Klaasen from Holland. He is slowly creeping up the rankings and when he gets into the top-thirty, which won't be long, he'll start winning things.

The game has changed so much since I started out, and most of the people I played with when I was fourteen or fifteen will be dead now. That's the trouble with having been a darts baby: I look back and all my friends of yesteryear who I played with are gone. The Arundel Arms league team have all died and pretty soon friends I made as a professional player will start disappearing. I'm still here, and that just doesn't make sense. The way I've lived my life I should've been gone long ago, but I'll continue plodding on, drinking, smoking, eating curries and probably getting in trouble with the law once or twice. I might even throw the odd dart or two.